Understanding the Corporate Annual Report: A User's Guide

University Edition

Understanding the Corporate Annual Report: A User's Guide
University Edition

Brian B. Stanko, Ph.D., C.P.A.

Thomas L. Zeller, Ph.D., C.P.A.

Loyola University Chicago
Associate Professors

John Wiley & Sons, Inc.

ACQUISITIONS EDITOR   *Mark Bonadeo*
MARKETING MANAGER   *Keari Bedford*
PROGRAM ASSISTANT   *Brian Kamins*
COVER PHOTO   © John Still/Photonica

This book was set in Times Roman by the authors and printed and bound by Malloy Inc.
The cover was printed by Phoenix Color Corporation.

This book is printed on acid free paper. ∞

ISBN 0-471-22991-1

Printed in the United States of America

10 9 8 7 6 5 4 3 2 1

Dedication

This book is dedicated to our families, for their encouragement and understanding, and for helping us keep life in perspective.

Julie, Brandon, and Justin (BS)
Mary, Lauren, and Jenny (TZ)

Preface

This book was written out of our findings in working with business students and a wide spectrum of professionals. We have found that most recipients of corporate annual reports do not use it to its fullest potential. Their attention is directed by the marketing strategy built into the glossy pictures and slick writing style prepared by public relations professionals. Little time and energy is devoted to the meat of the annual report, management's discussion and analysis (MD&A) of financial condition and results of operations, the notes accompanying the financial statements, and the quality of reported earnings. Further, most textbooks do little to assist this type of user. The majority of books are too focused on the financial statements, or too detailed to meet the needs of the business student or busy professional.

Our book, *Understanding the Corporate Annual Report: A User's Guide*, and our workbook, "Introduction to the Corporate Annual Report: A Business Application," address the needs of today's business students and other users of the annual report. We discuss not only what appears in a typical corporate annual report but explain its significance, analyze its substance in the context of the company's strategic initiatives, and then consider how this company is performing relative to its competition.

Our book has both a user and preparer focus. By this we mean that our book will help you capture the wealth of information that is provided in the annual report, put you in position to ask the right questions, and read between the lines. In order to accomplish this, you must first understand what the information means, how it evolved, and what factors influence its change. The strategic focus of our book provides an explicit framework showing first how the annual report serves as a tool to evaluate past performance and second to critically examine the linkage of corporate strategy and financial resources. By reading our book, the annual report user will be able to answer the fundamental question: Does the corporation have the resources to move forward and be successful with its corporate strategy?

Understanding the Corporate Annual Report: A User's Guide is divided into eight chapters and two appendices. Chapter 1 explains the importance of corporate annual reports and the problems that have recently emerged. Next we introduce the annual report structure and discuss the significance of each component. Chapters 3 to 5 discuss the balance sheet, statement of earnings, and statement of cash flows. Chapter 6 is devoted to the statement of change in stockholders' equity and notes accompanying the financial statements. The remaining two chapters are devoted to financial statement analysis and emerging issues in financial reporting. Appendix A reviews the regulatory environment and illustrates how and why the SEC, FASB, etc. are involved in accounting regulation. Appendix B recaps the theoretical framework of the accounting system and explains how it supports the annual report and financial reporting.

Much of our analysis is focused on The Home Depot corporate annual report. We selected The Home Depot because we believe that most readers have frequented the stores they operate and consumed the products they sell. We believe this is helpful when we discuss individual balance sheet and income statement elements. We do include excerpts from other corporate annual reports to help illustrate alternative reporting strengths and weaknesses.

Brian B. Stanko
Thomas L. Zeller

Acknowledgements

Many people and organizations have provided valuable assistance during the development, writing, revision, and production stages of our book.

First, we want to thank The Home Depot for granting us permission to use its annual report as a focal point throughout our book. Particular thanks goes to Carol Tomé, Chief Financial Officer, and Bob Burton, Vice President, Investor Relations, The Home Depot, for their commitment to the project and expert review of selected materials within our book.

In addition, we appreciate the efforts of our colleagues, Professors Ellen Landgraf and Lawrence Metzger, as well as Katherine Anichini, our research assistant, for their constructive criticism and developmental assistance. Without the contributions of these individuals, the project would have never reached completion.

Finally, we thank the professionals at John Wiley & Sons, particularly Mark Bonadeo and Sheck Cho, for providing support and timely guidance throughout the entire production process.

Table of Contents

Chapter 5: Statement of Cash Flows   73

Chapter 6: Statement of Stockholders' Equity
and Notes to the Financial Statements   89

Chapter 7: Analysis of The Home Depot's Annual Report   107

Chapter 8:   Emerging Issues in Financial Reporting   141

Appendix A: Regulatory Environment of Financial Reporting   161

Appendix B: The Building Blocks of Financial Reporting   171

Index   183

CHAPTER 1

Financial Reporting and the Annual Report

CHAPTER OUTLINE

Look Before You Leap

Baker Electronics specializes in the development and distribution of electronic components. The company's primary customers operate in the defense and auto industries. Recently, Baker Electronics, Inc. offered a newly created management position to Steve Ray, an electrical engineer employed with a major competitor.

Steve Ray was excited about this new position because of Baker's reputation for bringing quality products to the forefront of the industry. Baker's success is directly related to the quality of its engineering staff and the seemingly unlimited resources it dedicates to research and development and its engineering teams.

Although Steve Ray believed this engineering position was an outstanding opportunity, he knew little about the company itself. Moreover, a sluggish economy and recent high-profile accounting scandals impressed upon Steve the need to exercise caution when making this decision.

To learn more about Baker Electronics, he located the company's corporate annual report on the Internet. Steve knew the report would provide information to help him evaluate Baker's current position, strategic focus, and its potential to maintain long-term financial stability. The annual report began with a message from the president *that pointed to Baker's solid strategic initiatives positioning it well for continued success. He understood, however, that managers often use the annual report as a marketing tool and that a more detailed analysis was essential before he could decide. Further review of the company's financial information, found within the annual report, provided evidence that Baker Electronics was profitable, financially stable, and liquid. Based on his review, Steve accepted the management position.*

Nine months after joining Baker Electronics, Steve Ray was awarded his first company bonus: options to purchase 1,000 shares of Baker stock. Although Steve could not exercise the options for at least two years, he was pleased to see that within only a few months the company's stock price had increased 11 percent. Steve was pleased with his decision to join Baker Electronics and looked forward to many years of professional growth.

LEARNING OBJECTIVES

1. Understand what an annual report is and what it provides.
2. Recognize who is responsible for the content and accuracy of a corporate annual report.
3. Identify some examples of failure in financial reporting.
4. Understand the underlying pressures to inflate earnings.
5. Recognize what can be done to improve the current state of financial reporting.
6. Explain why education is the key to better understanding financial information.

The opening vignette highlights the importance of the company's annual report. Steve Ray looked to the annual report to provide evidence that (1) Baker Electronics, Inc. had a meaningful, long-term strategy for continued growth and (2) Baker possessed the financial resources to support this strategy. Without a careful review, Steve's decision might have resulted in disaster. Steve, however, was able to make a sound career decision because he knew where to find relevant strategic and financial information about Baker.

1.1 INTRODUCTION

Almost forty years ago (1963) Bob Dylan, a well-known recording artist, released a record titled "The Times They Are A-Changin'." Verse 3 includes the following lyrics:

> *Come senators, congressmen, please heed the call*
> *Don't stand in the doorway, don't block the hall*
> *For he who gets hurt, will be he who has stalled*
> *There's a battle outside, and it is ragin'.*
> *It'll soon shake your windows, and rattle your walls*
> *For the times they are a-changin'.*

Recent events in the business community might inspire the recording artist to release an updated version of this popular title. With corporate earnings carefully scrutinized, investor confidence at an all-time low, and chief executives of major corporations feeling pressure to explain to their shareholders, via Webcast, what their numbers mean and how they were constructed, the battle is indeed ragin.' Changes to the annual report and the financial reporting environment seem imminent, for the armor of the reporting framework has been pierced, and the evidence is there for all to see:

- "Xerox to Pay Record Financial Fraud Penalty, Investigation Turns to KPMG."[1]
- "Securities Exchange Commission Brings First Pro Forma Financial Reporting Case: Trump Hotels Charged with Issuing Misleading Earnings Release."[2]
- "Waste Management Founder and Five Other Former Top Officers Sued for Massive Fraud: Defendants Inflated Profits by $1.7 billion to Meet Earnings Targets…While Investors Lose More than $6 billion."[3]
- "AOL Time Warner Reports Biggest Loss [$54.24 billion] in History."[4]
- "Global Crossing: The Telecom Enron."[5]
- How a Titan Came Undone: Enron's Collapse Stunned the World."[6]

As a result, those who rely on the annual report and reported financial information might no longer be able to simply pick up a report and set of financial statements and feel confident that the company "walks the talk." No longer might those who rely on reported financial information feel secure in the decisions of a company's board of directors. And no longer might those who rely on reported financial information trust those who prepare the financial information (company management) or those who attest to its validity (auditors).

These developments have convinced many business insiders that revenue recognition rules must change, enforcement efforts by the Securities and Exchange Commission (SEC) must be stepped up, supplemental financial information must be improved, and auditors must become more critical during their periodic reviews. And while the jury (SEC, Financial Accounting Standards Board (FASB) and Congress) remains undecided on what decisions to render, one thing is clear: The financial reporting process will move forward and the corporate annual report will be the major vehicle for information transfer.

The objective of this book is to help you, the reader of a corporate annual report, become more knowledgeable of what lies within its glossy cover. This book will separate fact from fiction and enable you to understand whether management's strategic initiative is supported by the company's performance. That is, it will help you read between the lines. But before we move in that direction, let's briefly address the different types of annual reports, their complexities, and the current financial reporting environment. Having a background on these topics will enable you to become a more informed user of reported financial information.

1.2 CORPORATE ANNUAL REPORTS

Most U.S. companies prepare two types of annual reports. The first is called the *annual report to the Securities and Exchange Commission or Form 10-K*. The second is called the *shareholder annual report*. The major distinction between them is in their content. The annual report to the SEC provides a large amount of detailed financial and nonfinancial information. This type of disclosure is discussed further in Appendix A, "Regulatory Environment of Financial Reporting." The shareholder

---

[1] www.sec.gov/news/headline/xeroxsettles.htm.

[2] www.sec.gov/investor/pubs/proforma12-4.htm.

[3] www.sec.gov/release2002-44.

[4] Christopher Grimes "AOL Time Warner's Crown Jewel Loses Its Sparkle," *The Financial Times* (April 23, 2002).

[5] Robert Clark, "Global Crossing: The Telecom Enron," *Telecom Asia* (March 2002).

[6] J. Barnes, M. Barnett, H. Christopher, and M. Lavelle, "How a Titan Came Undone," *U.S. News and World Report* (March 18, 2002).

annual report, however, provides aggregated financial information plus sales and marketing information. The sales and marketing material alone can make up one-third to one-half of the pages in a shareholder annual report.

The most widely read annual report—and the subject of this book—is the shareholder annual report. In the simplest terms, the shareholder annual report is a booklet of quantitative and nonquantitative information prepared by management and provided to shareholders and other interested users. It often includes a wealth of company information, some required by the SEC and some not. It generally includes a statement of corporate mission and strategic focus, an executive message, product and/or service information, management's discussion of financial performance, comparative financial information, an audit report, and selected investor information. In the final analysis, the shareholder annual report is intended to meet the needs of many different users of company information.

1.3 NATURE AND EXTENT OF THE CORPORATE ANNUAL REPORT

The shareholder annual report (simply called the corporate annual report, or annual report from this point forward) can be an intimidating business document for anyone who is not familiar with its contents. The report can be lengthy, difficult to read, and quite confusing—much of which can be attributed to today's complex operating environment. For example, many companies operate across different industries and throughout foreign countries. Philip Morris Inc., for instance, owns Kraft Foods North America and Kraft Foods International.[7] It also owns the Miller Brewing Company. Pepsi Company operates worldwide and owns Frito-Lay Products, as well as Tropicana. As a result of such frequent business combinations, the nonfinancial and financial reporting framework of the annual report is no longer a 15-page booklet that summarizes the performance of a narrowly focused enterprise.

Accounting and reporting rules can also add to the complexity of the report. Because accounting rules guide business reporting and often pertain to complex business transactions, they are often disclosed in the notes to the financial statements or, on occasion, are discussed in the president's message or in management's discussion and analysis of the results of operations. Accounting information cannot be understood by just anyone. Understanding such rules and how they are applied can only be accomplished by someone the accounting profession called an *informed user* of financial information. To complete an evaluation and analysis of a company, the informed user must have fundamental accounting knowledge.

Knowing where to find useful information in an annual report and how to interpret the information can also be problematic. Some of the material in an annual report is required disclosure, while other material is included solely to improve the value of the company's information or simply to promote the company, similar to other marketing tools.

Adding to the actual complexity of financial reporting is how management places a positive spin on financial performance, regardless of actual performance. One would not have perceived financial concerns from a casual read of Enron, Xerox, Global Crossings, or Waste Management's annual report. The graphs, tables, pictures, and charts pointed to success, when in reality signs and signals of problems abounded. The lesson learned is that the investor or other user must carefully scrutinize annual reports, because management often tries to place a positive spin on negative business performance.

---

[7] Recently, Philip Morris sold to the public a portion of Kraft Foods as a means to improve its cash position. Much of the newly acquired cash will be used to pay down litigation losses that Philip Morris has sustained over the past years.

1.4 RESPONSIBILITY FOR CONTENT AND ACCURACY OF THE CORPORATE ANNUAL REPORT

Although management is responsible for the accuracy of the reported information, the *Securities and Exchange Commission (SEC)* and the *Financial Accounting Standards Board (FASB)* regulate much of what appears in the corporate annual report. The Securities Act of 1934, also known as the Continuous Disclosure Act, created the Securities and Exchange Commission and gave it the authority to administer federal securities laws and prescribe accounting principles and reporting practices. The SEC was also empowered to oversee the securities markets and to control brokers and dealers. One reporting requirement coming out of the Securities Act of 1934 was Form 10-K. A less detailed version of Form 10-K is provided to all shareholders and is the shareholder annual report.

The FASB, created in 1973, is responsible for establishing the current standards of financial accounting and reporting, as well as the financial information found in the annual report. FASB-issued standards and pronouncements are officially recognized as authoritative by the Securities and Exchange Commission (Financial Reporting Release No. 1, Section 101) and the American Institute of Certified Public Accountants (Rule 203, Rules of Conduct, as amended May 1973 and May 1979). The standards, also known as *generally accepted accounting principles (GAAP),* provide for consistency in financial reporting and comparability of financial information across firms. Imagine what financial reporting would be like if management chose not to follow GAAP. Because Enron was required to follow GAAP, the financial statements showed increased revenue but no cash flow from operations. This was a red flag to the analysts that something was wrong.

Other organizations, such as the *American Institute of Certified Public Accountants (AICPA)* and an affiliated organization, the *Auditing Standards Board (ASB),* act as advisors in the development of new accounting standards. The ASB also develops *generally accepted auditing standards (GAAS),* which are rules that govern the audit of a client company. Both of these organizations are discussed more fully in Appendix A.

1.5 CURRENT STATE OF FINANCIAL REPORTING

In mid-2001, Lynn Turner, chief accountant of the U.S. Securities and Exchange Commission, delivered a speech at the Third Annual SEC Disclosure and Accounting Conference titled *The State of Financial Reporting Today: An Unfinished Chapter.* During this speech, he identified a number of important issues:

- CFOs readily admit they are pressured to inappropriately manage the numbers, and have chosen to do so at an alarming rate.
- Corporate earnings restatements are increasing, with more than 200 cases in the year 2000.
- More reports of alleged financial frauds now involve companies with household names.
- Auditors contend that management fraud is the reason for undetected errors during the audit and, in some cases, during a number of audits.[8]

[8] www.sec.gov/speech/spch508

He went on to question the magnitude of the problem, unaware that in the coming months, recent events would provide the answer.

- *AOL Time Warner*: Considered by many to be immune to the economics of the Internet bubble, America Online stock fell by more than 50 percent during 2001-2002. A reduction in revenues, both from advertising and subscriptions, has limited AOL's operating performance. In addition, a $54 billion goodwill write-down in the first quarter of 2002 now indicates that AOL overpaid for Time Warner in January 2001. The write-off is approximately 30 percent of the $147 billion that AOL paid for the media giant.[9]

- *Global Crossing*: Once an investment favorite, Global Crossing filed for bankruptcy protection on January 28, 2002. At the time, the company listed more than $12 billion of debt. The action represents the largest telecom bankruptcy to date. Subsequent review uncovered improper revenue recognition practices, extensive trading of company stock by company executives, and an inordinate number of political contributions.[10]

- *Xerox*: The company announced an agreement with the SEC to restate 1997-2000 financials and adjust 2001 results. In addition, Xerox agreed to pay a $10 million penalty, the largest corporate fine imposed by the SEC in history. According to the SEC, Xerox was using a variety of accounting techniques to accelerate the recognition of more than $3 billion in revenue from 1997-2000. The moves boosted pretax profit by more than $1.5 billion during this period. If not for the accounting misrepresentation, earnings would have been below market expectations.[11]

- *Enron*: At one time the fifth largest company in America, Enron filed for bankruptcy protection on December 2, 2001. Approximately one month earlier, Enron said it had overstated earnings by $586 million since 1997. In addition, Enron had unreported liabilities in excess of $1 billion. Much of Enron's problems were the result of improper revenue recognition practices and special-purpose entities designed to remove high-risk assets and conceal debt.[12]

- *Waste Management*: On March 26, 2002, the Securities and Exchange Commission filed suit against Waste Management's founder and five other former top officers. The SEC alleged that six key Waste Management executives perpetrated a massive financial fraud that lasted from 1992 to 1997. According to the SEC, the defendants inflated the company's profits by more than $1.7 billion to meet earnings targets and defrauded investors by more than $6 billion. When the company filed its restated financial statements in 1998, the restatement was the largest in corporate history. The news release was followed by a 33 percent reduction in the value of Waste Management shares.[13]

- *Trump Hotels and Casino Resorts*: On January 16, 2002, the SEC, in its first pro forma financial reporting case, instituted cease-and-desist proceedings against Trump Hotels for making misleading statements in the company's third-quarter 1999 earnings release. According to the Commission, Trump Hotels issued a pro forma earnings statement but failed to disclose that the earnings were influenced by an unusual one-time gain and not

[9] Grimes.

[10] Clark.

[11] www.sec.gov/news/headline/xeroxsettles.htm.

[12] Barnes, Barnett, Christopher, and Lavelle.

[13] www.sec.gov/release2002-44.

attributable to operations. Utilizing non-GAAP, pro forma figures, the release announced that the company's earnings exceeded analyst's expectations. On October 25, the day the earnings release was issued, the price of the Company's stock rose 8 percent.[14]

These and many other reporting issues point to why it is important to be able to critically read and evaluate the annual report.

1.6 EARNINGS PRESSURE ON CORPORATE AMERICA

There are several reasons why corporate executives feel pressured to enhance reported earnings:

- *Analyst recommendations*—Analysts who follow selected companies estimate earnings from one quarter to the next. If the company fails to meet the street (analyst) estimate of earnings per share, oftentimes the analyst's recommendation to buy or hold the stock changes, and the company's stock value declines, sometimes dramatically.
- *High expectations*—Today's investors are more demanding than those of twenty or thirty years ago. The era to buy and hold and earn 5 to 6 percent per year now seems a distant memory. Investors who experienced the financial markets of the late 1990s and early 2000 want positive results immediately. They "vote with their feet," selling stock that does not meet expectations. Boards of directors, in turn, pressure CEOs and/or CFOs to explain the resulting fall in the stock price.
- *Stock options*—Company executives have an incentive to enhance earnings as a result of executive compensation agreements. Executive benefits often include stock compensation agreements whereby key individuals receive a predetermined number of stock options (or other incentives) should their company meet or exceed a certain earnings level. Occasionally if earnings increase beyond normal expectations, the options vest sooner.

Chapter 8 provides a more complete discussion of earnings management techniques used by selected companies.

1.7 IMPROVING FINANCIAL REPORTING

Various individuals and organizations have proposed a number of recommendations to improve the financial reporting system. Arthur Levitt, the former SEC chairman, suggests that an independent oversight board be established for the auditing profession. This would remove much of the power that the American Institute of Certified Public Accountants (AICPA) currently holds.[15]

Another initiative, proposed by Congress, seeks to prevent accounting firms from providing both audit and consulting services to the same client. The AICPA was once vehemently opposed to this recommendation but recently endorsed its passage. Several large accounting firms and corporations also support this limitation. For example, Walt Disney shareholders recently approved a proposal that now forbids company management from using one accounting firm for both audit and consulting services.

---

[14] www.sec.gov/investor/pubs/proforma12-4.htm.
[15] The recent passage of the Sarbanes-Oxley Act will be briefly discussed in Chapter 8.

A third initiative, sponsored by the SEC, would require accelerated disclosure on issues such as off-balance-sheet entities, corporate write-offs, and how the use of accounting methods affects reported results. According to current SEC chairman, Harvey Pitt, this action will help prevent another Enron debacle. Much of Enron's failure came from unreported liabilities that were associated with nonconsolidated entities.[16]

One additional proposal seeks "term limits" on how long an accounting firm can audit a specific company. The belief is that a mandatory rotation will prevent what some perceive as complacency during the audit process. The AICPA does not support this congressional initiative, however.

Some companies have attempted to improve financial reporting on their own. For example, executives from General Electric, IBM, and Tyco International Ltd. now hold teleconferences and Webcasts with analysts and investors to better explain their financial reporting practices and the results of their business operations.[17] Merrill Lynch has instructed its stock analysts to no longer rely on pro forma earnings. Instead, analysts have been advised to switch to GAAP-based analytics. This means they will focus on earnings prepared according to Generally Accepted Accounting Principles (official pronouncements issued by the accounting regulatory bodies).[18]

Improvements to financial reporting alone are not enough. The compensation structure for security analysts must also change. Before 1975, security analyst compensation was linked to trading commissions that their stock picks generated. That commission structure was outlawed in 1975, forcing investment banks to seek other compensation methods. The fallout was that analysts began to earn substantial bonuses based on the amount of new business they attracted to the investment bank, such as initial public offerings (IPOs) in the form of stocks and bonds. To attract this business, analysts often extended favorable ratings to a company's stock. As a result, investors have questioned the independence of analysts. Although this practice is flatly denied by the investment banking industry, one must question their position. According to a *Business Week* article, sell ratings now make up less than 2 percent of analysts' recommendation.[19] In the same article it is reported that security analysts who work for independent investment firms gain limited access to corporate America.

1.8 EDUCATION IS THE KEY

So how does one better understand a company's annual report? The simplest answer is education. Yet, educating oneself is a task that is easier said than done. Although much has been written on company analysis and the usefulness of financial ratios, little of this is valuable to the conventional reader. The material is either cursory in nature, written for the trained financial analyst, or tucked within a lengthy academic textbook. As a result, most readers of corporate annual reports gain little from the information they provide.

This book is designed to bridge the gap. It is written for those who intend to rely on reported financial information but have little understanding of an annual report. Upon completing this book, *you* will understand the nature and extent of the annual report, how to

---

[16] Barrett, Ante, Symonds and McNamee, "Slammed: Investors are Telling Companies that Creative Accounting Will Not Fly," Business Week (March 4, 2002), p. 34.

[17] Ibid.

[18] AccountingWEB US 07 (March 2002).

[19] Vickers and France, "How Corrupt Is Wall Street?" *Business Week* (May 13, 2002), p. 40.

fundamentally analyze financial statements, and know what questions to seek answers to when you review a company's performance.

What lies beyond Chapter 1 are the tools to help you understand and critically interpret the annual report and related financial statements. Chapter 2 provides an illustration and discussion of the annual report's structure. Chapters 3 to 6 provide a thorough review of the financial statements and their related notes. Chapter 7 examines some common techniques that can be used to better understand a firm's financial strengths, weaknesses, and opportunities for future success. Chapter 8 addresses emerging issues in financial reporting and includes earnings management, pro forma reporting, and supplemental disclosure. Two appendices are also included at the close of the book. These are provided for readers who seek a more thorough understanding of accounting systems and the regulatory environment of financial reporting.

Questions for Review

1. It has been said that relevant financial information is necessary for various decisions. Cite a specific decision that you have made or anticipate making that would be enhanced by your understanding of relevant financial information.

2. What recent circumstances have lead to an erosion of the confidence that individuals have previously placed on reported financial information?

3. Publicly held corporations in the U.S. prepare two types of annual reports. Describe and distinguish between the two reports.

4. Understanding the financial information included in the corporate annual report (also known as the shareholder annual report) requires an *informed user*. Describe in your own terms what an informed user is.

5. Define *forward-looking information*. Why should an investor be particularly careful when utilizing this type of information in the decision-making process?

6. What organizations are responsible for prescribing or regulating the content of corporate annual reports?

7. Who is primarily responsible for the accuracy and fairness of the information contained/disclosed in a corporate annual report?

8. What is meant by the term *earnings management*? What are some of the reasons that contribute to a perceived pressure to enhance or manage earnings?

Internet Exercises

1. Visit the Web site of Krispy Kreme Doughnuts (http://www.krispykreme.com/). Locate Investor Relations under the "Krispy Kreme" heading. From here you should be able to locate both types of annual reports prepared by Krispy Kreme. The annual report to the Securities and Exchange Commission (10-K) may be found by clicking on Financials/SEC filings. The annual reports to shareholders may be found by clicking on Annual Reports.

   Compare Krispy Kreme's 10-K to its annual report (both for the most recently reported on year). Describe five specific similarities and five specific differences in the information contained in the reports.

2. Visit the Securities and Exchange Commission Web site at http://www.sec.gov/. Locate the most recent 10-K for Starbucks. This is accomplished by going to "Filings and Forms (EDGAR)." Write a brief summary of the nonfinancial information disclosed about the business.

CHAPTER **2**

Structure of the Annual Report

CHAPTER OUTLINE

Getting to Know More about Baker Electronics from the Annual Report

Steve Ray has learned that a careful review of the annual report is time well spent. Early sections of the annual report are rich with product information and service offerings, past successes, future strategies, and more. This information is likely to be biased because it is prepared by management and is often written to make the company look attractive and prosperous. In the later sections of the report a user finds the financial statements and other financial reports. Management also prepares this information. Unlike earlier sections, however, the content and form must follow relatively strict guidelines set forth by accounting rules and the Securities and Exchange Commission. Still, a careful review is essential because management might twist and abuse reporting guidelines and ultimately present a picture that it wants you to see. This chapter frames for Steve a general structure of what to look for and where to find it, and it provides an introductory dose of how to critically consume the information found in the annual report.

LEARNING OBJECTIVES

1. Explain why annual reports have similar reporting structures.
2. Describe the typical components of a corporate annual report.
3. Discuss the importance of a company's mission statement or statement of corporate values.
4. Discuss the significance of MD&A of operations, the external audit report and the company's management letter.
5. Identify the four financial statements that are included in most annual reports.
6. Discuss the importance of a five or ten-year comparative information.
7. Explain why shareholder information is included at the close of the annual report.

2.1 INTRODUCTION

Users of financial information may notice that most corporate annual reports have similar reporting structures. There are two main reasons for this likeness. First, consistency in the reporting structure allows a seasoned or novice investor to easily locate information when moving from one report to the next. Understanding where to look improves the usefulness and value of the information. For example, an investor could easily compare the cash flows of two companies by simply finding the section devoted to a company's financial statements, or the investor could study a company's lease commitments by reviewing the section titled "Notes to the Financial Statements."

Second, disclosure rules require specific types of information to be included in the year-end report. This assures investors and other users that companies will address similar topics, as well as provide supplemental disclosure where necessary. For example, all annual reports must include *management's discussion and analysis (MD&A) of operating results*. In addition, the SEC requires that certain topics be discussed in the MD&A section. Required disclosures are necessary for investors and others to review essential financial facts and to analyze the company, the focus of this book.

Figure 2.1 identifies the separate components of most corporate annual reports. The placement of these components within the annual report is not necessarily in the same order.

Figure 2.1 Annual Report Components

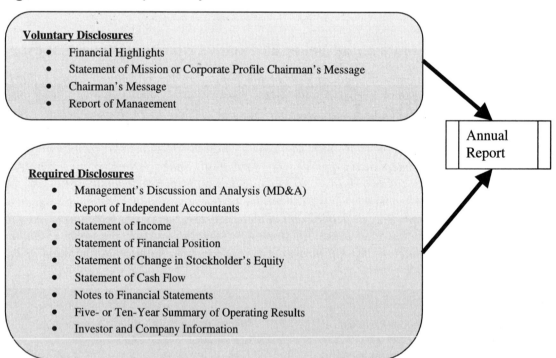

With no regulatory control, companies would report whatever and wherever. Soon all financial information comparability would be lost. This would create havoc for financial information users, the capital markets and ultimately eliminate all confidence in the annual report.

2.2 FINANCIAL HIGHLIGHTS

Annual reports generally open with a presentation of financial highlights or selected statistical data. This typically includes performance measures such as two-year comparative sales figures, net earnings reports, per-share information, and possibly some key financial ratios or other company statistics. Bar and pie charts also are used to visually enhance the company's financial information. A company's financial highlights represent a subset of more detailed information that follows in a later section of the annual report.

Financial highlights are presented early in the report in an effort by management to make the company look as good as possible. The message may or may not be a true reflection of the company. Therefore, do not rely on this information alone to make a decision about the company. View this information as a bias introductory summary for much more to come.

The Home Depot 2000 annual report includes the financial summary shown in Table 2.1. This highlight is designed to convey to the user that The Home Depot is a company that continues to grow. Notice the word *increase* is repeated three times across the heading. The percent and dollar amounts for each category increased for the period 1998 to 2000. Further analysis in subsequent chapters points to the financial resources available in support of The Home Depot growth strategy.

Table 2.1 **Financial Summary for The Home Depot, Inc. and Subsidiaries**

amounts in millions, except per share data	2000	Increase	1999	Increase	1998	Increase
Net sales	$45,738	19.0%	$38,434	27.2%	$30,219	25.1%
Gross profit	13,681	19.9%	11,411	32.6%	8,605	26.9%
Earnings before income taxes	4,217	10.9%	3,804	43.3%	2,654	32.6%
Net earnings	2,581	11.3%	2,320	43.7%	1,614	31.9%
Diluted earnings per share	1.10	10.0%	1.00	40.8%	0.71	29.1%

The first page of Enron's 2000 annual report is included in Figure 2.2. The charts convey a successful year with increasing revenues and income. Yet, subsequent to this annual report, Enron filed for bankruptcy protection. The message to the user of the annual report is to consume financial highlights with skepticism.

Figure 2.2 **Enron 2000 Annual Report Financial Highlights**

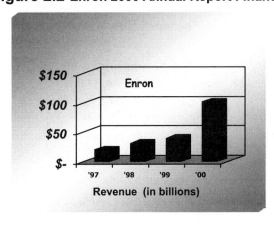
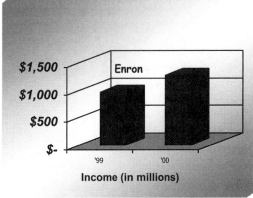

Often, a general discussion about products, services, and related information will follow introductory tables, charts, and graphs, and all of it will be designed to make the company look attractive. The Home Depot 2000 annual report does an excellent job at communicating the professional guidance it offers its customers. It also uses this section to recap stories about its employees and stores participating in community service programs. Unfortunately, some companies abuse this section and paint a picture of the company that is not representative of the current state. The Enron 2000 annual report is full of pictures and general promises about its wholesale energy, broadband, and transportation services that it simply could not deliver. Users should read this section of the annual report as an introduction to product and service offerings, past performance, and future market opportunities. However, they should also look to the numbers to support or refute the information found in this section.

2.3 MISSION STATEMENTS, CORPORATE PROFILES, AND STATEMENTS OF CORPORATE VALUES

Most companies include a mission statement in the opening pages of their annual report. A mission statement is viewed as a strategic communication tool and has become an important part of today's business reporting. It serves to publicly declare the purpose, goals, products, markets, and philosophical views of the organization.[1] It can also address an organization's commitment to its shareholders. A mission statement also provides the following important benefits:

1. *Communicates a sense of the firm's direction and purpose.* By reading a firm's mission statement, employees, stockholders, and customers should understand the direction of the firm, both short term and long term.
2. *Serves as a control mechanism to keep the firm on track.* A mission statement helps keep a firm from wandering into unrelated businesses and pursuing unrelated objectives. It serves as boundary lines for making decisions.
3. *Help in making a wide range of day-to-day decisions.* When new or non-routine decisions need to be made, a mission statement can be used as decision criteria, steering employees in the right direction.
4. *Inspires and motivates employees.* A mission statement helps workers realize the broader purpose of their efforts and encourage them to place that purpose ahead of their own self-interests.[2]

Some people confuse the words *mission* and *vision*. An organization's mission is what the organization is and its reason for existence, whereas vision is a forward-looking view of what the organization wants to become.[3]

Ben & Jerry's, Inc.'s (now owned by Anglo-Dutch conglomerate Unilever PLC) mission statement comprises three interrelated parts that help the user better formulate a basis for decision making. These are product, economic, and social (see Figure 2.3). Reading the mission

---

[1] Duane Ireland and Michael Hitt, "Mission Statements: Importance, Challenge, and Recommendations for Development," *Business Horizons*, (May/June 1992), pp. 34 - 42.

[2] Barbara Bartkus, Myron Glassman and Bruce McAfee, "Mission Statements: Are They Smoke or Mirrors?" *Business Horizons* 43, no. 6 (November 2000) pp. 23 - 28.

[3] Harrison and St. John, "Strategic Management of Organizations and Stakeholders."

statement tells the user that Ben & Jerry's is focused on providing the consumer with a quality product and generating wealth for its shareholders, all in an environment that meets the needs of the individual and community.

Figure 2.3 Ben & Jerry's Statement of Mission

Ben & Jerry's is dedicated to the creation & demonstration of a new corporate concept of linked prosperity. Our mission consists of three interrelated parts.

Product
To make, distribute and sell the finest quality all natural ice cream and related products in a wide variety of innovative flavors made from Vermont dairy products.

Economic
To operate the Company on a sound financial basis of profitable growth, increasing value for our shareholders, and creating career opportunities and financial rewards for our employees.

Social
To operate the Company in a way that actively recognizes the central role that business plays in the structure of society by initiating innovative ways to improve the quality of life of a broad community— local, national, and international. Underlying the mission of Ben & Jerry's is the determination to seek new & creative ways of addressing all three parts, while holding a deep respect for individuals inside and outside the Company and for the communities of which they are a part.

Some companies follow the financial highlights with a corporate profile rather than a statement of mission. An introductory corporate profile highlights the products it manufactures or the services it provides. Although the corporate profile is often brief, it introduces the organization to a first-time reader or unfamiliar investor. More significant details concerning the company's operations will follow in the president's message or MD&A section. Figure 2.4 shows The Home Depot's Corporate Profile from its 2000 annual report. The Home Depot corporate profile makes clear for the user that the company is in the retail home improvement business, with more than 1,100 stores.

Figure 2.4 The Home Depot Company's 2000 Corporate Profile

Founded in 1978, The Home Depot® is the world's largest home improvement retailer and the second largest retailer in the United States, with fiscal 2000 sales of $45.7 billion. At the close of fiscal 2000, The Home Depot operated 1,134 retail locations, including 1,029 Home Depot stores in the United States, 67 Home Depot stores in Canada and 7 Home Depot stores in South America. The Company also operated 26 EXPO Design Centers®, 4 Villager's® Hardware stores and 1 Home Depot Floor Store.[SM] In addition, the Company operated wholly owned subsidiaries Apex Supply Company, Georgia Lighting®, Maintenance Warehouse® and National Blinds and Wallpaper®. The Company employed approximately 227,000 associates at the end of fiscal 2000.

> The Company has been publicly held since 1981. The Home Depot trades on the New York Stock Exchange under the ticker symbol "HD" and is included in the Dow Jones Industrial Average and the Standard & Poor's 500 Index.

Other companies include a statement of corporate values in their annual report. Management uses this in much the same manner as a mission statement. It helps the reader understand the operating philosophy of the organization and corporate strategy. Figure 2.5 is Enron's statement of corporate values, taken from its 2000 annual report. As can be seen, corporate values on paper mean very little unless they are followed in practice.

Figure 2.5 Enron Corporation's Statement of Corporate Values

> Communication
> We have an obligation to communicate. Here, we take the time to talk with one another … and to listen. We believe that information is meant to move and that information moves people.
>
> Respect
> We treat others as we would like to be treated ourselves. We do not tolerate abusive or disrespectful treatment.
>
> Integrity
> We work with customers and prospects openly, honestly and sincerely. When we say we will do something, we will do it; when we say we cannot or will not do something, then we won't do it.
>
> Excellence
> We are satisfied with nothing less than the very best in everything we do. We will continue to raise the bar for everyone. The great fun here will be for all of us to discover just how good we can really be.

2.4 CHAIRMAN'S MESSAGE

The *chairman's message*, also referred to as the *letter to the shareholders*, follows the financial highlights and the company's statement of mission. This component of the report allows the chief executive to identify the company's strategy. A reader will learn about events that have unfolded throughout the year. Attention is often directed to revenue growth, capital improvements, dividend strategy, the impact of new accounting pronouncements, and new product information. Occasionally, new product information can make the chairman's message quite lengthy. Lucent Technologies' chairman's message in its 2000 annual report is 11 pages long, while The Walt Disney Company 2000 annual report includes an eight-page discussion. Tootsie-Roll Industries 1999 "message" is only one page long. Usually the length of the message will be influenced by the company's performance and its financial position. Keep in mind, however, that most chief executives attempt to make the company appear as good as possible.

As a user, always read the chairman's message with full knowledge that it is designed to communicate a robust and successful business. Sentences and phrases found in the 2000 Enron annual report message include:

- Enron has built unique and strong businesses. . .
- Enron is laser-focused on earnings per share, and we expect to continue strong earnings performance.
- Robust networks of strategic assets. . .
- Unparalleled liquidity and market-making. . .
- EnronOnline has enabled us to scale quickly, soundly and economically.

2.5 MANAGEMENT'S DISCUSSION AND ANALYSIS

Management's discussion and analysis of results of operations and financial condition is considered by many to be one of the most important components of the annual report. As a result, we have seen a significant increase in the length of this section. In fact, one study showed that the MD&A section increased from 7 pages in length to more than 12 pages over a recent 10-year period.[4]

The SEC requires management to discuss the company's past performance so that readers can gain insight into what management perceives the direction of the company to be. This is important to the user for two reasons. First, it makes explicit how successful leadership has been at achieving the corporate strategy and points to the company's future strategic focus. Second, the information forms a basis to critically consume measures that are the outcome of a comprehensive analysis. Chapter 7, the analysis chapter, uses The Home Depot's MD&A section to evaluate and interpret the most recent financial outcomes.

Specifically, the MD&A report should provide a meaningful analysis of the company's financial position and results of operations over the past three years. Included in the review management is expected to address three important areas. This includes capital resources, liquidity, and results of operations. Three of the SEC requirements regarding management disclosures are as follows:

1. *Capital resources.* Management must describe the company's significant commitments for capital expenditures as of the end of the latest fiscal period, and must indicate the general purpose of such commitments and the anticipated source of funds needed to fulfill such commitments. (Capital resources are debt and equity available for funding capital expenditures. Capital expenditures are the purchase of long-term assets, such as building and equipment.) Management must also describe any known material trends, favorable or unfavorable, in the company's capital resources. Indicate any expected material changes in the mix and give the relative cost of such resources. The discussion shall consider changes between equity, debt, and any off-balance-sheet financing arrangements.

2. *Liquidity.* Management must identify any known trends or any known demands, commitments, events, or uncertainties that will result in or that are reasonably likely to result in the company's liquidity increasing or decreasing in any material way. (Liquidity

---

[4] Ray Groves, "Financial Disclosure: When More Is Not Better," *Financial Executive* (May/June 1994).

is defined as the ability to pay short-term and long-term debt.) If a material deficiency is identified, management must indicate the course of action that the company has taken or proposes to take to remedy the deficiency. Also, management must identify and separately describe internal and external sources of liquidity, and briefly discuss any material unused sources of liquid assets.

For example, The Home Depot 2000 annual report MD&A section combines the disclosure regarding capital resources and liquidity. This section explains that much of The Home Depot growth will be funded by cash generated from its more than 1,100 existing stores. It also conveys that any shortage of needed funds can be mitigated by existing lines of credit. As a result, a user must closely monitor The Home Depot's ability to generate future cash flows from day-to-day operations. If the outcome of the analysis supports the availability of cash, then the user can agree with The Home Depot's growth strategy. However, if the signs are unclear, then the user is in position to critically question leadership's strategic focus.

3. *Results of operations.* Management must describe any unusual or infrequent events or transactions or any significant economic changes that materially affected the amount of reported income from continuing operations and, in each case, indicate the extent to which income was so affected. In addition, management must describe any other significant components of revenues or expenses that, in their judgment, should be described in order to understand the company's results of operations. For example, while The Home Depot 2000 annual report MD&A section recaps a three-year history of revenue and earnings growth. Management also indicates that operating expenses must be carefully managed as the company continues to grow and expand.

In addition, management must describe any known trends or uncertainties that have had or that management reasonably expects will have a material favorable or unfavorable impact on net sales or revenues or income from continuing operations. For example, information concerning acquisitions or divestitures is often discussed because this might affect all of these areas. Financial overviews are provided and generally include more specific information about operating segments within the organization. If management knows of events that will cause a material change in the relationship between costs and revenues (such as known future increases in costs of labor or materials or price increases or inventory adjustments), the change in the relationship shall be disclosed. You are likely to read about these issues in a section identified as the *forward-looking statement.*

The SEC regulation reads as follows: For the three most recent fiscal years of the company, or for those fiscal years in which the company has been engaged in business, whichever period is shortest, management must discuss the impact of inflation and changing prices on the company's net sales and revenues and on income from continuing operations.[5]

Like other sections of the annual report, the MD&A section should generally follow a consistent format. If a company deviates from this format, statement users should read the information with caution, as management might be attempting to conceal unfavorable information. As mentioned earlier, the SEC has recently released a report on its dissatisfaction with the type of information that is being included in the corporate annual report and more specifically the MD&A section. The proposed regulation, "Supplementary Financial Information," is intended to improve business reporting. This proposal, if passed, will require companies to enhance their disclosures in the MD&A section of the annual report.

---

[5] Regulation S-K, 17 CFR Sub-part 229.303, U.S. Securities and Exchange Commission.

At this point in reading the annual report you should have acquired a solid framework to evaluate and interpret the financial statements. Although potentially biased because they are prepared by management, the financial highlights, statement of mission, chairman's message, and other qualitative material tucked in the report should make clear the company's strategic focus. Next, the MD&A section should draw your attention to past performance and future opportunities. The advantage of reading this section is that the SEC regulates its content. The information points to leadership's successes and concerns in meeting it strategic targets and responses over a three-year time period. The user is now in position to critically evaluate the company's financial picture with knowledge of where the company has been and where it plans to go in the future. The essential question is: Does the company have the necessary resources to support its strategic initiatives?

2.6 REPORT OF MANAGEMENT

The *management report* or the *management letter* sometimes will follow the MD&A section. The purpose of this report is to highlight management's responsibility for what appears in the company's financial reports. This assumption of responsibility helps to clarify the role of management and the role of the independent accountants. The report is intended to help the user recognize that the contents of the annual report are the responsibility of management (Figure 2.6, in bold) and not the independent accountant. A company's financial information is audited only on a test basis, and because of this, an audit does not provide 100 percent assurance to the shareholders.

The management report also discloses that management has prepared the financial statements in accordance with generally accepted accounting principles, and within the report there are estimates that have some justifiable basis. Most importantly, however, is management's explanation of the internal control procedures used and their effectiveness. Generally, management states that the organization maintains an efficient internal control system, including an internal audit function that safeguards the enterprises assets. Most management reports close with a discussion of the interaction that occurs between the board of directors, the Internal Audit and Finance Committee, and the outside public accountants. These three groups ultimately work together to assure that the control systems are in place and are accomplishing their intended purpose.

Companies are not currently required to include a management report in the annual report. However, the SEC has considered making this a required disclosure, and if so would probably demand more information to be included in the report.

2.7 THE INDEPENDENT AUDITORS' REPORT

An outside accounting firm issues the independent auditors' report to the shareholders and board of directors of the client corporation. It must be signed and dated by the accounting firm that conducted the audit. And because there is no SEC requirement regarding placement, the audit report can be presented either before or after the company's financial statements. Regardless of its placement, however, the report provides important information and should be read before one interprets the financial statements. Any material reporting deficiencies would be disclosed in the report and should be taken into account before an analysis of the financial information is undertaken.

Most audit reports are divided into three paragraphs each addressing an important audit issue. The first paragraph is referred to as the *scope paragraph* and explains that the financial statements and the accompanying notes were audited by an outside accounting firm but that the reported information is the responsibility of management (Figure 2.7, in bold). The responsibility of the accounting firm is to express an opinion on the accuracy of the financial statements.

The second paragraph explains to the reader that the audit was performed in accordance with generally accepted auditing standards (GAAS). GAAS are established rules that must be followed when a firm conducts an audit. This helps to assure that the audit is performed in a responsible manner and can reasonably detect reporting inconsistencies.

The third paragraph is often noted as the *opinion* paragraph and, depending on the audit findings, can take several forms. First, and most common, is an "unqualified" or "clean" opinion. To the user this means that the audit found the company's financial results to be fairly presented under the rules of GAAP.

Figure 2.6 **Management's Responsibility for Financial Statements,**
The Home Depot Company

The financial statements presented in this Annual Report have been prepared with integrity and objectivity and are the **responsibility of the management** of The Home Depot, Inc. These financial statements have been prepared in **conformity with generally accepted accounting principles** and properly reflect certain estimates and judgments based upon the best available information.

The Company maintains a **system of internal accounting controls**, which is supported by an internal audit program and is designed to provide reasonable assurance, at an appropriate cost, that the Company's assets are safeguarded and transactions are properly recorded. This system is continually reviewed and modified in response to changing business conditions and operations and as a result of recommendations by the external and internal auditors. In addition, the Company has distributed to associates its policies for conducting business affairs in a lawful and ethical manner.

The financial statements of the Company have been audited by KPMG LLP, independent auditors. Their accompanying report is based upon an audit conducted in accordance with auditing standards generally accepted in the United States of America, including the related review of internal accounting controls and financial reporting matters. The Audit Committee of the Board of Directors, consisting solely of outside directors, meets quarterly with the independent auditors, the internal auditors, and representatives of management to discuss auditing and financial reporting matters.

The Audit Committee, acting on behalf of the stockholders, maintains an ongoing appraisal of the internal accounting controls, the activities of the outside auditors and internal auditors and the financial condition of the Company. Both the Company's independent auditors and the internal auditors have free access to the Audit Committee.

Dennis J. Carey, Executive Vice President and Chief Financial Officer
Carol Tome, Senior Vice President, Finance and Accounting

On occasion, the independent accounting firm will render a *qualified* opinion. To the user this means that the accounting firm is not in agreement with a specific accounting principle that was chosen by the company. This would be noted so that the statement user is aware of this limitation when conducting financial analysis. This limitation, however, does not have a material impact on the overall performance measure of the client company.

Independent accountants, on rare occasions, will issue an adverse opinion. This opinion highlights the fact that the auditor is not in agreement with a material component of the financial information. In this case, the limitation is so great that the auditor cannot offer even a qualified opinion and therefore concludes that the financial statements do not represent fairly the financial position of the company. Opinions of this nature are quite rare. While most opinions are unqualified, investors and other users of the financial information should exercise caution when the company's auditor presents an adverse opinion.

Figure 2.7 Independent Auditors' Report,
The Home Depot, Inc. and Subsidiaries

The Board of Directors and Stockholders

The Home Depot, Inc.:
We have audited the accompanying consolidated balance sheets of The Home Depot, Inc. and subsidiaries as of January 28, 2001, and January 30, 2000, and the related consolidated statements of earnings, stockholders' equity and comprehensive income, and cash flows for each of the years in the three-year period ended January 28, 2001. These consolidated financial statements are the **responsibility of the Company's management**. Our responsibility is to express an opinion on these consolidated financial statements based on our audits.

We conducted our audits in accordance with **auditing standards generally accepted in the United States of America**. Those standards require that we plan and perform the audit to obtain reasonable assurance about whether the financial statements are free of material misstatement. An audit includes examining, on a test basis, evidence supporting the amounts and disclosures in the financial statements. An audit also includes assessing the accounting principles used and significant estimates made by management, as well as evaluating the overall financial statement presentation. We believe that our audits provide a reasonable basis for our opinion.

In our opinion, the consolidated financial statements referred to above present fairly, in all material respects, the financial position of The Home Depot, Inc. and subsidiaries as of January 28, 2001, and January 30, 2000, and the results of their operations and their cash flows for each of the years in the three-year period ended January 28, 2001, in **conformity with accounting principles generally** accepted in the United States of America.

KPMG, LLP.
Atlanta, Georgia
February 19, 2001

As illustrated by the auditors' report in Figure 2.7, an unqualified, or "clean," opinion was rendered. Note that this does not suggest that the company's records are 100 percent accurate because an audit is performed using statistical sampling methodologies. Therefore, the auditor examines only a representative sample of accounts and business transactions (sometimes very few). It would be impossible and certainly cost-prohibitive to review all of the company's business transactions.

Sometimes management and the independent auditor disagree over certain accounting information. On occasion, the disagreement might be serious enough for the auditor to withdraw from the audit engagement. If this occurs, management is required to disclose this fact and the area of disagreement in the 10-K annual report filed with the SEC. According to Item 9 of the Home Depot Company 10-K "Changes in and Disagreements with Accountants on Accounting and Financial Disclosure," there were no material differences.

2.8 FINANCIAL STATEMENTS AND THE RELATED NOTES

A significant component of the annual report is devoted to a presentation of the company's financial statements, which normally includes a *consolidated statement of income,* a *consolidated balance sheet,* a *consolidated statement of cash flow,* and a *consolidated statement of change in stockholders' equity.* Extensive analysis is built from information reported in the respective reports. The purpose of each financial statement is addressed as follows:

1. *Statement of income.* Reports a company's financial performance over a period of time (may be one month, one quarter, or one year for example).
2. *Balance sheet.* Reports a company's financial position on a particular day.
3. *Statement of cash flows.* Reports a company's cash inflows and outflows over a period of time (may be one month, one quarter, or one year for example).
4. *Statement of change in stockholders' equity.* Reports changes to stockholders' equity accounts over a period of time (may be one month, one quarter, or one year for example).

Although the financial statements offer a significant amount of information, another section, *Notes to the Consolidated Financial Statements,* provides additional clarification and amplification of a company's performance for the user. This is the reason that beneath each financial statement is the caveat, "The accompanying notes should be read in conjunction with the financial statements." The notes section can include tables, schedules, and text disclosure to help enhance the meaning of the numbers that are presented in the financial statements.

Notes to the consolidated financial statements are included in the review by the independent accountant during the audit process. Each financial statement and their related notes will be thoroughly reviewed in Chapters 3 to 6.

2.9 FIVE- OR TEN-YEAR SUMMARY OF OPERATING RESULTS

The SEC requires a company to include a five-year summary of selected financial and non-financial information in the annual report. Summary information gives the investor and other users the opportunity to identify emerging trends and better understand where the company has been and where it is going, in one convenient location. Many analysts use this report to identify pending weaknesses or strengths. Often, companies extend the 5-year comparative to include 10 years of information.

Analysts and other users should exercise caution when they review these statistical summaries. This report is not covered by the auditor's opinion. In addition, management selects certain information included in this report. Information presented in the summary may be extensive for some companies and limited in others. The 5- or 10-year summary typically includes comparative sales and earnings information as well as measures of financial position such as total assets, working capital, total debt, and shareholders' equity. Occasionally, the report will include information on research and development costs or long-term capital expenditures. In addition, nonfinancial data is included in the summary. This information is not audited. As a result, most companies identify the summary information as unaudited.

Figure 2.8 provides useful information about The Home Depot. The Statement of earnings data section points to performance data, such as growth in net sales and in net income. This section shows the increase in whole dollars and percentage values. Whole dollars are useful in communicating the size of this business. Net sales in 2000 of $45,738 million are representational of a large business. The percentage increase measures let the user compare The Home Depot's increases to any business, large or small. Balance sheet data and financial ratios point to financial position. Here the user can see that The Home Depot has continually grown in Net property and equipment, yet maintained control over inventory, with turnover at approximately five times per year. This is a sign of a well-run business. The next section, "Store Data," points to an ever-increasing number of stores and the total square feet that leadership must manage. This tells the user that business growth is being accomplished by adding new stores. The last section, "Store Sales and Other Data," provides a detailed recap of business performance. Average store transactions for The Home Depot have grown slightly over time. The question is: What is management doing to increase this amount or increase the profit for each transaction?

To answer this and many other questions, the user needs a solid understanding of financial statements. Qualitative information spread throughout the early sections of the report gives a sense of company products, services, and future direction. The financial highlights and 5- to 10-year summary information point to the company's prior successes—and perhaps failures—in a general way. However, a clear understanding of financial statements and solid framework for financial analysis is required for making career, investment, and partnering decisions.

2.10 SHAREHOLDER INFORMATION

Annual reports close with a section devoted to investor and company information. Although this section is included at the back of the annual report, the placement should not diminish its importance. For example, this section includes stock information such as the company's trading symbol, listing exchange, number of common shareholders sold, and the stock transfer agent. Companies also discuss the upcoming annual meeting and invite all shareholders to attend the public event, as well as to meet company directors and officers. Financial statement users can also acquire copies of annual reports and SEC filings such as the form 10-K by contacting the corporate secretary that is identified in this section of the annual report (see Figure 2.9).

Figure 2.8 **The Home Depot—Five-Year Summary of Financial Information**
(Selected information, full summary found in the annual report)

5-Year Summary of Financial and Operating Results (unaudited)							
(amounts in millions, except where noted)							
	Compound Annual Growth Rate						
	5-Year	10-Year	2000	1999	1998	1997	1996 (1)
Statement of Earnings Data							
Net sales	24.2%	28.2%	$45,738	$38,434	$30,219	$24,156	$19,535
Net sales increase (%)	–	–	19.0	27.2	25.1	23.7	26.3
Net earnings (2)	28.7	31.8	2,581	2,320	1,614	1,224	938
Net earnings increase (%) (2)	–	–	11.3	43.7	31.9	30.5	28.2
Balance Sheet Data and Financial Ratios							
Net property and equipment	24.0	31.0	13,068	10,227	8,160	6,509	5,437
Inventory turnover	–	–	5.1x	5.4x	5.4x	5.4x	5.6x
Store Data (4)							
Number of stores	21.8%	22.8%	1134	930	761	624	512
Increase in square footage (%)	–	–	22.6	23.5	22.8	23.1	21.6
Store Sales and Other Data (4)							
Average sale per transaction ($)	3.1	3.7	48.65	47.87	45.05	43.63	42.09
Number of associates at year-end (actual)	23.0	26.6	227,300	201,400	156,700	124,400	98,100

[1] Fiscal years 1996 consisted of 53 weeks; all other fiscal years reported consisted of 52 weeks.

[2] Excludes the effect of a $104 million non-recurring charge in fiscal 1997.

[3] Diluted earnings per share for fiscal 1997, including a $104 million non-recurring charge, were $0.52.

[4] Excludes Apex Supply Company, Georgia Lighting, Maintenance Warehouse, and National Blinds and Wallpaper.

[5] Adjusted to reflect the first 52 weeks of the 53-week fiscal year in 1996

Figure 2.9 **Financial and Other Company Information**

A copy of the Company's Annual Report on Form 10-K for the fiscal year ended January 28, 2001, as filed with the Securities and Exchange Commission, will be mailed upon request to:

The Home Depot, Inc.
Investor Relations
2455 Paces Ferry Road, NW
Atlanta, GA 30339-4024
Telephone: 770-384-4388

In addition, financial reports, recent filings with the Securities and Exchange Commission (including Form 10-K), store locations, news releases, and other Company information are available on The Home Depot Web site.

For a copy of the 2000 Home Depot Corporate Social Responsibility Report, which also includes guidelines for applying for philanthropic grants, contact the Community Affairs Department at the Store Support Center, or access the Company's Web site.

Annual reports also identify the company's officers and board of directors. Officers generally include the CEO, CFO, company vice-presidents, and chief legal counsel. The board of directors comprises many current officers and a group of individuals outside the company. Internal stakeholders are essential as members of the board because they provide stability and an understanding of internal operations. External stakeholders provide a different perspective, often acquired from high-level positions held in other companies. Company shareholders appoint many of these board members. As a shareholder, you generally are granted one vote per share held. However, some of the director appointments are automatic and are tied to the positions they hold within the firm. Internal and external board members balance the bias of the many stakeholders of a business: shareholders, workforce, suppliers, customers, and the community.

The board of directors is often responsible for hiring, firing, supervising, advising, and compensating top managers within the firm. They also reserve the right to approve or reject major strategic initiatives such as mergers or acquisitions, or to initiate changes in the organization structure of the enterprise. Because of recent shareholder dissatisfaction, many director groups have been forced to become more active in the oversight of the enterprise. Companies such as General Motors, IBM, Time-Warner, American Express, and Westinghouse have experienced organizational changes due to board-of-directors shake-ups.

2.11 CONCLUDING REMARKS

The annual report contains a wealth of information. Financial highlights and nonfinancial information provide for the user a general view of where the company has been and where it is headed with its corporate strategy. The MD&A and financial statements provide quantitative and qualitative information for the user to critically evaluate prior performance and project future successes and concerns in respective to leadership's corporate strategy. Essential for the user is a firm grounding in financial statement analysis to refute, challenge and/or agree with leadership's strategic direction as a solid point of reference in business decision making.

Questions for Review

1. As stated in the chapter, annual reports must contain certain required disclosures. Suppose that you were a potential investor in the pharmaceuticals industry. Of what benefit to you are these required disclosures for deciding in which of the pharmaceutical companies to invest?

2. Why should the user of the information view the financial highlights section of an annual report with skepticism?

3. What is the primary difference between a company's mission and its vision? Why is this important?

4. Briefly summarize the SEC requirements for the information contained in the Management's Discussion and Analysis section of an annual report. Give one example of the importance of this information to a potential investor. A potential creditor.

5. Why is the information contained in the Management's Discussion and Analysis section of an annual report considered more credible than the information contained in the Chairman's Letter to the shareholders?

6. Who is primarily responsible for the financial statement information and related disclosures in an annual report? Why is this important?

7. Why is an independent audit of the financial statements necessary? Summarize briefly what the independent auditors are giving an opinion on.

8. Of what value to the user of financial information is the Five-Year Summary? What information is contained in this summary?

Internet Exercises

1. Visit the Web site of Krispy Kreme Doughnuts (http://www.krispykreme.com/.) Does Krispy Kreme have a mission or vision statement? If so, summarize briefly its content.

2. Pick two companies in the pharmaceuticals industry (e.g., Abbott Laboratories, Eli Lilly and Co., Merck and Co. or any SIC 2834) and visit their respective Web sites. Read the information contained in their respective Management's Discussion and Analysis sections and summarize similarities and differences in the information contained therein.

CHAPTER **3**

The Balance Sheet

Steve Ray is learning that the balance sheet is far more than a simple picture of Baker Electronic's financial position at a point in time. The balance sheet provides Steve a picture of what Baker owns (i.e., assets) and what it owes (i.e., liabilities) at a specific point in time. The stockholders' equity section of Baker Electronics measures the difference between assets and liabilities. Tucked within each section are the details necessary for rigorous financial analysis, such as inventory and payable balance information. Without this type of information, meaningful financial analysis is like batting in a dark stadium. An understanding of detailed information about cash, inventory, debt and more are necessary to determine whether Baker Electronics has the resources to support its strategic initiatives.

LEARNING OBJECTIVES

1. Discuss the primary purpose of the balance sheet.
2. Describe the relationship between the balance sheet and the accounting equation.
3. Identify two benefits associated with the balance sheet.
4. Discuss the limitations of the balance sheet.
5. Identify five users of balance sheet information.
6. Explain how a balance sheet is generally classified.
7. Discuss the meaning of assets, liabilities, and stockholders' equity.
8. Identify common elements found within the balance sheet.

This chapter concentrates on helping the reader understand the structure of the balance sheet and its related elements, also labeled the *statement of financial position.* Chapter 4 will focus on the statement of earnings, while Chapter 5 explores the statement of cash flows. Financial statements from The Home Depot 2000 annual report will be used to assist in our discussion of all financial statements. Open Home Depot's annual report to the balance sheet and follow along as each line item is discussed.

The consolidated balance sheet of The Home Depot accompanying this text reports the monetary values of the company's assets (resources), liabilities (claims against those resources), and stockholders' equity (residual ownership in the assets) at the close of the fiscal year. The word *consolidated* means the performance of several of The Home Depot businesses are combined in this financial report. The reports structure is based on the accounting equation where

$$\text{Assets} = \text{Liabilities} + \text{Shareholders' equity}$$

The purpose of the balance sheet is to provide a "snapshot" of The Home Depot's financial position at the close of its fiscal year. This is illustrated at the top of the balance sheet, where it identifies the financial statement, company name, and date of the report. The balance sheet for The Home Depot Company is dated January 28, 2001, and provides two years of comparative information, as required by the SEC.

As we review the report we can see that specific accounts (labeled financial statement elements) such as cash, receivables, building, equipment, accounts payable, and income taxes payable have dollar values assigned to them. These amounts represent the account's *carrying* or *book value* at January 28, 2001. Carrying values, in most cases, change constantly. Sales of lumber, millwork, tools, and so on occur, expenses like wages and income taxes are incurred, mortgage obligations are met, and cash is collected from customers or paid to vendors. This occurs because of the matching principle and the going-concern assumption.

For example, assume The Home Depot opens a new store and purchases 12 narrow-aisle forklift trucks for $40,000 each. The trucks represent assets that will benefit current and future years. Because of this long-term benefit, their cost is capitalized rather than expensed. Capitalization means that the equipment is recorded as an asset on the balance sheet. Each year the equipment's cost will be allocated to the income statement. This allocation of cost (depreciation expense) will cause the carrying values of the forklift trucks to decline. Eventually, the carrying value of the equipment can become quite low because depreciation expense reduces the original cost of an asset.

3.1 IMPORTANCE OF THE BALANCE SHEET

The user turns to the balance sheet for two pieces of information. The balance sheet provides information concerning a firm's *liquidity* and *solvency* on a particular day. These concepts are introduced in this chapter and fully developed in Chapter 7.

Liquidity analysis involves a comparison of a company's short-term assets and short-term liabilities. As mentioned earlier, the company is required to address liquidity issues in the management discussion and analysis (MD&A) section of the annual report. Liquidity measures provide an indication of a company's ability to meet its current maturing obligations, those obligations that must be satisfied in the next twelve months.

Liquidity concerns often involve creditors and potential creditors. Let's consider two questions asked by most bank loan officers: Does this company have the liquid resources (cash, cash equivalents, receivables, etc.) to pay back a twelve-month installment loan it recently applied for, and what is the liquidity position of a reputable competitor? To answer these questions we first place current assets and current liabilities into a ratio labeled the current ratio (current assets/current liabilities). Next we graph this information and compare across time. Companies with strong liquidity ratios, a high current asset to current liabilities index, have the financial means to meet this obligation. Weakness in this area can lead to loan default and ultimately business failure. Figure 3.1 shows that the current ratio of The Home Depot is slightly higher than that of Lowe's Companies. A loan officer would be satisfied that each company has the resources to satisfy its installment loans for the next 12 months. Enron, on the other hand, shows a very weak liquidity position. For every $1 in current assets it has $1 due in current liabilities. A loan officer in this case would question Enron's present level of liquidity. Analysts and others should have recognized this signal long before Enron's failure.

Figure 3.1 Liquidity Analysis

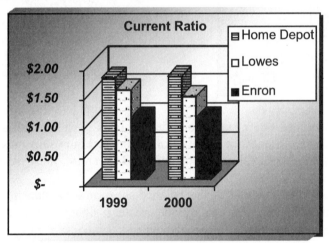

Measures of solvency refer to a company's ability to meet future principal and interest payments on its long-term debt. The greater the amount of debt (financial leverage), the greater the fixed cost (interest expense) associated with the debt. Many companies, over time, have shown an uncanny ability to manage this fixed cost. Success in this area can be advantageous to the shareholder. For instance, suppose The Home Depot raises $200 million through the sale of long-term bonds. Because the interest on the bonds is tax-deductible, the net cost of financing can be quite low. If The Home Depot Company can earn a higher rate of return on the investment of these funds than its after-tax cost of borrowing the funds, the company prospers. Ultimately, the position of the shareholder is improved by this strategy.

One measure of solvency involves a comparison of a company's total debt to total assets. As the proportion of total debt to total assets increases, so does the company's risk. This is true because most debt is interest bearing, which demands not only principal repayment but also interest payments. As interest costs rise, so does the pressure on the enterprise to generate more cash from its operations in a timely manner.

Comparing The Home Depot, Lowe's Companies, and Enron Corporation illustrates the insight offered by this ratio (see Figure 3.2). The Home Depot carries debt of approximately $0.30 for every $1 of assets and Lowe's carries approximately $0.50 for every $1 of assets. This means that Lowe's is more leveraged than The Home Depot but each company appears solvent. However, the amount of debt carried by Enron is questionably high. For every $1 of assets it holds, between $0.70 and $0.80 is financed with debt. Subsequent investigation shows that Enron failed to disclose further obligations. Much of its debt was hidden in the form of off-balance-sheet financing. The poor solvency and liquidity positions of Enron should have signaled that problems were on the horizon.

Figure 3.2 Solvency Analysis

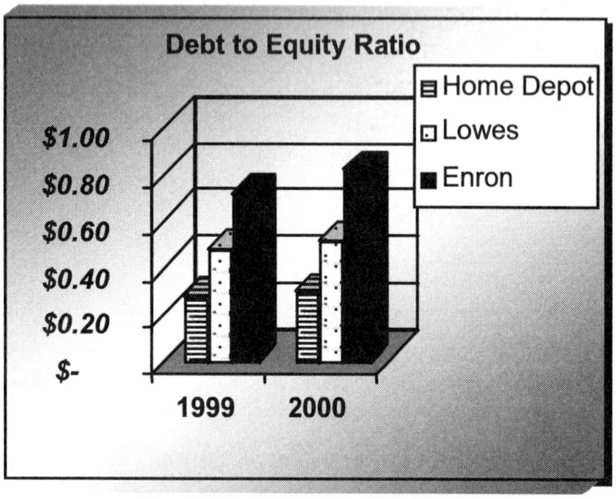

Always remember that the proportion of a company's total debt to total assets, as well as all other ratios, will vary from one industry to another. The information in Figure 3.2 must be considered with additional analysis to fully evaluate a company. The entire framework is constructed in Chapter 7.

Information from *two* financial statements, such as the balance sheet and the statement of income, can be analyzed as well. This type of review can provide greater insight into how well a company performed over the past year. For instance, a comparison of net income to total assets measures a company's return on assets (ROA), while a comparison of net income to shareholders' equity measures a company's return on equity (ROE). Both are useful measures for the company and for investors and analysts.

3.2 LIMITATIONS OF THE BALANCE SHEET

Although the balance sheet provides many important benefits to the reader, it does possess several shortcomings. First, account values within the balance sheet are not always measured according to the same rule. One example is the measurement of accounts receivable on the balance sheet. Accounts receivable are always reported at their net realizable value. Net realizable value is the amount the company believes it will ultimately collect from its customers. Essentially, the company understands that not all accounts receivable will be collected from its customers. This valuation approach offers a more conservative estimate of the asset's value. As of January 28, 2001, The Home Depot reports $835 million of "net" receivables at the close of its fiscal year. This number already includes the company's estimate of accounts receivable uncollectibility.

Another asset group, "furniture, fixtures, and equipment," is recorded on the basis of acquisition cost, also known as *historical cost*. The Home Depot, for example, has spent $2.877 billion over the years to acquire these assets. But with the passage of time and the subsequent depreciation recognition, the book value or carrying value of these assets no longer matches historical cost. As the balance sheet illustrates, there is a combined $2.164 billion of accumulated depreciation on all fixed assets including buildings, furniture, fixtures, and equipment. Further analysis of the related notes and supplemental SEC filings may identify the accumulated depreciation that specifically relates to each fixed asset group. Information users should note that depreciation expense is intended to capture the cost of using an asset. Although it reduces the carrying value of assets, it is not intended to reflect the fair-market value of assets.

Another fixed asset, land, is recorded at cost, but unlike buildings, furniture, fixtures, and equipment, land is not depreciated over time. This keeps the carrying value of land at cost until the company disposes of it. The logic behind this valuation approach is that the benefits associated with land do not decline with the passage of time, as would the benefits of furniture, equipment, buildings, and so on.

Some readers of financial information may ask the question: Do balance-sheet values approximate fair-market value? In some cases yes, but in many cases no. For fixed assets such as land and buildings, even though their market value may increase over time no adjustment is made to the assets book or carrying value. Upward adjustments to fixed assets are *not* made in practice, as this may lead to speculative values in the financial statements. Because there has been no arm's length transaction to establish the asset's market value, most valuations would be tied to market appraisals.

Fair-value accounting, or *mark-to-market*, is a valuation technique used in certain instances of financial reporting. Companies are required to use fair-value accounting when they invest in certain actively traded stocks or bonds of another enterprise. In these instances the investments are recorded at cost but adjusted to fair-market value as changes in market prices occur. A mark-to-market approach is allowed as long as the company's investment can be liquidated in an established market and the market price is identifiable. Investments such as these would be classified as short- or long-term in the balance sheet, as discussed in Section 3.4.

A question may be raised as to why fair-value accounting is used for a company's investment in stocks and bonds but not for its investment in building or equipment. The reason for this is the market mechanism that determines value. Stocks and bonds are traded in a highly efficient market and on a daily basis. The continuous trading makes current stock and bond prices very accurate. Equipment and buildings are not exchanged in a market of this kind. Without a current, clearly established price it would be difficult to support the valuation of fixed assets at their current exchange price.

Another limitation of the balance sheet (and related financial statements) is that certain values are based on management's best estimates. Estimates are used in accounting to provide for more effective reporting. For instance, the net realizable value of accounts receivable is determined by a percentage estimate of uncollectible accounts. Many companies prepare an aging schedule of their accounts receivable to help develop this estimate of bad debt expense. The rationale for estimating bad debt losses prior to their occurrence is to satisfy the matching principle of accounting. The matching of revenue and its related expense provides a better measure of performance for a given period.

Estimates in financial reporting also involve long-term, fixed assets. For example, rather than expense a fixed asset's acquisition cost, a company capitalizes it. The cost is then allocated to the income statement over an estimated useful life. This practice matches the revenues that the asset helps to generate with the cost or expense of generating the revenue. Estimating the lives of depreciable fixed assets directly impacts the allocation of depreciable cost to each reporting period. A shorter estimated life pushes a greater proportion of cost through the income statement, thus lowering reported income. A longer estimated life reduces the depreciation recognition and poses a lesser threat to the *bottom line* on a year-to-year basis.

Keep in mind that an estimated asset life should be appropriate. To expense an asset's cost over a shorter period of time yet have the asset contribute to the production of revenues beyond the period would create an imbalance or a mismatching of revenues and expenses. The SEC is investigating many companies for making arbitrary changes to the estimated lives of their fixed assets. To increase earnings, companies have extended the lives of assets, and to decrease earnings companies have shortened the lives of assets. This has led to what the SEC calls *abusive earnings management*. The SEC is proposing that companies better disclose changes to the estimated lives of long-term assets.

A final example of estimates in financial reporting involves *loss contingencies*. Loss contingencies are potential obligations that might arise from a past event. For example, suppose a company operates a refining operation within the city limits of Chicago. If the Environmental Protection Agency (EPA) concludes that years of refining operations have contaminated the soil beneath the plant with gasoline, diesel fuel, benzene, crude oil, and sulfuric acid, the company must develop a comprehensive soil-testing program and make sure the site is cleaned properly.

Loss contingencies of this nature involve a great degree of uncertainly. Typically, a situation such as this requires consultation between the company's attorneys, the EPA, and other environmental experts. Nonetheless, if a loss is considered probable and can be reasonably estimated, the financial statements should include an accrual for the loss contingency. This would require current period loss recognition (an expense) and the establishment of a liability for the future loss contingency. A disregard of the accounting for this event would overstate the company's performance in the current period, as well as overstate the company's equity position. In addition, the company would understate its impending obligations (liabilities). All loss contingencies are detailed in the notes to the financial statements. Figure 3.3 illustrates a statement made by the management of The Home Depot, found in the MD&A section of the annual report.

Figure 3.3 **Statement on Forward-Looking Information**

Certain written and oral statements made by The Home Depot, Inc. and subsidiaries (the "Company") or with the approval of an authorized executive officer of the Company may constitute "forward-looking statements" as defined under the Private Securities Litigation Reform Act of 1995. Words or phrases such as "should result," "are expected to," "we anticipate," "we estimate," "we project" or similar expressions are intended to identify forward-looking statements. These statements are subject to certain risks and uncertainties that could cause actual results to differ materially from the Company's historical experience and its present expectations or projections. These risks and uncertainties include, but are not limited to, unanticipated weather conditions; stability of costs and availability of sourcing channels; the ability to attract, train and retain highly - qualified associates; conditions affecting the availability, acquisition, development and ownership of real estate; general economic conditions; the impact of competition; and regulatory and litigation matters. Caution should be taken not to place undue reliance on any such forward-looking statements, since such statements speak only as of the date of the making of such statements. Additional information concerning these risks and uncertainties is contained in the Company's filings with the Securities and Exchange Commission, including the Company's Annual Report on Form 10-K.

These examples illustrate the many different ways estimates can be used in financial reporting. Obviously there are no guarantees that what a company estimates will become a reality. For this reason, many companies issue a statement of caution in the notes to their financial statements to alert the reader that estimates are a part of the normal reporting environment.

The following are some factors that could cause a company's actual results to differ materially from the expected results described in its forward-looking statements. This is taken from The Home Depot Form10-K report filed with the SEC:

- Adverse or unanticipated weather conditions, which might affect the company's overall level of sales and sales of particular lines of products, such as building materials, lumber, and lawn and garden supplies.
- Instability of costs and availability of sourcing channels, which might affect the prices that the company pays for certain commodity products, such as lumber and plywood, as well as the company's ability to improve its mix of merchandise. Our cost of sales is affected by our ability to maintain favorable arrangements and relationships with our suppliers. Our sources of supply may be affected by trade restrictions, tariffs, currency exchange rates, transport costs and capacity, and other factors affecting domestic and international markets.
- Our ability to attract, train and retain highly qualified associates to staff both existing and new stores.
- Conditions affecting the availability, acquisition, development, and ownership of real estate, including local zoning and land use issues, environmental regulations, and general conditions in the commercial real estate market.
- General economic conditions, which affect consumer confidence and home improvement and home-building spending, including interest rates, the overall level of economic activity, the availability of consumer credit and mortgage financing, and unemployment rates.
- The impact of competition, including competition for customers, locations and products, and in other important aspects of our business. Our primary competitors include chains of electrical, plumbing and building materials supply houses, lumber yards, home improvement stores and other local, regional or national hardware stores, as well as discount department stores and any other channel of distribution that offers products that we sell. Our business is highly competitive, and we may face new types of competitors as we enter new markets or lines of business.
- Changes in laws and regulations, including changes in accounting standards, tax statutes or regulations, environmental and land use regulations, and uncertainties of litigation.

3.3 USERS OF BALANCE SHEET INFORMATION

There are many internal and external users of financial information. One user is the company itself, which needs to monitor its current financial position as well as review changes in financial position from year to year. Decreased cash balances, receivable write-offs, increased debt, as well as reduced fixed asset carrying values may signal the need for increased management attention.

Investors are another group of financial statement users that demand balance sheet information. Company investors carry much more than a conventional interest in the success of the enterprise. They have committed personal financial resources to a company with no certainty of positive returns or recovery of investment. This user group is often referred to as the *residual owner* of the firm. They stand to gain the most if the company is successful but assume the greatest degree of risk if the company falters.

Other users of financial information would include lenders, investment analysts, the SEC, and the Internal Revenue Service (IRS). Each utilizes balance sheet information in different ways. Lenders are interested in a company's ability to generate cash flow from operations. Lenders are also concerned with the sustainability of net income levels over time because income is a predictor of future cash flows. Investment analysts and rating agencies, require a significant amount of detailed information, that which often is acquired through a company's SEC filings. These individuals or organizations are more concerned with disaggregated information rather than aggregated data. Their financial reviews are more comprehensive in nature than the traditional investors, in most cases. Finally, the IRS is a user of financial information but in a much different way. The IRS is not GAAP based; it requires economic transactions to be accounted for under IRS rules and regulations. This alternative accounting treatment often creates an imbalance between financial reported income and taxable income.

3.4 CLASSIFICATION OF THE BALANCE SHEET

Balance sheet accounts are generally classified to facilitate readability and analysis. The three major classifications include assets, liabilities, and shareholders' equity. As can be seen in The Home Depot balance sheet, assets and liabilities are divided into two categories: current and noncurrent. The purpose of this separation is to help the reader recognize the difference between assets and liabilities that will be consumed or satisfied in the upcoming year (current assets) and assets and liabilities that will influence the organizations operations for many years to come (noncurrent).

Equity is divided according to a different rule. Shareholders' equity is usually separated according to how it is developed. Is the equity generated from shareholder contributions or is it generated by the firm's operations? When the equity develops from investor contributions it is called *contributed capital*. When it emerges from the company's day-to-day operations, it is called *earned capital* and is combined over time in an account called *retained earnings*.

The Home Depot divides its assets, liabilities and owners' equity into the following subclassifications:

Assets
    Current assets
    Property and equipment (at cost)
    Long-term investments
    Notes receivable
    Intangible assets, including costs in excess of fair value of net assets acquired
Liabilities
    Current liabilities
    Long-term debt (excluding current installments)
    Other long-term liabilities
    Deferred income taxes
Minority Interest
Stockholders' Equity

3.5 ELEMENTS OF THE BALANCE SHEET

These subclassifications support what might be viewed as an aggregate approach to balance sheet analysis. For example, the current ratio requires the sum of current assets and the sum of current liabilities to enable its computation. Although aggregated financial information of this nature is a necessity, the balance sheet often includes multiple elements within a group. The understanding of each element enhances one's understanding of the subclassification, its associated group, and ratios in which it is a component.

3.5.1 Current Assets

Specific current assets for The Home Depot include cash, short-term investments, accounts receivables, merchandise inventories, and other current assets. They represent a company's resources that will ordinarily be consumed during the upcoming fiscal year. As shown, current assets are essential when evaluating a company's liquidity position.

Cash and Cash Equivalents
Cash in the balance sheet, and for the purpose of reporting cash in the statement of cash flows, includes cash on hand, cash in savings and checking accounts, and cash invested in highly liquid short-term instruments with original maturities of three months or less. Highly liquid instruments include high-grade commercial paper, money market funds, or U.S. government agency securities, each with original maturities of 90 days or less. Investments in these instruments are referred to as *cash equivalents* and are combined with cash in The Home Depot balance sheet. Companies take advantage of cash equivalents by exchanging excess cash for highly liquid investments. This maintains the company's liquid position and converts cash into an earning asset. At the close of fiscal year 2000 The Home Depot reports $167 million in cash.

Short-term Investments including Current Maturities of Long-term Investments
The balance sheet account *short-term investments* includes a company's investment in the stocks and bonds *of other companies*. These are investment opportunities that appeal to a company for the short-term or investments that were once classified as long-term but will mature in the upcoming year. Although it might appear that stock and bond investments can be held for an extended period of time, what controls this classification is *management's intent.*

Specific accounting rules require management to classify many investments into one of three groups: (1) trading, (2) available for sale (AFS), or (3) held to maturity (HTM). If an investment is classified as trading, it is management's intent to hold the investment for a very short period (generally a few weeks to a few months). These investments are shown on the balance sheet at their current market value with all unrealized gains and losses (based on changes in market value) reported in the income statement. Market value can be determined at the end of the reporting period by the closing price of a share of stock or bond on one of the major exchanges. If an investment is classified as available for sale, it is management's intent to hold the investment for more than a few weeks or months. *Available for sale* investments can be classified as a current asset or as a long-term investment in the balance sheet. AFS investments, similar to trading investments, are again adjusted to their fair-market values. However, changes in market values are reported in stockholders' equity (as a part of other comprehensive income, defined shortly), not in the income statement. The logic that underlies this accounting treatment is tied closely to the holding period of the investment. Since management intends to hold the investment for a longer period of time, all changes in market values can be reported in equity until the investment is liquidated. This way gains and losses can offset each other over time and in the end can reduce reported earnings volatility.

According to note 1, The Home Depot investments consist primarily of high-grade debt securities (generally bonds of another company) and are classified as available for sale. Therefore, any changes in market value would be reported in stockholders' equity as a part of *accumulated other comprehensive income.*

Long-term investments classified as held-to-maturity are debt investments that management intends to hold until they mature. An example of this would be an investment by The Home Depot in IBM bonds. This investment is generally carried at cost with no adjustment being made for changes in market value. Since management intends to hold the investment until the bonds mature, future changes in market value over the investment's holding period are irrelevant. Should management change its investment strategy at some point forward, certain investments might need to be reclassified and would then be influenced by other accounting rules.

Companies that actively seek to acquire additional shares of ownership in a particular company may, over time, acquire enough voting shares to gain significant influence over that company. When this occurs, the investing company can influence dividend payouts and other management decisions of the company. When this occurs, regulatory rules require a change in the accounting for the investment.

The investor company must employ the *equity method* of accounting, a departure from cost or fair-value accounting. The equity method requires the investor company to periodically adjust the carrying value of the investment based on its percent ownership of the investee company's profits and losses, as well as the investee company's dividend distributions. For example, the recognition of a percentage ownership in a company's profits increases the carrying value of the investment (and vice versa for a company's losses). Dividend distributions by the investee company decrease the carrying value of the investment for the investor company because dividends reduce investee equity.

The logic behind the equity method of accounting is in the name. If you own 40 percent of a company's common shares, then you essentially own 40 percent of the company or, conversely, have a 40 percent equity interest in the net assets of that company. As the investee company's position changes over time, so should the carrying value of the investment by the investor company. Generally, the threshold for the application of the equity method of accounting is 20 to 50 percent of a company's voting shares.

When a company's investment increases beyond the 50 percent threshold, the investor company is required to account for the investment under consolidation rules. Here, two or more companies' performances are merged and reported as one. They are still separate legal entities, but they are accounted for as if they were one.

Accounts Receivables, Net

Current assets, in addition to cash and short-term investments, will generally include amounts due from other companies or individuals. These amounts are identified as accounts receivable in the balance sheet and correspond to the sale of merchandise or services on credit. The granting of credit is a business decision made by the company to enhance sales revenue. Without this purchase alternative, many individuals or firms would shop elsewhere.

As the balance sheet illustrates, The Home Depot has $835 million due from its customers at the close of fiscal year 2000. Customers would include any business or individual that is purchasing goods or services using The Home Depot credit. Although this amount might appear substantial, most purchases of merchandise or services at The Home Depot Company are typically made by cash or by using bank credit cards. In either case, The Home Depot is receiving immediate payment for these goods and services and can utilize the funds for current operations or longer term, capital projects.

The Home Depot reports accounts receivable at its net realizable value. Net realizable value represents the amount of cash that it expects to collect from customers paying their receivable balance. The difference between gross accounts receivable and the net realizable value is identified as a bad debt expense on the income statement. The benefit of reporting net realizable value is that users can rely on this information to represent the approximate cash collections of receivables.

Merchandise Inventories

A company's inventory of goods is most likely the largest component of current assets but also the most illiquid. Inventories can be acquired from other manufacturers and then resold, as in the case of The Home Depot, or inventory can be manufactured and sold by a single company. When they are manufactured and sold by the same company the balance sheet may report three inventory accounts: raw materials, work in progress, and finished goods inventory. General Motors Corporation is an example of a company that would utilize three inventory accounts in its accounting system. Obviously, it can have an automobile at any stage of completion, from the raw material to the work in progress, to the finished good that remains unsold. As in the case of The Home Depot, the balance sheet simply reports $6.556 billion of merchandise inventories.

The 5- to 10-year summary typically provides the necessary data for analysis of significant balance sheet items. Figure 3.4 compares the 5-year compound annual growth rate in store square footage, number of stores and inventory for The Home Depot, Lowe's, and Kmart. The growth in inventory for The Home Depot and Lowe's can be explained by the growth rate in store square footage and number of stores. For Kmart, however, the data points show a very small negative growth in store square footage and number of stores, yet a slight increase in inventory. This is certainly a sign that the company is not growing and a signal for the user to inquire about leadership's strategic plans. The message to the user is that graphs and chats can be helpful tools in evaluating specific balance sheet items, and linking this information to non-financial measures drawn from the 5- to 10-year financial summary.

Figure 3.4 Inventory Analysis

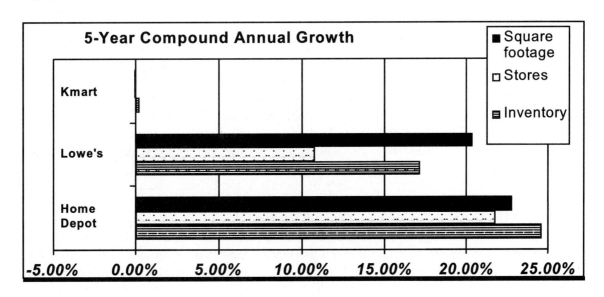

From a reporting perspective, merchandise inventories must be stated at the lower-of-cost or market (LCM). This approach requires companies to restate the value of their inventories when a permanent decline in the market value of specific inventory holdings has taken place. For this reason, companies must periodically review the carrying value of their inventory and recognize any losses on inventory write-downs in the period in which the decline takes place. The LCM is tied very closely to the conservatism principle in accounting, discussed in Appendix B. Inventory write-downs are common in the technology area as new technologies emerge. For example, a company could acquire digital cameras at a cost of $700 but a breakthrough in the industry might make the camera unmarketable even at the company's acquisition cost. If this occurs a company would be required to reduce the inventory value on the books and recognize a loss on inventory carrying value for the period.

Another somewhat unique accounting convention allows corporations great flexibility when they determine the value of their inventory at the close of the reporting period. For this reason, financial statement users must be knowledgeable of various inventory valuation approaches. For example, most companies utilize some type of cost-flow assumption when valuing inventory. Examples of cost-flow assumptions include first-in, first-out (FIFO), last-in, first-out (LIFO), and average cost. To illustrate, let's consider a simple example of goods purchased and goods sold.

Example: Assume The Home Depot buys a specific type of shovel three times a year from the same manufacturer. The first purchase of 30,000 shovels cost the Home Depot Company $11 each. The second purchase of 50,000 shovels cost $12 each, and the final purchase of 20,000 shovels cost $13 each. This suggests that The Home Depot had 100,000 shovels available to sell throughout the year and a total cost of $1,190,000 (30,000 x $11, 50,000 x $12, and 20,000 x $13).

If The Home Depot sells 80,000 shovels during the year, what value would it report in the income statement as cost of goods sold (COGS), and what value would it report in the balance sheet as merchandise inventory at the close of the year? *Note*: 20,000 shovels remain at year-end, but what is their value?

Some companies might use a specific identification approach and use the price paid for each remaining unit as the determining factor to establish value. Although this valuation approach seems quite logical at first, a system of this nature can be very expensive for a company to operate. Therefore, most companies prefer to use a product's cost flow as a means to valuation rather than physical flow. What this means is that a company views inventory as layers of cost that fluctuate over time. As each inventory unit is sold, even though the specific unit might have an $11, $12, or $13 cost (remember, the same model of shovel was purchased at three different prices), individual unit cost is not relevant for valuation.

Let's now consider The Home Depot example and assume it chooses a FIFO cost flow. Its cost of shovels sold would be reported at $930,000 (30,000 shovels at $11 plus 50,000 shovels at $12). In this instance, the earlier costs incurred flow through the income statement, while a more current replacement cost is reported in the balance sheet. Thus, having $1,190,000 of shovels available to sell would leave the inventory of shovels in the balance sheet reported at $260,000 (20,000 units at $13, or $1,190,000 - $930,000).

If The Home Depot chooses a LIFO cost flow rather than FIFO, cost of goods sold would be reported at $970,000 (20,000 at $13, 50,000 at $12, plus 10,000 at $11). In this instance, the more recent costs of shovels flow through the income statement, with the earlier shovel costs reported in the balance sheet. Having $1,190,000 of inventory available to sell would leave inventory in the balance sheet reported at $220,000 (20,000 units at $11). In other words, the remaining 20,000 units of cost would come from the first purchase of the year.

If The Home Depot used an "average" cost approach the balance sheet would report merchandise inventory at $238,000 (20,000 units x $11.90 per unit average cost). Average cost is calculated by dividing the total cost of goods available to sell by the number of units available to sell. According to the example, cost of goods available to sell is $1,190,000 and would be divided by 100,000 units, or shovels available to sell. The average cost method is simpler to use than FIFO or LIFO and is said to be a compromise between the two cost-flow assumptions. Table 3.1 illustrates the difference in reported before-tax income under the three approaches to inventory valuation.

Table 3.1 Differences in Reported Income under Three Cost-flow Assumptions

	FIFO Flow	LIFO Flow	Average Cost
Net Sales (assuming a $14 selling price)	$1,400,000	$1,400,000	$1,400,000
COGS	930,000	970,000	952,000
Gross Profit	$ 470,000	$ 430,000	$ 448,000

This example illustrates how particular layers of inventory cost leave the balance sheet and pass through the income statement as part of COGS, while other layers of cost remain and constitute end-of-year inventory. Determining what layers of cost leave the balance sheet and what layers remain is tied directly to the cost-flow approach chosen by a company's management. Cost-flow assumptions must be disclosed in the notes to the financial statements to help users understand the resulting differences in reported income when comparing multiple companies. Differences in net income can amount to millions or billions of dollars, depending on a company's chosen method of inventory valuation. In practice, many companies choose the LIFO approach because during periods of increasing prices the higher costs transfer to the income statement, thus creating lower reported profits. This reduces a companies tax obligation to the Internal Revenue Service.

3.5.2 Property and Equipment (at Cost)

Generally the most significant noncurrent asset in terms of value is a company's investment in property and equipment. These are the assets that companies commit millions of dollars to and when purchased are often referred to in the business press as a company's *capital expenditure*. Capital expenditures represent a company expenditure that will provide benefits over more than one period. The Home Depot 2000 balance sheet reports accumulated capital expenditures of $15.232 billion. This value represents the historical acquisition cost of many investments—not necessarily made in the most recent year but over several years and possibly decades.

When we consider The Home Depot balance sheet, we see that the property and equipment classification is comprised of land, buildings, furniture, fixtures, and equipment, as well as leasehold improvements, construction in progress, and capital leases. Most of the cost reported here will be allocated to future periods using some chosen method of depreciation or amortization.

A growth business will typically show a continued pattern of investing in property and equipment. Figure 3.5 compares the 5-year compound annual growth rate of property and equipment for The Home Depot and Lowe's. Both companies project a corporate growth strategy in the qualitative sections of the annual report and Figure 3.5 provides evidence that what they talk about is actually occurring. Interestingly, for each company property and equipment are growing at similar rates. Yet, The Home Depot is growing the number of stores at a much faster rate then Lowe's. This may signal to the user that Lowe's is either selectively entering markets where The Home Depot does not have a presence or it is being selective in the markets it wants to compete with The Home Depot, or both. Further inquiry would be necessary to answer this question.

Figure 3.5 Property and Equipment

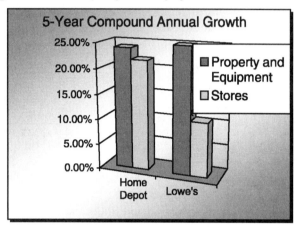

Land investment represents the only asset within the property and equipment group that will not be depreciated in current and future periods. Land is considered an asset that retains economic value as well as productive value. Therefore it does not need to be expensed over time. To date, The Home Depot balance sheet reports $2.164 billion in accumulated depreciation and amortization. The $13.068 billion that remains constitutes the net carrying value of the asset group: property and equipment.

Land
The cost of land includes all expenditures that relate to its acquisition and preparation for use. This amount typically includes purchase price, attorney fees, real estate costs, document filing fees, and so on. Special assessments levied by a government authority for sidewalks and streetlights or impact fees will also be included in the capitalized cost of land as well as general preparation costs such as grading, soil removal, drainage, and demolition of existing buildings.

Buildings
The cost of buildings can be determined in a number of ways. For example, let's say The Home Depot purchases a building previously owned by a competitor. The purchase would generally include both the land and building. If this occurs The Home Depot must allocate part of the purchase price to land and the remainder to the building. The allocation of cost is essential because land represents a nondepreciable asset while the cost of the building is depreciable. Once acquired, the building may need some additional expenditure to make the building ready for its intended use. These are often referred to as make-ready costs and are included in the cost of the building.

In many instances, The Home Depot constructs a new building. The determination of a new building's cost is simpler than that of a group purchase, as in the previous example. Here costs are more easily traceable to the asset. Contractor costs, architects' fees, building permit costs, and excavation costs are examples of costs associated with new construction.

Furniture, Fixtures, and Equipment

This category of noncurrent assets constitutes approximately 20 percent of The Home Depot's investment in property and equipment. Obviously a company that maintains more than 1,100 stores with an indoor lumberyard and warehouse merchandise displays must invest heavily in furniture, fixtures, and equipment. Narrow aisle forklift trucks, rental vehicles, customer shopping carts and flatbeds, and movable ladder systems are examples of The Home Depot's investment in equipment.

Probably the most significant investment in fixtures by The Home Depot is evident as customers walk between the product aisles. The heavy-gauge, steel storage systems throughout the store constitute an enormous investment in fixtures. This racking system not only has to be strong, but much of it has to be designed to be safe for consumers. For example, a steel shovel that can drop down and injure someone is set within a steel retaining system to prevent such an occurrence. Specially designed components of this nature are expensive to acquire.

Furniture, by contrast, would include The Home Depot's investment in checkout counters, desks, chairs, and so on that are needed throughout the store, as well as furniture necessary to support its administrative headquarters.

Since assets within the furniture, fixtures, and equipment category have varying useful lives, they must be depreciated individually. All companies maintain separate records of these assets for depreciation purposes but often combine these values when reporting to the public.

Leasehold Improvements

A lease is a contract between two or more individuals that authorizes the use of a specific asset (a building, for example) for an identified period of time. If a company needs to modify the leased asset for any reason, the cost of the modification is termed *leasehold improvements.* Leasehold improvements have a determinable period of benefit. Therefore, they are written off over the term of the lease or the life of the improvement whichever is shorter. The write-off of leasehold improvements is termed *amortization* rather than depreciation. Amortization, similar to depreciation, is a method of cost allocation. Generally leasehold improvements are viewed as intangible assets.

Construction in Progress

During any given year The Home Depot will have several, if not more, new facilities under construction. Therefore, throughout the year, The Home Depot is required to make periodic progress payments to their general contractors. When the books are closed at the end of the year much of their new construction will be at varying stages of completion. If this occurs, The Home Depot must report an asset under construction in its balance sheet. At some future time the costs associated with construction in progress will be transferred to the building account.

Capital Leases

The leasing of assets is common to most business organizations. One study conducted by the American Institute of Certified Public Accountants found that more than 90 percent of surveyed companies use one form of leasing or another.[1] Most lease agreements are classified into two general categories: operating leases and capital leases. On the one hand,

---

[1] Accounting Trends and Techniques, 1993, (New York: AICPA, 1993), Table 2-28.

operating leases are often viewed as temporary rentals, with rent expense being reported in the income statement of the company needing the asset. This company renting is referred to as the *lessee*. Operating leases can be short-term relative to the total life of the asset being rented. In addition, the rentals over the lease period do not provide a significant recovery of the asset's value over the term of the lease for the company providing the asset. Regardless of this fact, minimum lease payments under operating lease agreements often represent a substantial fixed charge awaiting the lessee.

A capital lease, on the other hand, is generally long-term. It requires rentals that are significant and approximate the value (excluding future interest) of the asset being rented. When this type of agreement is executed, the lessee must view the leased asset as if it were purchased using a long-term financing arrangement. The company that owns the asset is willing to receive installment payments over the lease term, and in this case, provides the financing. Keep in mind that there is not a transfer of title to the lessee. The transaction is simply accounted for as if it was a capital asset acquisition.

The rationale for this accounting treatment is to prevent companies from not reporting the liability that parallels a lease agreement of this nature. Since the lease agreement emulates a purchase with long-term financing, companies are required to account for them in a manner similar to a purchase. Therefore, leases of this nature require balance sheet recognition of a capitalized leased asset and the associated long-term liability.

According to its balance sheet, The Home Depot has capitalized leases that total $261 million. Since the leases are reported as assets, they will be associated with a related liability as well. Capital lease obligations are reported in both the current and long-term liability sections of the balance sheet.

As the leased assets are used in The Home Depot Company's operations, they will decline in usefulness similar to a purchased asset. Therefore, capitalized leased assets are depreciated as well. In most instances, assets of this nature are written off over the lease term. Upon the termination of the lease agreement, the leased asset should be fully depreciated and the lease obligation fulfilled by the lessee. At this point, the asset simply transfers back to the lessor, or is sold to the lessee at a bargain purchase price.

3.5.3 Long-term Investments

Long-term investments, discussed along with their short-term counterpart, are recorded when a company invests in another company's debt or equity. If management intends to hold these investments beyond one year, these investments must be categorized under the heading *long-term investments*. Occasionally management reclassifies long-term investments as market conditions change from one period to the next.

Long-term *stock investments* can be accounted for under the (1) cost, (2) fair value, (3) equity, or (4) consolidation approach. A careful review of the investments footnote (following the financial statements) may identify the types of investments and their related valuation. On occasion, if the reported investment is minimal, the note will provide little assistance.

According to the footnote, The Home Depot classifies its debt investments as available for sale (AFS) and accounts for them at their current market price. AFS investments are classified as short, or long-term investments, depending on management's intent. In either case, changes in market value are recognized in stockholders' equity as *unrealized gain or loss on AFS securities*. Upon careful review we find no mention of gain or loss under other comprehensive income. This suggests that no material change in the market value of the AFS securities has taken place.

Notes Receivable

A note receivable is a written promise to pay a specific amount or amounts at some point forward. Most notes receivable are loans but can result from a conventional sales arrangement that allows for extended terms. Occasionally, accounts receivable can be converted to a note receivable to extend the original terms of the agreement, generate a rate of return for the holder of the note, and strengthen legally the agreement between the parties. The Home Depot reports $77 million in notes receivable at the close of fiscal year 2000.

3.5.4 Intangible Assets, Including Costs in Excess of Fair Value of Net Assets Acquired

Previous classifications included assets that were generally tangible in nature. Intangible assets, however, generally lack physical substance and possess a greater degree of uncertainty in regard to future benefits than do tangible assets. They represent rights, privileges, and competitive advantages, backed by a legal agreement. Nonetheless, intangible assets, when properly created or acquired, can enhance the profitability of the enterprise for years to come. Once recorded, these assets operate no differently than tangible assets such as property, buildings, equipment, or fixtures. Their costs are capitalized and generally allocated to future periods through a method known as *amortization.* Amortization of intangible assets and depreciation of fixed assets both represent cost allocation processes that satisfy the matching principle. Examples of intangible assets include patents, copyrights, trademarks, organizational costs, and goodwill:

- *Patents* grant to the organization the exclusive right to manufacture, sell, or control a product or process for a specific period of time.
- *Copyrights* give the owner the right to reproduce and sell a published work or artistic creation.
- *Trademarks* are rights that relate to brand or trade names.
- *Organizational costs* include all costs incurred in the formation of the enterprise and would include attorney and accounting fees, federal and state filing costs, underwriting costs, and so on. They are regarded as expenditures that will benefit the organization over its life. These costs are capitalized and generally written off over a period of 5 to 10 years (5-year write-off period for taxable entities).
- *Goodwill* is recognized when one company acquires another company and pays more than the value of its net identifiable assets (assets less liabilities). It is often said that goodwill is the most intangible of the intangible assets group.

The Home Depot reports goodwill (cost in excess of the fair value of net assets acquired) at $314 million at the close of fiscal year 2000. Goodwill can only result from the purchase of another company and represents the expected value of better-than-normal future operating performance. It is measured as the difference between the purchase price of an acquired firm and the fair value of its identifiable net assets.

Goodwill has traditionally been written off over a period not to exceed 40 years. This write-off can place a significant drag on earnings for an extended period of time.[2] A recent change in accounting for goodwill by the Financial Accounting Standards Board (FASB) requires companies to no longer write off newly acquired goodwill. The FASB believes that companies should write down goodwill only when its value appears to be permanently impaired. The Board's rationale is

---

[2] As an example, AOL purchased Time Warner in January 2001 for $147 billion. The purchase took place when Time Warner net assets amounted to $51 billion therefore the remaining $96 billion was classified as goodwill. The subsequent amortization of goodwill (an expense) for AOL amounts to $1.5 billion per quarter.

that the synergistic benefits derived through business combinations often have indefinite lives. To arbitrarily write down goodwill does not follow the matching principle. In a sense, the FASB is suggesting that goodwill is similar to land in that it need not be written off unless its value becomes impaired.

3.5.5 Current Liabilities

Liabilities and stockholders' equity support a company's investment in assets. Liabilities must be recognized on the date the liability has been incurred. Liabilities, much like assets, can be classified according to when they will be satisfied. Current or short-term liabilities are obligations that will be satisfied in the upcoming year; noncurrent liabilities will be settled at some point beyond the current period. The Home Depot balance sheet reports a number of current liabilities:

- Accounts payable
- Accrued salaries payable and related expenses
- Sales taxes payable
- Other accrued expenses
- Income taxes payable
- Current installments of long-term debt

A pie chart can be used to quickly identify large liabilities. Figure 3.6 clearly shows that accounts payable is 45 percent and other accrued expenses are 32 percent of total current liabilities. Graphing this information over time, as demonstrated with inventory, will point to respective growth, stability or decline in these areas.

Accounts Payable
Accounts payable, also known as trade accounts payable, represent amounts owed to other companies as a result of goods, services, materials, supplies, etc. acquired throughout the year. Almost 50 percent of The Home Depot's current liabilities, or $1.976 billion, is tied to accounts payable. Obviously, to support the operation of more than 1,100 stores, The Home Depot must continually purchase significant quantities of goods from product supply houses. Conventional payment terms might require satisfaction of these obligations within 30 to 60 days of the invoice date depending on The Home Depot's relationship with the vendor.

Figure 3.6 Analysis of Current Liabilities

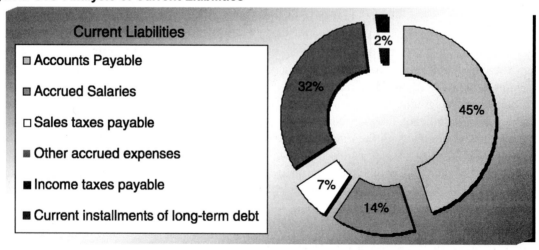

Accrued Salaries and Related Expenses

The recognition of accrued salaries and related expenses results from the application of accrual basis accounting. Accrual accounting requires revenues to be recognized when earned and expenses when incurred. The actual receipt of or payment with cash is not essential to the recognition of revenues and expenses in the accounting records. The key issue is whether product sales have occurred and what costs or expenses relate to the sale. Salaries are accrued because they are an expense that relates to the generation of revenue in the current period.

When an accrual takes place it is often related to a transaction that does not coincide with the close of the fiscal year or the exact amount is not yet known (in the case of a contingent liability). For example, The Home Depot may distribute compensation to a certain group of employees on a weekly basis and others twice a month, on the 10th and 25th. Because the distribution of wage does not cover services provided by employees through the close of the fiscal year an accrued liability for wages earned between the last payment date and the end of the year must be reported in the balance sheet. The accrued liability for salaries and other related expenses reported by The Home Depot amounts to $627 million. This amount would also include payroll taxes that the company is responsible for and would include FICA, FUTA, and SUTA payroll taxes. This amount was computed at the close of the business year and recorded via a year-end adjusting entry.

Sales Taxes Payable

State and federal mandates require corporations to collect sales tax when sales of tangible personal property are executed. Upon receipt from its customers, corporations have a legal obligation to remit these taxes to an appropriate government agency. Sales taxes are remitted periodically therefore any amounts collected represent a liability for the company collecting them.

The Home Depot reports $298 million of sales taxes payable at the close of the fiscal year. This is classified as a current liability because satisfaction of this obligation will take place in the following quarter.

Other Accrued Expenses

Other accrued expenses can include a variety of obligations. For example, this may include interest accrued on The Home Depot notes payable. The company presently has 6 percent senior notes outstanding that require interest payments each March 15 and September 15. Because the interest payment date does not fall at the end of The Home Depot's fiscal year, there must be an accrual of interest from the last interest payment date through the end of the fiscal year. The company has additional obligations in the form of leases and installment notes that would require similar accounting accruals.

Accrued expenses can also include estimated liabilities that will be settled in the upcoming year. This could include property tax expense that has been assessed for the current year but will be paid in the upcoming year, a litigation loss that has been accrued for but not yet settled, or bonuses that have been earned by key executives but will be paid in the upcoming quarter. Revenues received in advance (unearned revenue), such as deposits for goods ordered by The Home Depot customers, would also be recognized as a current liability.

Income Tax Payable

Income taxes payable represents an estimated liability that is generally satisfied with periodic payments by the corporation to several taxing authorities. Income tax payments are based on an estimate of corporate pretax income. As estimates change with the passage of time, so will the periodic installments paid by the firm. Any estimated liability should be reported at the close of the fiscal year.

To understand what constitutes pretax income one must first understand the difference between *before tax financial reported income* (income statement) and *pretax income* (tax return). Revenues and expenses for tax purposes are determined in accordance with the rules set forth by the Internal Revenue Code and other IRS regulations. Revenues and expenses for financial reporting purposes are based on generally accepted accounting principles (GAAP). The result can be a significantly different income measure depending on which set of rules is applied. Because of this, companies generally report future tax liabilities and/or assets. Any income tax obligation (benefit) due in the following year is reported as a current liability (asset).

The Home Depot reports a current liability of $78 million to various tax authorities at the close of the 2001 fiscal year. However, as will be seen later, The Home Depot has a noncurrent or deferred obligation to the income tax authorities of $195 million as a result of operations. The issue of deferred income taxes will be more thoroughly discussed in Section 3.5.8.

Current Installments of Long-Term Debt

The final item shown under current liabilities involves components of long-term debt that are due in the upcoming period. This is typically referred to as the current maturities of long-term debt and may include obligations such as installment notes, mortgages, leases and bond issues.

Upon review of The Home Depot notes to the financial statements we notice it has issued high-grade, commercial paper that bears an average interest cost of 6.1 percent. Commercial paper generally represents short-term debt. The Home Depot is also a party to a number of capital leases that require period payments of principle and interest. The portion of principle that will be settled in the coming year is reported as a current portion of that long-term debt. Mortgage notes or other installment notes operate in much the same way. The Home Depot has $4 million of long-term obligations that will be settled in the coming year.

3.5.6 Long-Term Debt (Excluding Current Installments)

Long-term liabilities generally represent the most significant obligation for the corporation. Although this obligation does not impact a firm's current liquidity, ultimately it becomes payable. Thus, there is significant concern with regard to the payment of ongoing interest and the ability to retire the obligation, either over time or when it becomes due as a single amount.

Long-term liabilities are obligations arising from past events that are not payable in the coming year. Generally, there is a much greater degree of formality when an organization incurs long-term debt. Long-term capital leases, mortgage obligations, pensions and other retirement benefit obligations are examples of long-term liabilities. Most of these examples, as was illustrated, require the recognition of both a short and long-term obligation.

According to note 2, The Home Depot's long-term debt comprises $754 million of commercial paper (usually short-term notes with original maturities of 30 to 270 days issued by highly rated corporations but classified by The Home Depot as long-term because of their rollover status), $500 million of senior notes due in 2004, $230 million of capital lease obligations payable in varying installments through 2027, and another $75 million in notes payable in varying installments through 2018. All of these obligations must be managed properly to prevent a decline in the company's credit rating.

3.5.7 Other Long-Term Liabilities

Other long-term liabilities outside of those discussed in note 2 are not clearly identifiable from the notes to the financial statements. Companies that raise capital through the issuance of bonds would recognize a long-term obligation: bonds payable. Additionally, many companies provide to employees pension and health-care benefits upon retirement. Generally, these employee benefits are not earned until the employee has been with the company for a number of years, known as a *vesting period*.

From an accounting perspective, companies that provide employee retirement benefits must accrue for them with the passage of time. If companies fund less than 100 percent of the accrued pension or other post-employment expense, a liability for the future obligation must be recognized. Obligations relating to pension plans and other post-employment benefit (OPEB) programs are reported under long-term liabilities as accrued pension cost obligation or accrued other post-employment benefit obligation. Table 3.2 illustrates the magnitude of pension and other post-employment benefit obligations for Abbott Laboratories at the close of its 1998 fiscal year. Four components are of special interest:

1. *Projected benefit obligation* is the actuarial present value of employee benefits earned using projected salary levels and present years of service.
2. *Pension or OPEB plan assets* are placed in trust by the company, invested, and then distributed to employees upon retirement. Their value fluctuates with the stock market and the economy.
3. *Prepaid (accrued) benefit cost* is the pension or OPEB asset or liability being reported in the balance sheet.
4. *Net cost* is the pension or OPEB expense for the current reporting year.

Although it is beyond the scope of this book to discuss the calculations that led to the following numbers, it is necessary to highlight two important points. First, Abbott Laboratories reported 1998 pension and OPEB expense (or cost) in the amount of $62.1 million and $69.5 million. The expense comprises four items.

1. *Service cost* increases pension expense because of an additional year of service benefits (pension and OPEB) earned by Abbott Laboratories employees.
2. *Interest cost* is the cost of the projected benefit obligation, measured on a present value basis. The mere passage of time increases the projected benefit obligation and pension expense.
3. *Expected return on plan assets* is used in the calculation of pension and OPEB expense to reduce its potential volatility. The reduction of pension and OPEB expense by an expected return on plan assets yields *net* pension or OPEB expense (or cost).
4. *Net amortization* relates to the actuarial adjustments (changes in discount rates, mortality rates, etc.) are made periodically, thereby increasing or decreasing the projected benefit obligation. Rather than adjust pension or OPEB expense dollar for dollar, the resulting gains and losses (known as *liability gains/losses*) are often amortized over time.

   A second adjustment often involves *asset gains/losses*. Asset gains/losses result from the difference between the expected return on pension or OPEB plan assets and the actual return on plan assets. Because of the potential for large swings in the stock market, the use of an average expected return over time reduces volatile reporting.

Next, Abbott Laboratories reports plan assets in excess of the projected benefit obligation of $202 million for its defined benefit pension plan. This means that Abbot currently has more assets in its plan than the projected benefit obligation. However, for OPEB obligations, the projected benefit obligations are in excess of plan assets by $632 million.

Table 3.2 Note 5: Post-Employment Benefits, Abbott Laboratories

(in thousands)	Defined Benefit Plans	Medical and Dental Plans
	1998	1998
Projected benefit obligations, January 1	$2,000,329	$646,448
Service cost — benefits earned during the year	108,754	30,664
Interest cost on projected benefit obligations	140,287	43,770
Actuarial loss (gain), primarily changes in discount rate and lower than estimated health care costs	182,829	18,057
Benefits paid	(85,722)	(23,993)
Other, primarily translation	2,143	-----------
Projected benefit obligations, December 31	$2,348,620	$714,946
Plans' assets at fair value, January 1, principally listed securities	$2,192,486	$86,600
Actual return on plans' assets	426,023	18,656
Company contributions	18,945	1,265
Benefits paid	(85,722)	(23,993)
Other, primarily translation	(761)	-----------
Plans' assets at fair value, December 31, principally listed securities	$2,550,971	$82,528
Projected benefit obligations less than (greater than) plans' assets, December 31	**$202,351**	**($632,418)**
Unrecognized actuarial (gains) losses, net	(143,876)	137,701
Unrecognized prior service cost	6,134	---------
Unrecognized transition obligation	(21,015)	---------
Prepaid (accrued) benefit cost	$43,594	($494,717)
Service cost - benefits earned during the year	$108,754	$30,664
Interest cost on projected benefit obligations	140,287	43,770
Expected return on plans' assets	(179,194)	(7,211)
Net amortization	(7,728)	2,290
Net pension or OPEB cost	**$62,119**	**$69,513**

3.5.8 Deferred Income Taxes

Deferred income tax liabilities and assets represent future income tax obligations or future income tax benefits as a result of past events. They arise when GAAP and the Code conflict with regard to the timing of revenues, expenses, gains, and losses. The resulting timing differences are temporary (in most cases), but nonetheless create a reporting difference between taxable income and financial income. Timing differences result when revenues, gains, expenses, or losses affect financial reported income in one period but taxable income in another period.

Table 3.3 Example of Timing Differences

Year	Tax Depreciation	Book Depreciation	Difference
1	$25,000	$10,000	$15,000
2	15,000	10,000	5,000
3	10,000	10,000	---
4	---	10,000	(10,000)
5	----------	10,000	(10,000)
	$50,000	$50,000	

As an example, let's assume The Home Depot depreciates a $50,000 asset over five years for financial reporting purposes but uses a 3-year accelerated cost recovery schedule for tax purposes. Table 3.3 illustrates depreciation expense timing differences.

As noted, depreciation expense in year 1 is $25,000 for tax purposes and $10,000 for financial reporting purposes. The $15,000 difference is called an *originating temporary difference*. When we move to year 2, another $5,000 originating temporary difference results. The combination of the two differentials then becomes a future reversing difference. While no reversals occur in year 3, years 4 and 5 show a combined total of $20,000 reversing differences. What this means is that The Home Depot would report a deferred income tax liability in anticipation of greater taxable income down the road when compared to financial reported income. Keep in mind that while depreciation expense differences exist *within* periods, they are equal in amount over the life of the asset. In either reporting, $50,000 of depreciation expense is recognized. This is why these originating differences are noted as temporary differences.

If we take this example one step further and assume that this company has $80,000 of income before depreciation, Table 3.4 illustrates what would be reported as taxable and financial reported income (ignoring taxes).

Table 3.4 Year 1 Income before Depreciation

	Tax	Book
Income before depreciation	$80,000	$80,000
Less: Depreciation expense	25,000	10,000
Income after depreciation	$55,000	$70,000

Therefore, in years 1 and 2, taxable income will be lower than financial reported income and reduce that year's income tax obligation. In year 3 there will be no difference in reported income and in years 4 and 5 taxable income exceeds financial reported income. Nonetheless, because greater tax benefits were achieved in year 1, a *deferred* tax liability is reported in the balance sheet based on the difference in year 1. Ultimately, deferred tax liabilities become current tax liabilities.

Depreciation timing differences are often the largest contributor to the magnitude of deferred tax liabilities. Because most companies take advantage of the accelerated depreciation schedules, deferred tax liabilities appear in the long-term liabilities section of corporate balance sheets. However, another expense related to health-care benefits upon retirement give rise to a deferred income tax benefit (an asset). Companies that provide for employee healthcare coverage upon retirement must recognize an expense and a related liability (if not funded) with the passage of time. The IRS does not allow the recognition of this expense until the distribution of benefits takes place. When companies accrue for this expense, they create future deductible amounts for tax purposes. Ultimately these expenses will lower taxable income and reduce future income tax obligation. Future deductible amounts are reported as deferred tax assets.

Common examples of temporary (timing) differences include

- *Depreciation*—Generally results in a deferred tax liability
- *Bad debt expense*—Generally results in a deferred tax asset
- *Prepaid or deferred expenses*—Generally results in a deferred tax liability
- *Unearned revenues*—Generally results in a deferred tax asset
- *Accrued warranty liabilities*—Generally results in a deferred tax asset
- *Other post-retirement benefit expenses*—Generally results in a deferred tax asset

3.5.9 Minority Interest

Because The Home Depot reports a minority interest of $11 million between the liability and stockholders' equity sections of the balance sheet, this indicates that it has an ownership interest of more than 50 percent but less than 100 percent in another company. When this situation occurs, 100 percent of the assets of the subsidiary company are included in the asset section of The Home Depot's balance sheet. The amount reported as minority interest is the amount of the assets The Home Depot does not own. The $11 million amount is reported neither as a liability nor equity but simply represents another investor's (company's) interest in the consolidated net assets of a Home Depot subsidiary.

3.5.10 Stockholders' Equity

Assets are financed both by debt and equity. Equity represents the net assets of a corporation. This concept can be compared to owning a house (asset) with an outstanding mortgage note (liability). If the house is valued at $200,000 and the payoff on the mortgage note is $140,000, then the equity in the house is $60,000. A company's balance sheet is viewed in much the same way. It is composed of many assets, a variety of liabilities, and a residual interest (equity) in those assets. The relationship between the three defines the balance sheet equation.

Furthermore, there continues to exist an inverse relationship between a company's debt and its equity. If equity increases relative to total assets, then debt decreases proportionally. The greater the equity component in a balance sheet, the less pressure on the organization to cover related interest costs and generate a profit. Stockholders' equity is generally divided into two categories: contributed capital and earned capital.

Contributed Capital
Contributed capital is recognized when a company acquires assets through the sale or exchange of common stock. When this occurs, companies recognize additional contributed capital in the balance sheet as well as an asset or reduction in an existing liability. Most often the asset received is cash, but occasionally a building and/or equipment can be received as well. Companies also have the flexibility to settle existing debt obligations with the issuance of common shares. In all of these cases, the net assets of the companies change because of management's decision.

The Home Depot balance sheet shows that contributed capital consists of common stock and additional paid-in-capital. Alongside these elements is The Home Depot's disclosure of authorized common shares, issued common shares and outstanding common shares. Authorization establishes the ceiling on the total number of shares that may be issued by the company. The Articles of Incorporation identify this number and can only be exceeded if the corporate charter is amended. The issued number of shares are the shares sold over time, while the number of shares outstanding can be less than or equal to the number of shares issued. If the number of shares outstanding is less than the number of shares issued, the company has reacquired some of its own common stock. Companies do this to enhance future earnings per share, reduce total future dividends paid, support executive compensation programs, or help fend off hostile takeovers. Reacquired shares are called treasury stock.

At the close of 2000, The Home Depot reported approximately 2.323 million shares of common stock at a par value of $.05 per share. Understand that par value and fair market value are unrelated measures. Multiplying the number of shares outstanding by a par value of $.05, a value of $116 million is recorded in The Home Depot balance sheet. The $116 million also constitutes the legal capital of the firm. Legal capital is used as a protective means to prevent companies from distributing dividends in excess of earnings and additional paid-in-capital. It provides some measure of value to creditors in case of liquidation.

The paid-in-capital account represents the excess of selling price per common share over par value per share. Because company stock is sold periodically, the selling price will often vary depending on market conditions. Thus, paid-in-capital can accumulate in different amounts with each public offering of the firm. To date, The Home Depot has been paid $4.81 billion in excess of par value by its shareholders.

Earned Capital

The other component of shareholders' equity is called *earned capital* or *retained earnings*. Earned capital represents the accumulated earnings of that company since its inception, less any dividends paid to the company's shareholders. Many newly established companies pay limited dividends and instead concentrate on growth. Rather than acquire capital externally at an additional cost, they can use these internally generated funds in a more efficient way. Established companies, on the other hand, attract a different type of investor who looks to dividends as a source of periodic revenue.

When a company first begins operations, accumulated or retained earnings are zero. With the passage of time however, earnings are reported and dividends are distributed. As a result, retained earnings may be positive or negative. A positive measure indicates that the company has attained some level of profitability (net income) and has distributed less than those earnings to shareholders. Negative retained earnings suggest that the company has sustained net losses over time or paid out dividends in excess of profits achieved. There is no relationship between retained earnings and a company's cash position. Remember that retained earnings are a subset of equity, and equity supports all assets.

Accumulated Other Comprehensive Income

An additional component of stockholders' equity is *accumulated other comprehensive income*. Accumulated other comprehensive income includes gains and losses related to certain events that have historically bypassed the income statement for income smoothing reasons. Therefore, for many years, the only reported measure of a company's performance was net income. A recent change in financial reporting now requires companies to report a more complete measure of income called *comprehensive income*. In essence, comprehensive income includes not just net income but other comprehensive income. As increases and decreases in other comprehensive income occur *during the reporting period*, these are reported in the statement of change in stockholders' equity or in a separate statement of comprehensive income. But any *accumulated balance* of these unrealized gains and losses is reported under stockholders' equity in the balance sheet. These items normally include unrealized gains and losses on available for sale securities, translation gains and losses on foreign currency and excess of additional pension liability over unrecognized prior service cost.

According to The Home Depot's balance sheet, the only item of accumulated other comprehensive income is foreign currency translation adjustments. These arise when assets and liabilities denominated in a foreign currency are translated into U.S. dollars. Careful review of The Home Depot annual report discloses that the company operates 67 stores in Canada, 5 stores in Chile, 2 stores in Argentina, and 2 stores in Puerto Rico. When consolidation takes place, the assets and liabilities denominated in foreign currencies must be combined with the assets and liabilities denominated in U.S. dollars. Note 1 to the financial statements provides additional disclosure of this action, as well as what rates are used in the translation process.

Shares Purchased for Compensation Plans

The last element that appears on the balance sheet is the *cost of shares reacquired for compensation plans*, also known as a company's *treasury stock*. Treasury stock represents stock that has been repurchased by the issuer for some intended purpose. For example, companies buy back their shares do the following:

- *Take advantage of current market conditions and lower stock prices*. Reacquisition of shares at low prices eliminates future dividend payments to existing shareholders, therefore enhancing future cash flow.
- *Support ongoing executive compensation programs*. If key executives exercise stock options the company must have existing shares to issue to these individuals. A stock option gives the holder the right to buy company stock at a predetermined price oftentimes at a great discount. Essentially stock options represent a form of deferred compensation.
- *Enhance future earnings per share*. If shares of stock are no longer outstanding, they are removed from the computation of earnings per share. Fewer outstanding shares increases earnings per share in subsequent accounting periods. Companies often seek opportunities to enhance this number.

According to The Home Depot's balance sheet, the cost of their reacquired treasury shares is $6 million. Most companies use the cost method to account for the acquisition of treasury stock. This means that they measure treasury stock based on the current market price at the time of acquisition. For example, if The Home Depot reacquires 100,000 shares to be held in treasury and pay $30 per share, treasury stock is reported at $3 million. On the balance sheet, treasury stock is a contra-equity account and is therefore deducted from stockholders' equity. Some users of financial information believe treasury stock should be considered an asset but fail to recognize that a company cannot own itself.

3.6. CONCLUDING REMARKS

The balance sheet provides important information regarding a company's liquidity and solvency. Shortcomings, however, involve a myriad of valuation approaches and management estimates. This chapter was designed to help the reader understand the structure of the balance sheet and its related elements. Financial statements from The Home Depot 2000 annual report were used for illustrative purposes. As we proceed to Chapter 4 and Chapter 5 and discuss the *statement of earnings* and the *statement of cash flow*, you should begin to better understand the interrelationships that exist between the mandatory financial statements.

Questions for Review

1. How does the classification of assets and liabilities on the balance sheet aid in analyzing a company's liquidity? Solvency?

2. What type of information for decision makers is provided by the balance sheet? What type of users would be primarily interested in this information? Does the balance sheet provide information on a company's profitability?

3. What is meant by *historical cost*? How does the use of historical cost effect information contained on the balance sheet?

4. What is meant by fair value accounting? For which assets on the balance sheet is this valuation method utilized?

5. How are customer accounts receivable valued (shown) on the balance sheet? Why?

6. What is the logic behind the equity method of accounting? When and where is this method utilized in the financial statements?

7. Distinguish between LIFO, FIFO, and average cost. In periods of inflation, which method will lead to a higher reported net income? Can management freely change cost-flow assumptions from year to year? Why or why not?

8. Distinguish between current and long-term liabilities. Why is this distinction important?

Internet Exercises

1. Locate the balance sheet for Timberland (http://www.timberland.com.) For the most recent report, list the amounts for current and noncurrent assets as well as current and noncurrent liabilities. As a potential supplier, would you extend it credit? (Note: Limit your analysis to the liquidity and solvency measures discussed in this chapter.)

2. Locate the most current balance sheet for Amazon.com. Critically assess its assets and liabilities, as above and compare your findings.

CHAPTER 4

Income Statement

CHAPTER OUTLINE

Study the Income Statement with a Critical Eye

Steve Ray cannot believe the wealth of information tucked into the company annual report. The previous chapters of this book have given him much greater understanding of a company's financial status, and now he is looking forward to studying the income statement. Upon studying this chapter, he will be able to tell whether Baker is generating profits from day-to-day operations. Operating income (loss) is a separate line item on an income statement and much different than net income (loss). Net income (loss) includes profits or losses from day-to-day operations plus several other transactions, such as taxes, interest, gains/losses on equipment sales and more. It is becoming clear to Steve how a business can report losing money from day-to-day operations and still show a robust net income.

LEARNING OBJECTIVES

1. Explain the primary purpose of the income statement.
2. Discuss the strengths and weaknesses of an income statement.
3. Describe the format of the income statement.
4. Identify three irregular items often found in the income statement.
5. Discuss the elements of an income statement.
6. Distinguish between the operating and non-operating sections of the income statement.
7. Explain the meaning of earnings per share and its calculation.
8. Distinguish between basic and diluted EPS.

The income statement, also labeled the statement of operations, measures a company's performance over a specified period of time. For this reason, the statement is titled for a period of time—for example, year ending January 28, 2001. The statement is different from the balance sheet because it is a cumulative record of activity for a month, quarter, multiple quarters, or for one year. Creditors, investors, and many others use the income statement as a measuring stick of how a company has performed, where it appears to be heading, and what its future cash flows will be. Open the Home Depot's annual report to the income statement (statement of operations) and follow along as each item is discussed.

In Chapter 7 we explore the numbers and evaluate The Home Depot's income statement. To complete a through analysis of The Home Depot, it is necessary to have a solid understanding of the income.

4.1 IMPORTANCE OF THE INCOME STATEMENT

Creditors, employees, suppliers, investors, and more use the income statement. The report serves as a measuring stick of how a company has performed, where it appears to be heading, and what future cash flows are likely to be. For example, Figure 4.1 compares the performance of The Home Depot and Kmart. The Home Depot amount and trend in net income points to future success. Success appears to have eluded Kmart for the most recent periods and is questionable in the future. Kmart is losing money, and its performance is inconsistent. This information certainly sends a signal to question management's strategic focus in an effort to position Kmart for long-term success. The 5-year financial summary in the annual report serves as the source of this information.

Figure 4.1 also provides clues regarding future cash flows. Operating cash flows are generated from day-to-day operations. This type of cash flows is essential for success. Although further analysis is required, The Home Depot trend points to the ability to generate future cash flows. This does not seem to be the case for Kmart. In the final analysis, only a company's operating activities provides continuous cash flow. Cash received from selling assets, loans (debt), and sale of its stock (equity) may be significant on an occasional basis but cannot be relied on as a year-to-year source of funds.

Figure 4.1 Net Income (Loss) Analysis

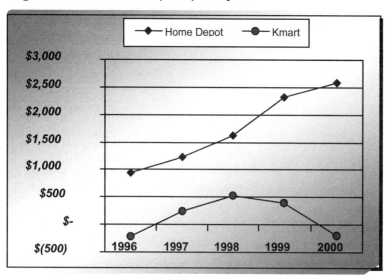

4.2 LIMITATIONS OF THE INCOME STATEMENT

The income statement provides a measure of performance that can be challenged on certain grounds. First, some believe that the organization's performance should be measured as its increase/decrease in net assets (equity). This economic theory of income measurement is premised on an organization's change in wealth and is referred to as a *capital-maintenance approach*. The weakness of this measure is that it fails to identify the specific elements of income and thus removes a company's flexibility to include or exclude certain events from income. Accountants generally use a *transactional approach* to measure performance (excess of revenues and gains over expenses and losses) from one year to the next. This model has been expanded recently to include items of other comprehensive income previously discussed in Chapter 3. The popularity of the transactional approach will likely continue.

A second income statement limitation is closely tied to a manager's accounting choice. For example, one manager might depreciate an asset using a straight-line approach, while another selects an accelerated approach. The end result is different reported expenses and different reported earnings. Because various methods of cost allocation exist, companies are required to disclose their choice(s) in the notes to the financial statements. This allows informed users to better compare companies.

Third, in some cases accounting rules are more specific, yet management intent drives the accounting. To illustrate, assume that two companies invest $3 million in the stock of a third, unrelated company. Current accounting rules require managers to disclose whether they intend to hold the investment for the short term or for an extended period. A manager's decision in this case changes the accounting for the investment. For one assumption, a change in market value is recognized in the income statement, the investment held for trading. Here the unrealized gains and losses are reported as part of net income. Under the second assumption, unrealized gains and losses are reported outside income, as a component of other comprehensive income, the investment held as available for sale (AFS). Financial statement users must realize that earnings outcomes often influence management's accounting decisions. The subject of managed earnings and earnings quality will be more formally discussed in Chapter 8

The fourth weakness of the income statement is its basis of preparation. Accrual accounting, while it provides a better measure of performance, includes noncash expenses in the calculation of income. For example, depreciation expense is an allocation of cost that has no associated cash outflow, yet it decreases net income.

Fifth, net income ignores when future cash receipts tied to current revenues will be received and when future cash payments tied to current expenses will be paid. This occurs because accounting rules require the recognition of earned revenue prior to the cash receipt. Accounting rules also require the recognition of an expense prior to its cash payment. An example of this would be a company that recognizes pension and other post-employment expenses. Some companies may contribute to this expense immediately while others may not. Therefore, cash flow from operations in the early years for a non-contributing company will be much higher than reported income because of these accruals. This is an important point from an employee retirement perspective. A company can expense the cost of funding a retirement, yet not set aside all the cash necessary to pay the benefits to the recipients. For the interested reader, Appendix B carefully explains the accounting rules regarding the recording of transactions before the cash flows have occurred.

4.3 FORMAT OF THE INCOME STATEMENT

The income statement is generally divided into two sections: operating and nonoperating. The *operating* section of the income statement includes revenues and expenses that correspond to the principle operations of the company (i.e., day-to-day operations). The combination of operating revenue and operating expenses leads to a reported measure of operating income or operating loss.

The *nonoperating* section of the income statement, on the other hand, includes income/expense items and gain/loss items that are routine to most any type of business entity but are viewed as peripheral to day-to-day business operations. Examples include interest earned on investments, interest incurred on borrowings, and gains and/or losses associated with the disposal of assets and/or elimination of liabilities. An example of a peripheral activity would be the sale of a piece of equipment. If the equipment has a book value of $20,000 and it is sold for $15,000, there is a realized loss of $5,000. While the loss is reported on the income statement, it is recognized in the nonoperating section under *other expenses and losses*. This loss is excluded from operating income because it is related to a support activity rather than an operating activity.

The sum of operating income (loss) and nonoperating income (loss) is simply *income (loss) before income tax expense.* Once income tax expense or benefit is considered, net income (loss) is the residual. The level of detail disclosed between operating income and net income varies among companies. We will show in Chapter 7 that when evaluating a company a study of operating income from one year to the next is much more meaningful than a study of net income from one year to the next.

Often, the nonoperating income or loss and tax expense components provide subtle signals of a company's financial complexity that deserve careful study. Figure 4.2 shows a difference between operating income and net income for The Home Depot ranging between $1,000 to $1,500 million. A careful review of the income statement shows that much of the difference is due to income taxes. This is not the case for Enron. Figure 4.2 shows a difference between operating income and net income ranging between $1,000 and $1,500 million, as well. A careful review of the income statement shows this difference is attributable to a host of complex economic events and taxes. This level of detail is a signal that the financial backbone of the company is complex and deserves careful study. In addition, how can the difference between operating income and net income be so different in 1998 and 2000, yet have very similar values in 1999? The user should read these as signals that professional guidance is necessary to untangle the intricacy and understand the implications surrounding the many different financial transactions underway at Enron.

4.3.1 Irregular Items

Three items of special importance are also included in the conventional income statement but are reported beyond the operating and non-operating sections: discontinued operations, extraordinary events, and changes in accounting principles. Accounting professionals view these events as irregular items and generally prefer that their effects be removed from the main body of the income statement. Lucent Technologies' comparative income statement (Table 4.1) illustrates the effects of a discontinued operation and an accounting principle change on net income. Net income decreased in 2000 and increased due to restructuring in 1999 and 1998.

Figure 4.2 Operating and Net Income Analysis

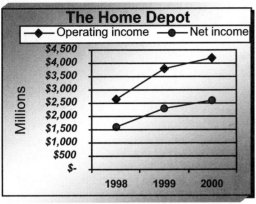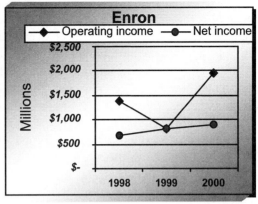

4.3.2 Discontinued Operations

One of the most-often-occurring irregular items is the gain/loss associated with the disposal of a business segment. Just as many companies have recently expanded operations through business acquisitions, many of these same companies have disposed of other operating segments along the way. For a disposal to qualify as a discontinued operation, the assets, results of operations, and activities of a business segment must be clearly distinguishable, physically and operationally, from the balance of the enterprise. Table 4.1 shows Lucent lost $462 million from discontinued operations in 2000.

Table 4.1 Lucent Technologies Three-Year Comparative Income (loss) Information

Results of Operations (in millions)	2000	1999	1998
Revenues	$33,813	$30,617	$24,367
Gross margin	14,274	15,012	11,429
Depreciation and amortization expense	2,318	1,580	1,228
Operating income	2,985	4,694	1,953
Income from continuing operations	1,681	3,026	769
Income (loss) from discontinued operations	**(462)**	**455**	**296**
Income before cumulative effect of accounting change	1,219	3,481	1,065
Cumulative effect of accounting change	—	**1,308**	—
Net income	$1,219	$4,789	$1,065

An example of a discontinued operation would be the elimination of an automobile line by General Motors. The economic substance of this event (revenues and expenses related to the Oldsmobile line, for example) would be removed from the upper portion of the statement of operations and reported separately. This method of segregated reporting highlights the significance of the event and illustrates the business unit's profitability or lack thereof. Furthermore, assets that are being sold by a company generally receive fewer economic commitments from the organization and have a tendency to under-perform. A seperate reporting of the discontinued operation prevents its measure of performance from contaminating the record of performance of the ongoing enterprise when the organization is under review by outside analysts.

4.3.3 Extraordinary Items

A second irregular item that gets special accounting consideration is an *extraordinary event*. An extraordinary item is a transaction or event that is both unusual *and* infrequent in occurrence, taking into account the environment in which the company operates. For example, assume two companies sustain significant flood loss damage. One company might classify the loss as extraordinary, yet the other might not. Flood loss sustained by an enterprise located in a flood plain would not constitute an unusual occurrence and would not warrant extraordinary classification. Nor would an earthquake loss for a company located in California.

One extraordinary item addressed by the FASB is the economic affect of the September 11, 2001, terrorist attack on the World Trade Center and the Pentagon. Certain businesses, as a consequence of the attack, have sustained significant personnel losses and severe economic damage. Many of these companies, as well as associated businesses, were forced to report extraordinary losses in their 2001 current year financials.

Another item, known as a *corporate restructuring charge*, may appear to be unusual or infrequent but is still reported as a component of continuing operations. The FASB considers organizational restructuring a part of today's normal business environment. However, restructuring charges, if material, can be shown as a separate line item. Many companies use pro forma reporting techniques as a means of softening the effects of reported restructuring changes. They essentially highlight what earnings would have been had they not experienced a corporate restructure. Many believe that this type of reporting is misleading and helps to disguise management shortfalls. Table 4.2 highlights the magnitude of a corporate restructure. As you can see, Sara Lee Corporation experienced a $2,040 million restructure in fiscal year 1998.

Table 4.2 Sara Lee Corporation 1996 to 1998 Consolidated Statement of Income

	June 27, 1998	*Years ended* June 28, 1997	June 29, 1996
Net sales	$20,011	$19,734	$18,624
Cost of sales	$12,331	$12,267	$11,470
Selling, general and administrative expenses	$5,907	$5,824	$5,603
Interest expense	224	$202	228
Interest income	(48)	(43)	(55)
Restructuring charge	**$2,040**	---------	---------
	$20,454	$18,250	$17,246
Income (loss) before income taxes	(443)	1,484	$1,378
Income taxes	$80	$475	$462
Net income (loss)	($523)	$1,009	$916

4.3.4 Change of Accounting Principle

A third irregular event that requires special accounting treatment is an *accounting principle change*. A change in accounting principle results when a company switches from one generally accepted accounting principle to another or when the FASB issues a new accounting pronouncement. A change in an accounting principle often requires an adjustment to specific asset or liability accounts, as well as an adjustment to net income or retained earnings (prior year changes where necessary). When income is affected, the firm is said to be applying the "current approach." When retained earnings are affected, the firm is said to be applying the "retroactive approach." Firms may not select one method over the other. Each new accounting standard specifies which approach to use in a given situation. Most changes in accounting principles are accounted for under the current approach, with a cumulative effect of the change reported in current-year income.

Cumulative prior-year differentials often occur when companies switch depreciation methods or change inventory cost-flow assumptions. Essentially, the cumulative effect is the total income difference between what was reported using the current depreciation method versus what would have been reported under the newly adopted depreciation method. Most often these changes target assets acquired over, let's say, the past five years, rather than those assets acquired in the current year. This allows management to report an outcome that might have a favorable impact on earnings. This is referred to as a discretionary change by a company and is not the result of a new accounting rule.

Retroactive adjustments generally pertain to changes in a company's revenue recognition practices or changes in inventory cost-flow assumptions that involve LIFO. Rather than take the cumulative differentials to reported earnings of the current year as with the current approach, the effect is recognized as an adjustment to retained earnings. This allows the effect to bypass current year income but requires restatement of related prior year information. Most users of financial information dislike this approach because of the changes to previously reported values.

The economic consequence of a mandatory change in accounting principle can also have a dramatic effect on reported earnings.[1] General Motors, for example, recorded a $20.8 billion accounting charge in 1992 as a result of a new accounting rule issued by the Financial Accounting Standards Board. The rule, FAS 106 "Employers Accounting for Postretirement Benefits Other than Pensions" required companies to change their accounting for postretirement benefits from a pay-as-you (cash) basis to an accrual basis. According to the Board:

> "a defined postretirement benefit plan set forth the terms of an exchange between the employer and employee. In exchange for the current services provided by the employee, the employer promised to provide, in addition to current wages and other benefits, health and other welfare benefits after the employee retires. It follows from that view that postretirement benefits are not gratuities but are part of an employee's compensation for services rendered. Since payment is deferred, the benefits are a type of deferred compensation. The employer's obligation for that compensation is incurred as employees render the services necessary to earn their postretirement benefits."

The Board's objectives in issuing this FAS was to improve employers' financial reporting for postretirement benefits in the following manner:

a) To enhance the relevance and representational faithfulness of the employer's reported results of operations by recognizing net periodic postretirement benefit cost as employees render the services necessary to earn their postretirement benefits.

---

[1] When then FASB issued FAS No. 106 "Accounting for Postretirement Benefits Other than Pensions" in 1990 with an effective date of December 15, 1992, many organizations were required to accrue enormous obligations and recognize current period expenses for future post-employment costs.

b) To enhance the relevance and representational faithfulness of the employer's statement of financial position by including a measure of the obligation to provide postretirement benefits based on a mutual understanding between the employer and its employees of the terms in the underlying plan.

c) To enhance the ability of users of the employer's financial statements to understand the extent and the effects of the employer's undertaking to provide postretirement benefits to its employees by disclosing relevant information about the obligation and cost of the postretirement benefit plan and how those amounts are measured.

d) To improve the understandability and comparability of amounts reported by requiring employers with similar plans to use the same method to measure their accumulated postretirement benefit obligations and the related costs of the postretirement benefits.[2]

As a result of General Motor's $20.8 billion accounting charge, it lost close to $23 billion in 1992. The balance of this chapter is devoted to a discussion of the elements of The Home Depot consolidated statement of earnings.

4.4 ELEMENTS OF THE HOME DEPOT'S STATEMENT OF EARNINGS

The Home Depot's statement of earnings can be divided into two sections: operating and nonoperating. The operating section includes sales revenues, cost of goods sold, and other operating expenses.

4.4.1 Operating Section

Net Sales
The operating section begins with The Home Depot's *net sales* of goods and services, reported at $45,738 million. The figure includes revenues generated from the sale of merchandise, tool and equipment rental, and product installation service revenue. Net sales result when the Home Depot Company deducts from gross sales:

* Cost of goods returned by customers
* Cash discounts earned by contractors when they pay within the discount period
* Allowances granted to customers when goods are defective

These items generally are not disclosed in the annual report but are tracked for internal reporting purposes. Information about returned merchandise, allowances granted to customers, and discounts taken by contractors are important for managing suppliers, customers, and cash flow.

Net sales in whole dollars and percentage growth are often included in the financial highlights and 5- to 10-year summary. These measures are designed to provide the user a perspective of company size and growth. Figure 4.3 shows that The Home Depot is substantially larger than Lowe's in terms of sales, yet both are growing at the same approximate rate of 20 percent. This growth rate appears reasonable given management's historical track records. Most interesting will be to see what happens next year with the growth rates of each company. For

---

[2] FAS No. 106 "Accounting for Postretirement Benefits Other than Pensions" Financial Accounting Standards Board, Stamford, Ct., 1990.

Enron, the signals are different. Note, we had to graph sales dollars and growth rates separately for Enron because of the magnitude of the values. Any and all users should question a business that goes from $40,000 million to $100,000 million in one year, at a growth rate in excess of 150 percent. The message is simple: If it looks too good to be true, it probably is!

Figure 4.3 Net Sales in Dollars and Growth Percent

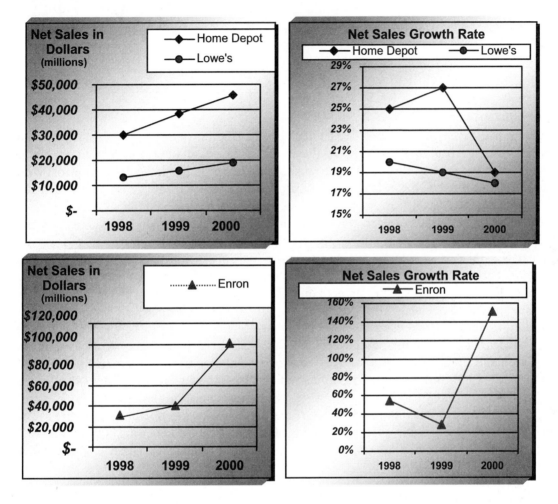

Cost of Merchandise Sold
The next line item, cost of merchandise sold, is generally the most significant expense reported in the income statement. Cost of goods sold is only recognized when a sale of merchandise has taken place, $32,057 million for The Home Depot.

Cost of goods sold as a percentage of net sales is an important measure of a firm's performance. The percentage can be compared from year to year as well as across firms within the same industry. Figure 4.4 shows that the percentage of cost of goods sold is very similar for The Home Depot and Lowe's, with both resting near 70 percent. However, a small percentage difference can have a larger impact on the bottom line when sales are in the billions of dollars. For example, reducing The Home Depot cost of goods sold by 1 percent would contribute approximately 400 million to operating profits. Remember that cost of goods sold is directly related to the cost-flow assumption that is chosen by the company to value its inventory (i.e., FIFO, LIFO, weighted average). Inventory valuation was previously discussed in Section 3.5.1.

Figure 4.4 Comparative Analysis of Cost of Goods Sold, Percent of Net Sales

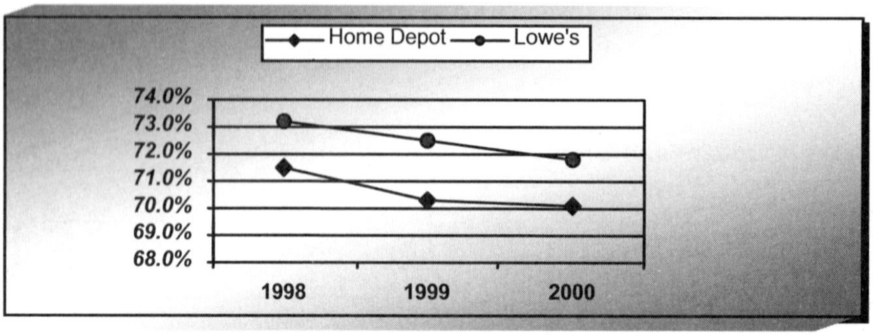

Gross Profit

The difference between net sales and cost of goods sold is a company's *gross profit,* or *gross margin.* A reported gross profit is essential to cover operating expenses that a company incurs during the operating year. Management's effective control over inventory acquisition cost can lead to an improved or at least stable gross profit measure from one year to the next.

Companies that report lower operating profits often have been quoted as saying, "Product price increases could not be passed along to the consumer in a timely manner." Circumstances like these create a squeeze on gross margins that ultimately filters down to a company's bottom line. Many times price increases cannot be passed along because of existing market conditions such as an economic downturn. To increase prices would simply create less product demand.

According to The Home Depot's 2000 income statement, gross profit is $13,681 million and has increased by more than 60 percent over the past three years. Likewise, gross profit as a percentage of net sales has steadily improved and is currently 30 percent ($13,681 million/$45,738 million). The decline in cost of goods sold as a percent of net sales shown in Figure 4.5 translates to an increase in gross profits. For The Home Depot, 30 cents ($1.00 - .70) of every sales dollar is used to meet current-period operating expenses. The improvement of gross profit as a percentage of sales (29.9 percent in 2000 versus 29.7 percent in 1999), according to management, is the direct result of three company-wide initiatives:

- A lower cost of merchandise as a result of product line reviews
- Benefits from global sourcing programs
- An increase in revenue from tool rental centers

Additional insight is available to a user who has a solid understanding of the relationship between costs of goods sold and sales revenues. When costs of goods sold are compared to revenue, a company's product mark-up percentage becomes more visible. During 2000, The Home Depot had an average mark-up on product costs and services of approximately 43 percent ($45,738/$32,057 minus 1). A sufficient mark-up is essential for a company to maintain a consistent bottom line.

Selling and Store Operating Expenses

Selling expenses are expenses that directly relate to the selling of goods and/or services. For example, The Home Depot employs thousands of sales personnel whose job is to assist customers throughout the store and monitor inventory levels. These employee salaries represent a significant selling expense for a company of The Home Depot's size. As a result, these costs will increase as the company opens new locations or as employees become "more seasoned." A careful review of The Home Depot's MD&A section of the annual report illustrates this point. According to management, a higher payroll expense was realized in 2000 as a result of market wage pressures and an increase in employee longevity. In addition, medical costs increased due to higher family enrollment in the Company's medical plans, rising health care costs, and higher prescription drug costs.

Television and radio advertising production costs, as well as media placement costs, are other examples of selling expenses for The Home Depot Company. Most of these costs are initially capitalized but become an expense as the advertising occurs throughout the year. Selling expenses for The Home Depot as well as other companies might include sales commissions, sales office salaries, travel and entertainment, and depreciation expense on a sales office or sales training facility.

Store operating expenses or occupancy expenses are another significant cost for The Home Depot. Once again, as desirable growth rates are achieved, total occupancy expenses should increase proportionately to the number of stores that are opened. On average, however, expenses should remain the same. For example, average depreciation expense per store should remain relatively constant from one year to the next (assuming a straight-line depreciation method). But should new construction prices increase, the average expense per period accelerates. This is the result of a greater capitalized cost being allocated to a consistent useful life (say, 45 years). This causes the average depreciation expense per store and in total to increase.

In certain instances, operating expenses will rise regardless of expansion. Consider, for example, a company's utility costs and property taxes. Typically, these expenses increase because of utility industry conditions and government budgetary pressures. As local taxing authorities and utility service providers increase rates, a company's income statement is adversely affected. The Home Depot management addresses these issues in the MD&A section of the annual report and states that "store occupancy costs such as property taxes, property rent, depreciation and utilities, increased in year 2000 as a result of new store growth and energy rate increases."

Pre-Opening Expenses

Consistent with management's initiative to aggressively expand its operations, The Home Depot opened 204 new stores and relocated 8 others during fiscal year 2000. In advance of these store openings, new personnel were hired, trained, and required to assist in the organization of the new facility. Expenses associated with these activities are called *pre-opening expenses*. These expenses can be incurred over a few weeks or a much longer period, depending on the complexity of the operation. Accounting rules do not allow for these costs to be capitalized; therefore they are expensed as they are incurred, generally in the year in which the store opens for business. Within the MD&A section management explains that preopening costs were higher during fiscal year 2000 due to the opening of more EXPO Design Centers and the expansion of The Home Depot stores into new markets, including international locations, which involve higher training, relocation, and travel costs. This expense amounted to $142 million in 2000, as opposed to only $88 million in fiscal year 1998.

General and Administrative Expenses

A company's general and administrative expenses often include a variety of costs that relate to other than its sales operations. For example, the depreciation of a company's corporate headquarters constitutes a general and administrative expense. Depreciation of a sales training center, conversely, would constitute a selling expense. Management salaries, utility costs, and property taxes are further examples of general and administrative expenses.

An explicit comparison of the above operating expenses deserves careful study on an individual company basis. The expense titled: Store selling and operating expense as a percent of sales can be drawn from The Home Depot 10-year summary. The summary shows this expense category has recently increased to 18.6 percent of sales from 17.8 percent the previous year. This is a signal to management that store selling and operating expenses must be carefully controlled. Comparability of general, selling and operating expenses across different companies is difficult because each will likely have a different definition and classification system. To overcome this comparability obstacle the user can simply graph total operating expenses as a percent of sales.

Operating Income

Operating income (or loss) is the difference between operating revenues and operating expenses. Operating income is essentially the most useful measure of a company's performance from one year to the next. The reason for this is that it excludes nonoperating gains and losses that oftentimes can distort measures of performance.

Home Depot Company generated $4,191 million of operating income in 2000, an increase of $383 million over its 1999 reporting year. Even with the increase, however, operating income as a percentage of sales had fallen from the preceding year as shown in Figure 4.5. The percentage decrease can be attributed to an increase (27 percent) in operating expenses during 2000, which management discusses in the MD&A section.

Figures 4.3 to 4.5 point to a comprehensive view of financial operating performance. At this point in our study of The Home Depot and Lowe's income statements we see solid growth in sales and a stable operating income percent of sales. Good management teams will stabilize and work to decrease operating costs in an effort to maintain and grow the operating revenue and income in total and percent of sales. The Home Depot and Lowe's leadership teams have successful track records thus sound management is expected in the future.

Figure 4.5 **Operating Income as a Percent of Sales**

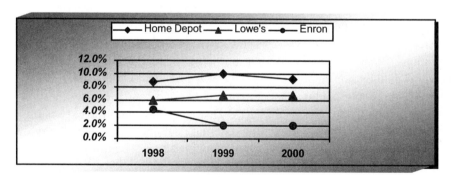

The Enron story is quite different. Figure 4.3 shows substantial sales growth, yet Figure 4.5 shows a poor operating income of just 2 percent and no increase in the current year when sales grow from $40,000 to $100,000 million. This is a signal that any student in a beginning financial analysis class should question. The immediate reaction is that the upbeat and positive qualitative discussion spread throughout the Enron annual report is not worth the paper it is written upon. Figures 4.3 and 4.5 point to a situation that simply does not appear reasonable, a substantial increase in sales, yet a decline in operating performance.

4.4.2 Nonoperating Section

Interest and Investment Income

Interest and investment income is earned and reported when a company invests in certificates of deposits, treasury bills or notes, or in the stocks and bonds of other companies. The success of these investments will be measured in the form of dividend, interest, or investment income. These returns will ultimately be reported on the company's income statement under nonoperating income (expenses).

As an aside, institutions that report interest and investment income as a part of operations include banks and other financial institutions. Their business purpose is to attract capital at a predetermined cost, invest the acquired capital, and achieve a higher rate of return. Therefore, a financial institution's gross profit is controlled by the percentage difference.

Interest Expense

Interest is a payment that companies make for the use of another company's money and is directly related to the passage of time. Interest is associated with a company's notes, mortgages and bonds or embedded as part of a lease obligation or pension obligation. In most cases, a company's long-term liabilities (and some short-term liabilities as well) will have some related interest expense. Once again, however, interest expense (and revenue) falls outside operating income.

Interest expense for The Home Depot declined considerably in 2000, to $21 million. This number will rise sharply in 2001 because of the substantial increase in long-term liabilities during 2000 ($1,545 million versus $750 million in 1999).

Income Taxes

Most corporations are responsible for a variety of taxes. These can include federal, state, and foreign income-tax obligations. Because many of these taxes are revenue based, they must be accrued for and paid in a timely manner. Income tax expense, the number reported in the income statement, is essentially the federal statutory rate multiplied by a company's income before tax. This rate varies, depending on taxable income and political agenda. The number is further adjusted to include any state or foreign income tax obligation (or income tax benefits). Once all of these effects are considered, income tax expense is reported. Therefore income tax expense, as a function of income before taxes, can vary from year to year. According to the notes to the financial statements, The Home Depot had an effective tax rate of 38.8 percent in 2000.

As a concluding point, keep in mind that a company's income tax expense is often different than its income taxes paid. Current-year income tax expense may be partially satisfied with payments to the taxing authorities, but often payments are made in the forthcoming quarter (current income tax payable) or possibly years beyond (deferred taxes payable). The current income taxes payable is a result of the tax-filing deadline falling in the next year, and represents the cash needed to meet the obligation. The deferred income taxes payable (or income tax asset), on the other hand, is the result of differences between revenue and expense recognition rules under the Internal Revenue Code and GAAP.

By reviewing The Home Depot's statement of cash flows, you see that the current period income taxes paid amount to $1,386 million. This number might include cash payments for income tax expense from the 1999 fiscal year as well as for income tax expense from the current year. Any differences between income taxes paid for this year's expense can be reconciled with reported current and future income tax liabilities and future income tax assets (benefits).

Net Earnings

A company's net earnings (or income) are often referred to as its *bottom line*. Net earnings, as we have seen, remain after a company deducts operating and nonoperating expenses from operating and nonoperating revenues. The result can be compared to a company's net sales in order to calculate its *net profit margin, calculated [net income (loss)/net sales]*. A company's net profit margin is often compared across years or across firms within the industry.

Figure 4.6 shows a comparison of the net profit margin for The Home Depot, Lowe's and Enron. The Home Depot and Lowe's represent stability in the range of 5.5 percent to 6.0 percent and 3.7 percent to 4.3 percent respectively. Enron shows a low and declining net profit margin of approximately 2 percent in 1998, dropping to less than 1 percent in 2000. Again, with sales increasing by greater than 150 percent (Figure 4.4) and a decline of the net profit margin to less than 1 percent in the same period should be a cause for alarm for any Enron stakeholder—employees, customers, investors and more.

Figure 4.6 Net Profit Margin Analysis

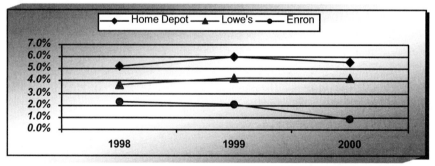

4.4.3 Basic and Diluted Earnings per Share

Earnings per common share must be computed and reported by all publicly traded companies in their corporate annual report and annual report 10-K. The reason for this is that it measures performance on a per share basis and helps to standardize earnings. Standardized earnings allow two companies to be compared side by side by investors without being unduly influenced by the magnitude of earnings. For example, if Company A achieves $5 billion in net earnings while Company B achieves half that amount, Company A would appear to be more attractive as a shareholder investment. If, however, Company B had only half as many shareholders, Company B's earnings per share would be equal to Company A's.

Because of a variety of equity-related instruments that exist within a company's capital structure, companies are often required to report two measures of earnings per share. Examples of equity-related instruments that may lead to common stock include

- Convertible bonds or notes
- Convertible preferred stock
- Stock options or warrants

Each of these instruments, if converted into common stock by their holders, could lower a company's earnings per common share because the number of shares outstanding will increase. Therefore, accounting rules and the conservatism principle require companies to report two measures of per share performance: basic earnings per share and diluted earnings per share.

Figure 4.7 recaps the basic earnings per share for The Home Depot, Lowe's and Enron. Notice than Lowe's has the highest earning per share, yet is the smallest of the three companies. The reason being is that Lowe's has less stock outstanding, thus even though its earnings are lower, the earnings per share are greater and growing at a steady rate. The Home Depot basic earning per share did not change between 1999 and 2000. Although earnings increased, the number of shares outstanding increased at the same rate for the 2000. Enron's earnings per share decreased slightly in the most recent period.

Figure 4.7 Basic Earnings Per Share Recap

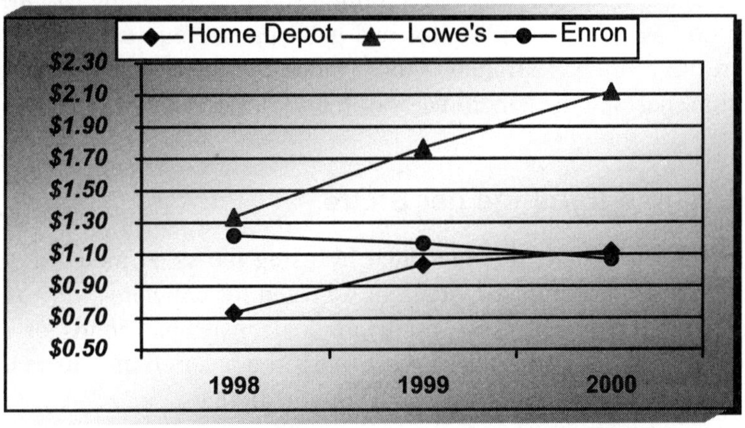

4.4.4 Calculation of Basic Earnings per Share

Basic earnings per share (EPS) is generally calculated by taking net income less any preferred dividends and dividing it by a company's weighted-average shares outstanding. The model in its mathematical form is

$$\frac{\text{Net Income - preferred dividends (if applicable)}}{\text{Weighted average shares outstanding}}$$

But according to The Home Depot's balance sheet, no preferred stock has been issued to date. Therefore, preferred dividends are not applicable when calculating The Home Depot's basic earnings per share. As a result, basic earnings per share is simply net income divided by weighted average shares outstanding. The remaining two variables, net income and weighted average shares outstanding, are found at the bottom of the income statement. Net income amounts to $2,581 million and weighted average shares outstanding are 2.315 billion. The Home Depot's basic EPS amounts to $1.11 ($2,581 million divided by 2.315 billion shares).

In the preceding basic EPS computation, we utilized the weighted average number of shares outstanding presented to us by The Home Depot. In practice, however, the calculation of weighted average shares outstanding may be quite complex. To understand this calculation, we must recognize that net income in the numerator of the EPS model represents a company's performance over an entire reporting period. Therefore, to compare apples with apples, the denominator (shares outstanding) should represent the entire reporting period as well. As a result, each share outstanding must be representative of a full year. The following example simplifies the understanding of weighted average shares.

> Example: Assume that Company A has 3 million shares of common stock outstanding at the start of the year. If no additional shares are issued during the year by Company A and no outstanding shares are repurchased by Company A during the year, the weighted average number of shares outstanding for the year is 3 million shares. The reason for this is that each share is outstanding for one full year.
> Now assume that Company B has 3 million shares of common stock outstanding at the start of the year. If Company B issues 3 million shares of *additional* common stock on July 1st and does not repurchase any other outstanding common shares, the weighted average number of shares outstanding now changes. Company B now has 3 million shares outstanding for a full year and 3 million shares outstanding for one-half year. The 3 million shares outstanding for one-half year are equivalent to 1.5 million full-year shares (3 million multiplied by 6/12 months). Therefore, Company B would use 4.5 million shares in the denominator of the EPS model.

4.4.5 Calculation of Diluted Earnings per Share

A company's diluted earnings per share are calculated by using the same model as above except that the numerator and the denominator would be adjusted for any *potentially dilutive securities*. Dilutive securities are securities—for example, convertible bonds or notes, convertible preferred stock, or stock options or warrants—that if converted may increase the numerator and will increase the denominator of the EPS computation.

According to the notes, The Home Depot Company's 2000 capital structure includes company-issued stock options (there were no convertible notes outstanding in 1998 and 1999). As a result of the stock options, the denominator in the EPS model increases to 2.352 billion, with no numerator adjustment. Therefore, The Home Depot reports *diluted* earnings per share of $1.10. The reported diluted earnings per share is a hypothetical number based on the conservatism principle of accounting. Essentially, it provides investors with the most conservative estimate of earnings on a per-share basis. Although the difference between basic EPS and diluted EPS for The Home Depot is very small, you might find a wider difference in other company annual reports.

As illustrated, a company's weighted average shares outstanding must be used in the calculation of both basic and diluted earnings per share. If the weighting effect were not required, companies might purchase their own shares at or near the close of the year to arbitrarily inflate earnings per share.

4.5 CONCLUDING REMARKS

The income statement serves as a measuring stick of how a company has performed, where it appears to be heading, and, in addition, as a predictor of future cash flows. Shortcomings involve a clear definition of income and management accounting choices that influence income statement measures. This chapter was written to help the reader understand the structure of the income statement and its related elements. As in Chapter 3, the statement of earnings from The Home Depot 2000 annual report assisted our analysis. As we move forward to Chapter 5 and discuss the statement of cash flow, a clearer understanding of the relationship between earnings and cash flow emerges.

Questions for Review

1. What does an income statement measure? How does this differ from the balance sheet? In terms of predictive ability, how do creditors and investors utilize the income statement?

2. Compare the capital-maintenance approach to the transactional approach to income measurement. Which is utilized for financial reporting purposes? Why is this deemed beneficial?

3. Suppose that B Co. and T Co. are exactly alike in all material financial respects (assets, liabilities, ability to generate earnings, and so on). B Co. shows a lower net income than T Co. due to the use of an accelerated depreciation method in the current year. Which company would you invest in? Why?

4. An income statement contains various categories of income (gross profit, operating income, nonoperating income, net income...). When comparing one company to another, which measure of income is most beneficial? Why? When comparing past performance to current performance of the same company, which measure is most useful? Why?

5. Describe briefly what *discontinued operations*, *extraordinary items* and a *cumulative effect* of a change in accounting principle mean. Where are the financial effects of these items disclosed on the income statement? Why? Is the loss of a plant due to an earthquake considered an extraordinary item in California? In Illinois? Why or why not?

6. BS Co.'s gross profit has declined 20 percent over the past year. What are some plausible explanations for this?

7. TZ Co.'s gross profit has risen 20 percent over last year; its operating expenses have remained constant, yet its net income has declined over 30 percent. What are some possible explanations for these changes?

8. What is the difference between basic and diluted earnings per share? Why are these measures important to users of financial information?

Internet Exercises

1. Search the Internet for a recent example of a company who experienced a change in net income due to a change in accounting principle. In a well-developed paragraph, describe the circumstances surrounding this event. Locate the financial information prior to this event and after this event (if possible) for the company. Was the event preshadowed in the previous annual report? How was the event disclosed in the most recent 10Q, 10K, or income statement?

2. Search the Internet for a company that experienced a restructuring in the recent past. In a well-developed paragraph describe what you found and how this restructuring is expected to affect the financials. How and where are restructuring costs shown on the income statement? Why?

CHAPTER 5

Statement of Cash Flows (SCF)

CHAPTER OUTLINE

This chapter clarified for Steve the three different types of cash flows (operating, investing, and financing). Armed with an applied knowledge of different types of cash flows, he was able to determine why Baker Electronics' cash balance changed from the beginning of the year to the end of the year. Further, Steve is now able to critically evaluate and interpret Baker's cash flows. Having read this chapter, Steve Ray now understands why cash flows are different than net income.

LEARNING OBJECTIVES

1. Know Statement of Cash Flows terms and concepts.
2. Understand and evaluate the three major components of the SCF:
   - Operating activities
   - Investing activities
   - Financing activities
3. Read and interpret the individual SCF line items.

5.1 INTRODUCTION

The statement of cash flows (SCF) measures different aspects of a company's health than do the balance sheet and income statement. The balance sheet measures financial position at a point in time, and the income statement measures financial performance for a period of time. The SCF provides a clear picture of how cash flows into and out of the business (see Table 5.1). Open The Home Depot's annual report to the SCF and follow along as each item is discussed.

Table 5.1 **Summary of The Home Depot SCF, January 28, 2001 (in millions)**

Net cash provided by operations	$ 2,796
Net cash used in investing activities	(3,530)
Net cash provided by financing activities	737
Effect of exchange rate changes	(4)
(Decrease) increase in cash	(1)
Cash balance, beginning of year	168
Cash balance, end of year	$ 167

The SCF captures three types of cash flows over a period of time. First measured is cash that flows into and out of the business from day-to-day operations, labeled *net cash provided by operations*. Examples include the cash inflow from the sale of goods and the cash outflow from the purchase of inventory or payment of interest. As of January 28, 2001, The Home Depot net cash provided by operations amounted to $2,796 million.

Measured next is *net cash used in investing activities*. Purchasing for cash the land and building for a new store would be an example of an investing cash outflow. Selling for cash the land and building of a store or equipment would be an example of investing cash inflow. As of January 28, 2001, The Home Depot net cash used in investing activities amounted to $3,530 million. Bracketed amounts in Table 5.1 mean a cash outflow.

Measured next is *net cash provided by financing activities*. A loan to The Home Depot from a bank is an example of a financing cash inflow activity. When The Home Depot repays the loan, this is an example of a financing cash outflow activity. As of January 28, 2001, The Home Depot net cash provided by financing activities amounted to $737 million.

The last SCF measure in Table 5.1 is to accommodate a foreign currency translation adjustment. This line is typically a small value, yet necessary to reconcile the actual cash flows for the year. The SCF shows explicitly for the user why and how the cash balance changed from the beginning of the year to the end of the year (Table 5.1). For the year ending January 28, 2001 The Home Depot generated $2,796 million from day-to-day operating activities, invested $3,530 million in new stores and borrowed $737 million. In addition, a $4 million adjustment was necessary for currency fluctuations. The net result was that total cash flows for the period decreased by $1 million, thus decreasing beginning of the year cash balance of $168 million to an ending year cash balance of $167 million. The balance sheet dated January 28, 2001, shows a cash balance of $167 million, and the user is provided through the SCF an explanation of why the cash balance decreased by $1 from the beginning of the year to the end of the year.

A brief history about the SCF is helpful to gain the maximum insight offered by cash flow reporting. In 1987, the FASB initiated specific cash flow reporting guidelines with Financial Accounting Standard (FAS) No. 95. The new accounting standard requires corporations to include a statement of cash flows in their periodic reporting.[1] The SCF became the fourth

---

[1] Statement of Financial Accounting Standards, No. 95, Statement of Cash Flows" (Stamford, Conn.: Financial Accounting Standards Board, November 1987).

required financial statement. The FASB designed the SCF to provide information to help the user assess the amount, timing, and uncertainty of an enterprise's cash receipts and disbursements in an accounting period. Cash flow information, combined with other financial statements and disclosures, helps the user evaluate the following:

- The enterprise's ability to generate positive future net cash flows
- The enterprise's ability to meet its obligations and pay dividends and assess its needs for external financing
- Reasons for differences between net income and associated cash receipts and payments
- The effects on the enterprise's financial position of its investing and financing transactions during the period[2]

This chapter shows the user how to use the SCF. We do so by working through The Home Depot SCF. Chapter 7 integrates cash flow data with other financial statement information in conducting a complete evaluation and analysis of The Home Depot financial position and financial performance.

5.2 SCF CONCEPTS, STRUCTURE, AND TERMS

Cash flows are the lifeblood of any business. For the successful business there is a distinct balance among operating, investing, and financing activities. Over time there will be a pattern of financing and investing activity, followed by the initiation or continuation of sufficient operating cash flows. The operating cash flows are used to purchase replacement assets and grow the business, as well a pay-off loan balances. The recap provided in Table 5.1 of The Home Depot SCF shows that sufficient operating cash flows are available to fund a substantial portion of its expansion and the remaining, approximately $737 million, comes from financing activities.

For the business that is having difficulty, signs and signals usually surface in its inability to generate sufficient operating cash flows to purchase new assets and repay loans. Over time there will be a pattern of financing cash inflow and investing cash outflow activity, followed by the initiation or the continuation of inadequate operating cash inflows. The lack of cash flows forces the business to seek additional financing to support day-to-day operations and to reinvest into the business.

For example, 2001 was a challenging year for the airline industry, and UAL Corporation in particular. UAL is the parent company of United Airlines. UAL's SCF is summarized in Table 5.2. The SCF reports that day-to-day operations consumed $160 million, and $1,969 million was used in investing activity. Financing activity provided the funding for operations and investing cash outflow in the amount of $2,139 million. As a result, even though the company had a poor year regarding performance, the cash flow balance increased by $9 million. The cash balance at the beginning of the year was $1,679. At the end of the year it was $1,688 million. The reason it increased was because it generated more cash inflow from financing activities than it used in day-to-day operations and investing activities. If this pattern continues for UAL or any business, financing sources will dry up and liquidation or bankruptcy will result. Certainly, leadership must put into action a strategic plan that changes this pattern of operating cash flows. Day-to-day operations must generate sufficient cash flows to support acquisitions and pay-off long-term debt.

---

[2] SFAS No 95, paras 4 – 5.

Table 5.2 Summary of UAL's SCF, December 31, 2001 (in millions)

Net cash used by operations	$ (160)
Net cash used in investing activities	(1,969)
Net cash provided by financing activities	2.138
Effect of exchange rate changes	0
(Decrease) increase in cash	9
Cash balance beginning of year	1,679
Cash balance end of year	$ 1,688

5.2.1 Net Cash Provided (Used) by Operating Activities

Net cash provided (used) by operating activities represents the source and use of cash in day-to-day operations. Illustrative operating cash inflows include:

- Cash inflow from the sale of goods
- Cash inflow from service revenue, such as retail income from equipment
- Cash interest income received on investments
- Cash dividends received on investments

  Illustrative operating cash outflows include:

- Cash payment for inventory
- Cash payment for operating expenses, such as heat, wages, supplies, and maintenance
- Cash payment for taxes
- Cash payment for interest

You are likely to encounter two different reporting methods for net operating cash flows. Table 5.3 recaps the details of The Home Depot net operating cash flows section of the SCF found in its annual report. The Home Depot follows the indirect method of reporting net operating cash flows. It is labeled the indirect method because the computation starts with net income, followed by several adjustments resulting in net operating cash flows. Adjustments are necessary to remove (1) the impact of noncash transactions and (2) accrual-based changes to current asset and current liability accounts from net income.

Table 5.3 The Home Depot, Operating Cash Flow section of the SCF, January 28, 2001

Cash Provided from Operations (amounts in millions)		Adjustment Source or Type
Net earnings	$ 2,581	
Depreciation and amortization	601	Noncash transaction
Increase in receivables, net	(246)	Current asset adjustment
Increase in merchandise inventories	(1,075)	Current asset adjustment
Increase in accounts payable and accrued expenses	754	Current liability adjustment
Increase in income taxes payable	151	Current liability adjustment
Other	(4)	Unknown
Net cash provided by operations	$ 2,796	

Table 5.4 recaps the UAL Corporation net operating cash flow section of the SCF. UAL also reports the operating section using the indirect method. The types of adjustments to net income will be similar for companies using the indirect method of reporting net operating cash flows. Observe in Tables 5.3 and 5.4 that The Home Depot and the UAL Corporation add back to net income, depreciation, and amortization amounts. These are noncash transaction. Each also adjusts current asset and liability accounts for operating cash flows associated with earnings.

Table 5.4 UAL Corporation, Operating Cash Flow Section of the SCF, December 31, 2001

Cash Provided from Operations (amounts in millions)		Adjustment Source or Type
Net earnings (loss)	$ (2,145)	
Cumulative effect of accounting change, net of tax	8	Noncash transaction
Gain on sale of investments	(261)	Noncash transaction
Pension funding less than expense	391	Noncash transaction
Deferred postretirement benefit expense	214	Noncash transaction
Depreciation and amortization	1,932	Noncash transaction
Provision (credit) for deferred income taxes	(1,144)	Noncash transaction
Undistributed losses of affiliates	30	Noncash transaction
Decrease (increase) in receivables	165	Current asset adjustment
Decrease (increase) in other current assets	170	Current asset adjustment
Increase (decrease) in advance ticket sales	(271)	Current liability adjustment
Increase (decrease) in accrued income taxes	(60)	Current liability adjustment
Increase (decrease) in accounts payable and accrued liabilities	589	Current liability adjustment
Amortization of deferred gains	(66)	Noncash transaction
Other, net	288	Unknown
Net Cash Used by Operations	$ (160)	

The differences between Tables 5.3 and 5.4 are (1) the level of detail and (2) the names of the accounts used by the respective company. You will encounter many different levels of detail and accounts in the operating section of the SCF. For example, Table 5.4 shows a gain on sale of investments as a $261 million reduction of operating cash flows. The reduction in operating cash flows is indicated by brackets. It is removed from operating cash flows because the cash inflow associated with a sale of an asset is an investing cash inflow, yet the gain portion is included in the net earnings (loss) computation. The Home Depot does not report this type of transaction for the period presented. It may be too small and simply lumped into the Other category of operating cash flow activity. For the interested reader, further details and mechanics behind operating section adjustments are found later in this chapter.

Table 5.5 recaps The Home Depot operating section of the SCF, if it had used the direct reporting format method. The direct method reports operating cash flows directly associated with day-to-day operations. Although a very logical presentation of operating cash flows, only a small percentage of companies use this method. The reason being is that the accrual accounting system does not readily capture cash flow data in this format.

Table 5.5 The Home Depot, Operating Cash Flow section of the SCF, January 28, 2001

Direct Method of Reporting (Approximated by the authors from available data.)

Cash Provided from Operations (amounts in millions)

Cash provided from customers	$ 45,490	
Cash used for merchandise	(33,141)	
		All computed from accounting records.
Cash used for selling and store operations	(7,821)	
Cash used for general, administration, and other	(200)	
Cash used for interest	(21)	
Cash used for taxes	(1,511)	
Net Cash Provided by Operations	$ 2,796	

The direct method begins with a row measuring operating cash inflows. The Home Depot reports in Table 5.5 that cash provided from customers amounted to $45,490 million. This represents cash that flowed into the business from (1) sales, (2) customers paying on accounts receivable, and (3) equipment rentals for the calendar year ending January 28, 2001.

Cash was used for the period (1) to purchase merchandise inventory amounting to $33,141 million, (2) for selling and store operations amounting to $7,821 million, (3) for general, administrative, and other operating expenses amounting to $200 million, (4) for interest payment amounting to $21 million, and (5) for taxes amounting to $1,511 million. This level of detail makes explicit the source and use of cash for The Home Depot for the calendar year, with net cash provided by operations amounting to $2,796 million.

The informed consumer should be aware of two issues regarding the direct method of reporting. FAS No. 95 requires separate line items to disclose cash flows associated with interest paid and taxes paid, as shown in Table 5.5. This information is needed for financial analysis.

When the FASB compromised and allowed for two methods of reporting operating cash flows, the direct method was recommended because of the explicit sources and uses of cash in day-to-day operations, as shown in Table 5.5. If a business elects to report operating cash flows under the direct method of reporting, then a separate schedule is required that reconciles the difference between net income and net operating cash flows. The reason for the reconciliation is to show the user why net income is different from operating cash flows.

Noteworthy for the user is that regardless of the method of how the company reports net operating cash flows, directly or indirectly, the evaluation and interpretation of net operating cash flows is exactly the same. Operating cash flows represents the amount of cash generated by (used in) day-to-day operations.

5.2.2 Net Cash Provided (Used) by Investing Activities

Net cash provided (used) by investing activities measures the source and use of cash in selling and purchasing assets. Illustrative investing cash inflows include:

- Cash from the sale of property, plant, or equipment
- Cash from the sale of land
- Cash from the sale of stock or bonds investments
- Cash from a vendor or other party when they repay a loan

Illustrative investing cash outflows include:

- Cash used to purchase plant and equipment
- Cash used to purchase land
- Cash used to purchase stock or bonds of another company
- Lending of cash to a vendor or others for greater than 90 days

Table 5.6 recaps The Home Depot investing section of the SCF. This section shows explicitly where and how much cash flowed into and out of the business from investing activities. This recap shows that The Home Depot continues to invest a significant amount of money into new stores, $3,558 million. Only one reporting method is permitted for investing cash flows.

Table 5.6 The Home Depot, Investing Cash Flow section of the SCF, January 28, 2001

Cash Flows from Investing Activities (amounts in millions)		
Capital expenditures	$	3,558
Payments for business required, net		(26)
Proceeds from the sale of property and equipment		95
Purchase of investments		(39)
Proceeds from maturities on investments.		30
Advances secured by real estate, net		(32)
Net cash used in investing activities	$	(3,530)

5.2.3 Net Cash Provided (Used) by Financing Activities

Net cash provided (used) by financing activities measures the source and use of cash to finance a business. Illustrative financing cash inflows include:

- Cash inflows from a bank loan
- Cash inflows from a bond issue
- Cash inflows from the issuance of preferred or common stock
- Cash inflows from the sale of treasury stock

Illustrative financing cash outflows includes:

- Cash used to repay the bank loan principal
- Cash used to repay the redemption of a bond principal
- Cash used to purchase the company's own stock (treasury shares)
- Cash used to pay dividends[3]

Table 5.7 recaps The Home Depot financing section of the SCF. This section shows explicitly where and how much cash flowed into and out of the business from financing activities. This recap shows The Home Depot is financing its growth for this period by debt to the extent of $754 million and equity to the extent of $351 million. Combining this information with operating and investing activities shows that operating cash flows are funding the majority of its growth. The recap also shows that it paid shareholders $371 million in dividends. Only one reporting method is permitted for financing cash flows.

---

[3] One may question why dividends paid is a financing activity. How to classify dividends paid was a controversial issue when the FASB voted on FAS no. 95. The compromise was to classify dividends paid as a financing activity because a business may elect to pay or not to pay dividends. Cash dividend payments more closely match a financing decision.

Table 5.7 The Home Depot, Financing Cash Flow section of the SCF, January 28, 2001

Cash Flows from Financing Activities (in millions)		
Increase in commercial paper obligations, net	$	754
Proceeds from long-term borrowings		32
Repayment of long-term debt		(29)
Proceeds from the sale of common stock, net		351
Cash dividends paid to stockholders		(371)
Net cash provided by financing activities	$	737

5.2.4 Cash and Cash Equivalents

In addition to defining the structure of cash flow reporting, the FASB defines specifically the term *cash*. Interestingly, prior to FAS No. 95 the term *cash* was not defined in the authoritative accounting literature and, as a result, carried a wide spectrum of interpretations. FAS No. 95 defines cash to include cash and *cash equivalents*. The definition of cash is clear. Cash equivalents are financial instruments that are (1) readily convertible to a known amount of cash and (2) so near maturity that they present an insignificant risk of change.

Typical cash-equivalent instruments include treasury bills, commercial paper, money market funds, and like investments where the original maturity is 90 days or less.[4] Thus, when the user encounters the term *cash* in the annual report, it actually represents the sum of cash and cash equivalents.

5.3 THE SCF: A DETAILED LOOK

The value of the SCF to the user becomes very clear at this point. Focusing on each line of operating, investing, and financing cash flow activity explains specifically why total year ending cash increased or decreased.

5.3.1 Net Cash Provided (Used) by Operating Activities

At this point, we want to make a special note to the reader. This book was designed to meet the needs of different users. The following section goes into the details and mechanics of how to compute each value reported in the operating cash flow section of the SCF. For those who do not need this level of detail, this section can be skipped without losing the flow of the remaining sections.

All businesses generate operating cash flows. See UAL, Table 5.2, for example. A business will report a net operating cash outflow when day-to-day operations consume more cash than generated in sales activities (i.e., when day-to-day cash flow needs simply out-pace cash flow generated from sales). When this occurs in consecutive years, it is time to question the long-term viability of the business.

---

[4] SFAS No 95, pars 8-10.

Let's work through each line of The Home Depot operating cash flow section to experience the thinking and mechanics behind the indirect method of reporting. The Home Depot operating section of the SCF for January 28, 2001, begins with net earnings of $2,581 million (Table 5.3). The logical question at this point is to ask, "How much of net earnings are actual operating cash flows?" To answer this question, net earnings must be adjusted to represent operating cash flows.

Typically, the first adjustment is for depreciation and amortization expenses. Depreciation and amortization reduce earnings, yet there is no cash flow associated with these expense items. Therefore, the first step is to add back to net earnings $601 million to reflect that cash did not flow out of The Home Depot for depreciation and amortization expenses. You will identify this line item on the vast majority of businesses that follow the indirect method of reporting. In fact, if you do not see an add-back for depreciation or amortization or both, it would be logical to ask why.

"(Increase) decrease in receivables, net" is the next line item. The brackets around $246 million means that this amount is subtracted from net income. The reason for subtracting is because the net balance in accounts receivable on the balance sheet increased by $246 million during fiscal year 2000. The balance sheet shows that the row labeled "Receivables, net" was $835 million on January 28, 2001, and $587 million on January 30, 2000, resulting in an increase by $246 million ($835 - $587 = $246), confirming that, in fact, receivables increased during the current period.

Now we explain why an increase in the balance sheet from "receivables, net" is a subtraction to net earnings of $246 million on the SCF. An operating cash inflow occurs when (1) customers pay in cash and (2) when customers pay-off any receivable balance due the company from a sale. Cash inflow from customers that pay at the time of sale is reflected in net sales and thus net income. No further adjustment is necessary.

For a credit sale to a customer, we need to evaluate carefully two transactions in computing operating cash flows. First, when customers purchase goods on account, the accounts receivable account on the balance sheet increases and the sales revenue account increases. Notice, however, that no operating cash flow has occurred with this transaction, yet the sales amount is part of net income for the period reported. Second, when a customer makes payment on an accounts receivable balance, the cash account balance on the balance sheet increases and the accounts receivable account decreases. This transaction is labeled an operating cash inflow.

Taking this a step further, we can infer that when the balance in the accounts receivable account changes from the beginning of the year to the end of the year, this means the amount recorded into accounts receivable for sales is different from the amount paid by customers. This is a natural occurrence in business because it is common for a charge sale in one accounting period to be paid in another.

The operating cash flow adjustment associated with sales revenue is computed by taking the difference in the balance sheet account labeled accounts receivable, or in The Home Depot case "Receivable, net." The difference between the beginning and the ending year balances signals the necessary subtraction or addition to net earnings in measuring operating cash flows. When the accounts receivable balance increases, this means more sales have been recorded into the accounting system than cash flowing into the business from collections. Notice, the beginning and ending period receivable, net balances on The Home Depot's balance sheet. Therefore, sales in terms of operating cash inflows is overstated by the increase in the accounts receivable balance. In The Home Depot case, a subtraction from net earnings in the amount of $246 million is necessary to reflect actual cash inflows from sales. When the accounts receivable balance decreases, this mean more cash flowed into the business from collections than sales recorded into the accounting system. Therefore, sales are understated in terms of operating cash flows by the decrease in accounts receivable. If this occurs, an addition to net earnings is necessary to reflect actual cash inflows for the period.

Please note, however, that for two reasons it is unlikely that the user can explain the exact SCF adjustment for all rows in the operating section when a business follows the indirect reporting method. First, for readability this section aggregates several accounts from the accounting information system. Second, small, immaterial adjustments to these accounts are made throughout the year that typically are not disclosed for the reader. Not being able to reconcile to the exact adjustments should not concern the user. Research indicates that most annual reports do not provide sufficient information to reconcile many operating cash flow adjustments when a business uses the indirect method of reporting. What is important is to be able to see the reason for the majority of the dollar adjustments. We demonstrate this in the follow paragraphs.

Merchandise inventories is the next row. Similar mechanics are used in adjusting for operating cash flows. The brackets around $1,075 million mean that this amount is subtracted from net income. The reason for subtracting is because the balance in the merchandise inventory account on the balance sheet increased by $1,067 million during 2000. The balance sheet shows that the row labeled "merchandise inventories" was $6,556 million on January 28, 2001, and $5,489 million on January 30, 2000 ($6,556 - $5,489 = $1,067). We can use this information, along with the cost of goods sold section on the income statement, to explain the majority of the $1,075 million merchandise inventory SCF adjustment.

Again, two transactions can be used to explain this adjustment. First, when a business sells merchandise the cost of goods sold account in the income statement increases and the inventory account on the balance sheet decreases. Notice that no operating cash flow has occurred at this point, and the cost of goods sold account is an income statement account that reduces net earnings. For the year ending January 28, 2001, the cost of goods sold account on the income statement shows cost of goods sold at $32,057 million and thus the inventory account decreased by the same amount. Second, operating cash outflows occurs when the business purchases merchandise inventory. When this takes place, the cash account balance decreases to pay for the inventory and the merchandise inventory account balance increases. When we continue with The Home Depot, we see that the balance sheet merchandise inventories account began the year with a balance of $5,489 million. We also know that the merchandise inventory account was decreased by $32,057 million during the year as a measure of cost of goods sold. For the merchandise inventory account to end the year with a balance of $6,556 million, The Home Depot must have made cash purchases for inventory in the amount of \$33,124 million. (\$32,057 + [\$6,556 - \$5,489]) As a result, \$1,067 million must be subtracted from net earnings for the actual cash flow associated with the increase in merchandise inventory for the period. Another approach to the SCF adjustment is to simply take the difference in the balance sheet account labeled Merchandise inventory (\$6,556 - \$5,489 = \$1,067 million) on the SCF. This means \$1,067 million more cash was used for inventory purchases than what is measured by net earnings; thus, it is a subtraction on SCF.

The next line item in the SCF is the increase in accounts payable and accrued expenses. In this case, \$754 million is added back to net earnings in operating cash flows. Similar to above, looking at the changes in the current liability section of the balance sheet is used to explain the adjustment. In general, when balance sheet accounts labeled payables and accrued expenses increase, an amount is added to the SCF. When these accounts decrease, an amount is subtracted from the SCF.

When The Home Depot records an expense on the income statement, the expense account increases and the accounts payable account increases. For instance, when the telephone bill arrives in the mail, The Home Depot will increase the telephone expense account and increase the amount due to the phone company in the accounts payable account. Notice that no operating cash outflow has yet to occur. When The Home Depot pays the telephone bill, the cash account balance decreases and the accounts payable account balance also decreases. The payment is an operating cash flow event. Reading The Home Depot's SCF tells us that \$754 million more was recorded for all expenses for the period than what was paid. That is, \$754 million was added back to net earnings because expenses recorded on an accrual basis were \$754 million greater than actual operating cash that flowed out of the business. If more cash is paid out in a period than was recorded as an expense, reflected when balance sheet payable accounts decrease, then the account's payable and accrued expense adjustment on the SCF would show a decrease, reducing net operating cash flows.

The next line item in the operating section of the SCF is the increase in income taxes payable. In this case, \$151 million is added back to net earnings in operating cash flows. Similar to above, looking at two transactions can explain why this amount is added to net earnings.

When The Home Depot records income tax expense on the income statement, the expense account increases and the income taxes payable account increases. No operating cash outflow has yet to occur. When The Home Depot pays the income tax obligation (i.e., writes a check to pay the tax bill), the cash balance decreases and the income taxes payable balance also decreases. This would be labeled an income tax operating cash flow transaction. An add-back of \$151 million tells the user that \$151 million more was recorded as an income tax expense for the period than was actually paid. If more cash is paid out in a period for income taxes than is recorded as an expense, then the SCF will show a decrease to net operating income in the SCF for income taxes.

The last line item in the operating section of the SCF is labeled "Other," showing \$30 million is added back to net earnings. An *other* account simply represents the net change of several current asset and current liability accounts combined. Details explaining why and how much are not typically provided in the annual report, nor are they necessary. An amount added back to net earnings means that less cash flowed out of the business in miscellaneous expenses than is reflected in net earnings. An amount subtracted from net earnings in the other category means that more cash flowed out of the business in miscellaneous expenses than is reflected in net earnings. The authors suggest that you only inquire about large unexplained "Other" account increases or decreases.

In summary, The Home Depot SCF shows that $2,796 million operating cash flows were generated from day-to-day operations in the fiscal year ending January 28, 2001. Clear for the user to see is that a substantial amount of cash was used in stocking the new stores with inventory, consuming approximately $1,075 million of cash. The Home Depot substantially offset this use of cash by allowing accounts payable and accrued expenses to increase by $754 million. An increase in merchandise inventory and payable accounts is logical, given that approximately 200 new stores were added in this accounting period. Chapter 7 provides a complete evaluation of operating cash flows, along with traditional accounting measures and analysis.

5.3.2 Net Cash Provided (Used) by Investing Activities

The investing cash flow section measures how much cash was (1) generated and (2) consumed with the sale and purchase of equipment, property, and investments in another business. The Home Depot engaged in seven types of investing activities for the years ending January 2001, 2000, and 1999.

1. *Capital expenditures, net of $16 million, $37 million, and $41 million of noncash capital expenditures in fiscal 2000, 1999, and 1998.* Capital expenditures are the purchases of long-term assets. This line on the SCF explains to the reader that The Home Depot has made substantial capital expenditures in cash amounting to $3,558, $2,581, and $2,053 million during the respective fiscal periods. The brackets indicate a cash outflow has taken place. The interpretation of, "net of $16, $37, and $41 million of non-cash capital expenditure" is not as clear. The words noncash capital mean assets were exchanged for some form of a liability. However, the annual report does not provide any further information. This lack of detail is relatively unimportant because the numbers are small. Lacking further details on this is not something to be concerned about and would not affect the financial analysis and overall evaluation of The Home Depot.

2. *Purchase of remaining interest in the The Home Depot Canada.* Most companies will report separately on the SCF a substantial capital acquisition of a business for cash. During the year ending January 31, 1999, The Home Depot completed the purchase of The Home Depot Canada, for $261 million.

3. *Payments for business acquired, net.* During the respective periods, The Home Depot purchased existing, ongoing businesses in the amount of $26 million, $101 million, and $6 million. The word *net* in this situation means that when The Home Depot purchased the businesses, the purchase included assets and liabilities for the net amounts reported. Typically, the annual report does not provide further information about small business transactions.

   This type of activity is important in financial analysis. The Home Depot is following a growth strategy. One way to implement this strategy is to purchase ongoing business ventures. The SCF investing section provides evidence to the reader that some of The Home Depot growth is being purchased. However, as mentioned above, the vast majority of its growth is through new stores, as identified by the substantial capital expenditure dollars.

4. *Proceeds from sales of property and equipment.* During the respective periods, The Home Depot sold existing assets. The cash inflow associated with the sales amounted to $95 million, $87 million, and $45 million. Notice the amounts are not bracketed, meaning a cash

inflow. The annual report does not identify the specific assets that were sold, but additional information could be gained by reviewing the SEC 10-K report. It is not unusual for a company to dispose of assets as business needs change.

5. *Purchases of Investments.* During the respective periods, The Home Depot made investments in stocks and bonds in the amount of $39 million, $32 million, and $2 million, respectively. Once again additional information describing the purchases could be gained from the notes to the financial statements or the SEC 10-K. The Home Depot annual report does not provide a specific identification on what was purchased.

6. *Proceeds from Maturities of Investments.* During the respective periods, The Home Depot sold investments that matured in the amount of $30 million, $30 million, and $4 million, respectively. Most investments have a well-defined maturity structure and therefore lead to an eventual cash inflow. The annual report does not provide a specific identification on the specific investments sold.

7. *Advances Secured by Real Estate, net.* During the respective periods, The Home Depot made net deposits on real estate in the amount of $32 million and $25 million. The $2 million inflow may have been the result of a sale of real estate that may have been purchased for a store location and management subsequently changed plans. The annual report does not specifically identify what was purchased or sold. However, it appears logical that this line represents real estate acquired for future store locations.

The Home Depot Company's SCF shows that $3,530 million was used as investing cash flows for the year ending January 28, 2001. A substantial amount of cash was used in building new stores, indicated by the line labeled Capital expenditures of $3,558 million. Spending this amount of cash should not alarm the reader of The Home Depot annual report. Previous messages to the shareholders have pointed to an aggressive growth strategy through store expansion. This level of growth also justifies why $1,075 million of operating cash flow was consumed in building product inventories. Chapter 7 expands the evaluation of investing cash flows, along with traditional accounting measures and analysis. The essential question to ask is, Are the amounts of investing activity reasonable for The Home Depot growth strategy?

5.3.3 Net Cash Provided (Used) by Financing Activities

The financing cash flow section measures how much cash was generated from loans and the original issuance of stock. The financing section also measures how much cash was consumed in the repayment of loans and the repurchase of stock. The Home Depot engaged in six types of financing activities for the years ending January 2001, 2000, and 1999.

1. *Issuance (repayment) of commercial paper obligations, net.* The Home Depot increased cash flows through the sale of commercial paper. In 2001 it generated $754 million through this instrument, paid back $246 million in 2000, and raised $246 million in 1999. The details behind this financing activity are identified in the accompanying note No. 2 to consolidated financial statements and discussed in Chapter 6.

2. *Proceeds from long-term borrowings.* The Home Depot increased cash flows by $32 and $522 million in fiscal years 2000 and 1999, respectively, via long-term borrowings. When a company borrows money, the cash account balance increases and the long-term debt account

increases.   Long-term borrowings are often a necessary component of any business operation. These funds are used to build new stores that will generate operating cash inflows for many years into the future.   Therefore, it is logical to borrow long term to finance expansion.

3. *Repayments of long-term debt.* The Home Depot used cash to repay long-term debt in the amounts of $29 million, $14 million, and $8 million, respectively.   This is important information for the user. As The Home Depot continues to grow, so will the amount of principal obligation. A successful company will generate sufficient operating cash flows from the investments to pay principal and interest on long-term loans. We will see in Chapter 7, how certain financial ratios can help to estimate a business' ability to pay interest and principal obligations.

4. *Proceeds from sale of common stock, net.* The Home Depot generated $351 million in cash flow by issuing 19,430,000 shares of common stock. The number of shares is computed by subtracting the number of shares outstanding on January 28, 2001, listed in the equity section of the balance sheet (2,323,747,000), less the number of shares outstanding on January 30, 2000 (2,304,317,000).

You can also identify this activity by carefully reviewing the consolidated statements of stockholders' equity and comprehensive income statement. This statement is discussed in the next chapter. The vast majority of this cash came from the sale of The Home Depot stock to employees. The first row for the reconciliation between January 30, 2000, and January 28, 2001, shows $349 million was sold to employees in "Shares Issued Under Employee Stock Purchase and Option Plans." The difference between the amount listed in the financing section on the SCF, $351 million, and the amount identified on the consolidated statements of stockholders' equity and comprehensive income, $349 million, is typically due to minor transactions that are not disclosed in the annual report.

5. *Cash Dividends Paid to Stockholders.* The Home Depot paid cash to its shareholders in the amounts of $371 million, $255 million, and $168 million, respectively. You can also identify the cash dividends paid on the consolidated statements of stockholders' equity and comprehensive income statement. For instance, the second to last row on this statement lists cash dividends at $0.16 per share, for a total of $371 million. The amount of $371 million is included on consolidated statements of stockholders' equity and comprehensive income to show the reconciliation of retained earnings from the beginning of the year to the end of the year.

6. *Minority Interest Contributions to Partnership.* For the years 2000 and 1999, The Home Depot owned greater than 50 percent of one or more subsidiaries. The exact amounts are not available in the annual report. The subsidiary partners must have made cash contributions in the amounts of $7 and $11 million, respectively. Further details of this transaction are not provided in the annual report, and it is impossible to interpret the exact nature of these transactions. If, however, the amounts were material, the user would search the notes to the financial statement or the SEC annual report 10-K for additional insight.

In summary, The Home Depot SCF shows $737 million was generated from financing activities. Clear for the user to see is that a substantial amount of financing cash inflow in 2001 came from two sources: $754 million was generated from a commercial paper transaction and

$352 million from the sale of common stock to employees. Chapter 7 expands our evaluation of financing cash flows, along with traditional accounting measures and analysis. Once again, the important question is, Is this amount of financing reasonable, given The Home Depot's growth strategy?

5.3.4 Effect of Exchange Rate Changes on Cash and Cash Equivalents

The impact of fluctuating currencies must be included in the SCF to reconcile the change between the beginning cash to the ending cash balance reported. For the year ending January 28, 2001, $4 million of net cash was consumed to cover foreign currency transactions. That is, The Home Depot had to use $4 million to cover the drop in the value of the dollar, in the form of decreased cash receipts or increase cash payments. The specific reasons why this occurred are not available in the annual report.

5.4 CONCLUDING REMARKS

The user can clearly see from The Home Depot SCF the many sources and uses of cash flow. A review of the balance sheet shows a $1 million decrease from the beginning of fiscal year 2000 to the end of fiscal year 2000. The Home Depot began the fiscal year with $168 million and ended the year with a $167 million cash balance. The details of the SCF illustrate the dynamics of where cash flowed into the business and where cash was consumed. A careful review of why shows substantial cash inflows from operating activities, cash outflow from investing activities, and cash inflows from financing activities.

GAAP requires a separate and total cash flow reporting for interest and income taxes when the indirect method of reporting operating activity cash flows is employed. The "Supplemental Disclosure of Cash Payments Made for" schedule at the bottom of The Home Depots SCF meets this requirement. The row labeled Interest, net of interest capitalized tells the user of the report that $16 million, $26 million, and $36 million, respectively of cash was used to pay interest. The wording *interest, net of interest capitalized* means that some interest payments are included as a cash outflow for investing activities. This occurs when interest is paid on a loan during the construction period of an asset. For The Home Depot this is the interest paid while new stores are being built. Thus, the amount shown in the supplemental disclosure schedule is for interest paid on all borrowings, except those related to new construction. The row labeled "Income taxes" means $1,386 million, $1,396 million and $940 million of cash was used to pay taxes, respectively. GAAP requires specific information regarding interest and taxes paid because this information is used in the financial analysis of a company.

The study of The Home Depot SCF is now complete. Notice the SCF is different from the balance sheet and income statement. The balance sheet measures the financial health of the business at a point in time and the income statement measure financial performance for a period of time. The SCF measures the flow of a very valuable resource, cash. An evaluation of all three statements along with the notes to the financial statement puts the user in an excellent position to project the financial success and identify concerns the business will face in the future. Chapter 7 shows how to complete this task.

Questions for Review

1. How are the balances shown for cash on the balance sheet and the SCF statement related? What information does a SCF provide about cash that comparative balance sheets do not?

2. Describe what is meant by *net cash provided (used) by operating activities*. If this number is negative (cash used less than cash provided), how does this affect your assessment of the company?

3. Describe what is meant by *net cash provided (used) by investing activities*. Explain how a company might end up with a positive number (cash provided greater than cash used) for this category? If this number is negative (cash used greater than cash provided), how does this affect your assessment of the company?

4. Describe what is meant by *net cash provided (used) by financing activities*. What circumstances lead to a positive net cash flow in this category? Negative net cash flow?

5. In general, what is the difference between net income from operations (as shown on the income statement) and net cash provided (used) by operating activities (as shown on the SCF)?

6. Explain how a company could have a positive cash flow from operations on its SCF and a net loss on its income statement.

7. Give specific examples of the types of circumstances found on a SCF that would indicate concerns about a company for investors and/or creditors.

8. Give specific examples of the types of circumstances found on a SCF that would indicate future success of a company.

Internet Exercises

1. Locate the most recent annual report for Starbucks (www.http\\starbucks.com). What is Starbucks' net income for the year? Its net cash provided (used) by operations for the year? Explain the differences in these two numbers. Explain the net change in cash balance for Starbucks for the year. Where did cash come from? Where did it go?

2. Search the Internet for articles on the importance of cash flows to a company. Write a brief summary on two such articles of your choice.

CHAPTER 6

Statement of Stockholders' Equity and Notes to the Financial Statements

CHAPTER OUTLINE

6.1 Statement of Stockholders' Equity
    6.1.1 Importance of the Statement of Stockholders' Equity
    6.1.2 Limitations of the Statement of Stockholders' Equity
6.2 The Home Depot's Statement of Stockholders' Equity and Comprehensive Income

6.3 Notes to the Financial Statements
    6.3.1 Note 1: Summary of Significant Accounting Policies
    6.3.2 Other Significant Note Disclosures
6.4 Concluding Remarks

Steve Ray is looking forward to reviewing the Statement of Stockholders' Equity and the notes to the financial statements. He has been told that the statement of stockholders' equity will show him why and how an equity account balance, such as common stock, changes from one period to the next. The notes to the financial statements discuss how Baker Electronics employed significant accounting policies for inventory valuation, depreciation expense, research and development costs, and much more. Steve knows the first note will provide him with a great deal of general information about Baker Electronics and its application of GAAP. The remaining notes will address specific qualitative issues regarding the numbers in the financial statements.

LEARNING OBJECTIVES

1. Explain the purpose of the statement of stockholders' equity.
2. Discuss the strengths and weaknesses of the statement of stockholders' equity.
3. Identify the elements typically within the statement of stockholders' equity.

4. Discuss the purpose of the notes to the financial statements.
5. Explain the significance of Note 1 to the financial statements as a whole.
6. Discuss the significance of each note to the financial statements.

6.1 STATEMENT OF STOCKHOLDERS' EQUITY

The statement of stockholders' equity (or statement of *change* in stockholders' equity) identifies the changes in all balance sheet equity accounts over a specified period. For this reason, the statement is titled, for example, fiscal year ended, January 28, 2001.

In a sense, one might contend that the purpose of the statement of stockholders' equity is similar to that of the statement of cash flow. To a degree, this is true. But rather than explain the change in one balance sheet element (cash), the statement of stockholders' equity explains the changes in *all* equity accounts.

Three points are noteworthy about the statement of stockholders' equity. First, similar to the statement of cash flow, three years of information are presented in the report. Second, tucked within the statement of stockholders' equity is a reconciliation of retained earnings from beginning balance to ending balance for the period. This reconciliation is a required disclosure and is identified as the fourth required financial statement. Third, FASB requires that significant changes in the equity accounts must be disclosed, to include comprehensive income. The statement of stockholders' equity fulfills this requirement.

6.1.1 Importance of the Statement of Stockholders' Equity

Creditors and investors use this report to better understand the changes in a company's equity position over a specific period of time. Keep in mind that this category—stockholders' equity—presents the net assets of *a* company (excess of assets over liabilities). As the makeup of assets and liabilities changes from one period to the next, so will stockholders' equity. The statement of stockholders' equity, therefore, helps the user to focus on the changes that occur.

In general, as a company becomes more financially complex, a statement of stockholders' equity becomes a necessity for external reporting. In their infancy, companies have few events outside of earnings and dividends that impact equity. When this is the pattern, a stand-alone statement of retained earnings is acceptable for external reporting. Most statements of stockholders' equity are included as a separate schedule, along with the other three financial statements in the corporate annual report. Occasionally, the statement will be separately included in the notes to the financial statements.

6.1.2 Limitations of the Statement of Stockholders' Equity

The statement of stockholders' equity has few limitations, simply because it is a summary financial statement used to explain equity changes. Because of this, the statement of stockholders' equity is not well suited for financial analysis. Most relevant equity information can be drawn specifically from the balance sheet stockholders' equity section and the income statement. One exception is a company's dividend payments. Dividend distributions are not reported in the balance sheet and fall outside the income statement. They are, however, reported in the statement of stockholders' equity.

6.2 THE HOME DEPOT'S STATEMENT OF STOCKHOLDERS' EQUITY AND COMPREHENSIVE INCOME

The Home Depot's statement of stockholders' equity and comprehensive income accompanying this text is prepared using a row/column format. The columns identify the respective elements of stockholders' equity. The statement of stockholders' equity includes the following categories:

- Common stock (in number of shares and dollars)
- Paid-in-capital
- Retained earnings
- Accumulated other comprehensive income
- Other
- Total stockholders' equity
- Comprehensive income

The rows identify the event that caused a change in the stockholders' equity account balance. These events, along with a brief discussion, follow:

- *Shares issued under employee stock purchase and option plans:* The issuance of additional common shares for employee stock purchase and option programs has multiple effects on the statement of stockholders' equity. First, the number of common shares outstanding will increase. Second, par value of the common stock is recognized based on the number of shares issued and the shares' related par value. According to The Home Depot, 20 million shares of common stock were issued with a .05 per share par value. This caused the $1 million increase in common stock. Finally, additional paid-in-capital must increase. The increase in additional paid-in-capital ($348 million) is based on the difference between the selling price of the common stock and its related par value (previously discussed in Chapter 3). The resulting effect is a total increase in stockholders' equity of $349 million.

- *Tax effect of sale of option shares by employees:* The exercise of selected stock options (i.e., nonqualified options) provides the issuing corporation with certain tax advantages. However, GAAP accounting treats the recognition of the tax advantage differently than the Internal revenue service. Under financial reporting guidelines, compensation expense is measured (if using a fair value approach) using this formula:

(Shares' market price - Option price on the *date the options are granted*) x Number of options granted

The amount is then allocated to expense over a required service (vesting) period.

Under tax law, however, compensation expense is measured and reported when the options are exercised. This timing difference results in the recognition of a deferred tax asset. As a result, when the options are executed, compensation expense is measured by using this formula:

Number of options x (Option price - Fair market value of the stock on the *date the options are exercised*)

Any expense differential between the two sets of rules results in an adjustment to a paid-in-capital account. As can be seen from The Home Depot's reported information, the tax benefit associated with the options exercised exceeded the previously reported deferred tax asset.

- *Net earnings:* Net income has a positive effect on a company's retained earnings from one year to the next. The Home Depot's $2.581 billion in earnings increases both retained earnings and total comprehensive income.

- *Translation adjustments:* Foreign currency translation adjustments ($40 million loss) reduced total stockholders' equity and comprehensive income for The Home Depot by $40 million in fiscal year 2000. Strength in foreign-denominated currencies relative to the U.S. dollar was responsible for this adjustment.

- *Stock compensation expense:* During fiscal year 2000 The Home Depot issued 750,000 deferred stock units and 2.5 million nonqualified stock options to a "key officer" (disclosed in note 4).

  Deferred stock units are options that allow an officer to exchange one stock unit for one share of common stock. No price is paid for the share received. Deferred stock units vest at 20 percent per year, and their fair value is amortized based on the vesting dates. This incentive plan resulted in the recognition of stock compensation expense on the income statement and an addition of $6 million to paid-in-capital and total stockholders' equity. Compensation expense is recognized over five years and is measured as the difference between the market value of the shares on the date the options were granted and the option price to acquire the shares (which is zero in the case of a deferred stock unit).

  The 2.5 million nonqualified stock options resulted in no compensation expense because the exercise price of $40.75 was equivalent to the fair market value of the shares on the date of grant.

- *Shares purchased for compensation plans (assets in trust):* In fiscal year 2000, holdings in assets in trust, a contra-equity account, decreased from $7 million at the close of fiscal year 1999 to $6 million at the close of fiscal year 2000. The decrease in the assets in trust balance of $1 million was primarily due to cancellations and vesting of restricted stock. Companies commonly use assets in trust accounts to reflect shares set aside for certain stock compensation plans.

  Often when stock prices decline, a company will acquire its own stock at the reduced price. When the market rebounds and stock prices have increased, the company can either reissue the shares or retain the shares in treasury. The result is an increase to paid-in-capital, treasury stock, or enhanced earnings on a per share basis. The increase to paid-in-capital, treasury stock, also increases overall stockholders' equity. The effect is similar to that of a gain. Keep in mind, though, that companies might not recognize gains or losses on the sale of their own stock. Nonetheless, the impact of the transaction may be positive, as if a gain was the result.

- *Cash dividends ($0.16 per share):* Dividends declared or paid by a company reduce retained earnings and total stockholders' equity. The Home Depot paid $371 million in dividends during fiscal year 2000; therefore, total stockholders' equity was reduced by that amount.

- *Comprehensive income for fiscal year 2000:* The comprehensive income of $2.541 billion is simply a summation of realized and unrealized income. (See Chapter 3 for a complete explanation of comprehensive income.)

Most statements of stockholders' equity and comprehensive income appear to be incomplete (missing values) at first glance. This is not the case, however. The reason for this "unique" appearance is that each reported event might only affect one, two, or even three components of stockholders' equity (therefore, the adjustments only influence a few columns in the report).

Because the components that make up the statement of stockholders' equity were reviewed individually in Chapters 3 and 4, we now move our discussion to the notes to the financial statements.

6.3 NOTES TO THE FINANCIAL STATEMENTS

The accounting profession has adopted the full-disclosure principle, which emphasizes the reporting of any information that would influence the judgment of an informed reader. Although the balance sheet, statement of operations, and statement of cash flows provide significant economic substance, additional clarification and amplification provided in the notes can improve the understanding of the financial statement information. Furthermore, *FASB Concept Statement Number 1* states that useful information can be provided within the financial statements or by some alternative approach where available. Companies that provide extensive note presentation are simply complying with Generally Accepted Accounting Principles (GAAP), and in certain cases, with the Securities and Exchange Commission (SEC). Notes provide this additional support and represent an integral part of the reported financial statements. They are a means of clarifying what is being presented in the financial statements and are audited along with the general financial statements.

The Home Depot annual report includes 10 notes to help enhance a user's understanding of its financial statements. The broadest and most generally read note is the first, "Summary of Significant Accounting Policies." Accounting policies are the accounting principles and methods used by the reporting entity. For that reason, users of financial information can look to this note to gain a general understanding of the business and related accounting applications and establish a framework for comparing two or more companies.

6.3.1 Note 1: Summary of Significant Accounting Policies

A careful review of note 1 provides an exceptional amount of quality information. The note begins with a description of the company and its operations and includes the name of the company, where it operates and what types of products and/or services it renders. For instance, you will find in note 1 that The Home Depot operates 1,134 stores.

Subsequent to the introduction of the company is a presentation of significant accounting policies that includes a brief presentation on a wide range of accounting principles and the methods of applying these principles. Much of this information, however, is more thoroughly discussed in the adjoining notes. The balance of this chapter provides illustrations and explanations of The Home Depot's significant accounting policies.

Fiscal Year
The Home Depot's fiscal year does not follow the calendar year. Generally, retail companies prefer to close their fiscal year at some point beyond the close of the calendar year. This allows companies to include peak holiday revenues as well as report reduced inventory holdings. Although the home improvement industry historically has not seen peak revenues during the holiday season, it reports under the same year-end for consistency with other retailers.

Basis of Presentation

The Home Depot prepares consolidated financial statements at the close of each fiscal year. This means that its financial statements reflect the position and results of all operations controlled by The Home Depot as if they are a single entity. The reports, therefore, include all wholly owned subsidiaries and majority-owned subsidiaries. Inter-company transactions between the parent and subsidiary are excluded because of the single-entity concept.

Cash Equivalents

Cash and cash equivalents are combined for reporting purposes in the balance sheet and the statement of cash flows. Cash equivalents are similar to cash but are not cash because these instruments are not in negotiable form. They are defined as investments in short-term, highly liquid instruments that have an original maturity of 90 days or less. Examples of cash equivalents are investments in commercial paper, treasury bills, and money market funds.

Merchandise Inventories

Recall from Chapter 3, inventory valuation is often based on a specifically chosen cost-flow assumption. The Home Depot uses a FIFO cost-flow assumption. Inventories are stated at the lower of cost (first-in, first-out) or market, as determined by the retail inventory method. This means that the earlier costs incurred for a specific product are the costs used to determine cost of goods sold. This also means that the reported value of merchandise inventory at the close of the year is calculated using the most current prices. In other words, an FIFO cost-flow assumption establishes a more realistic balance sheet value. The Home Depot calculates its margins based on the retail inventory method. Many companies like The Home Depot use the retail method because it is a more feasible method for companies that report a large volume of inventory.

Investments

Investments in equity and debt securities can be recorded at cost, at fair market value, or at amortized cost. The appropriate investment valuation model is based on its classification. Investments are generally categorized as *trading investments*, *available-for-sale investments*, or *held-to-maturity investments*.

For example, equity investments are carried at cost if market value is not readily determinable. Alternatively, they can be carried at fair-market value, and classified as *trading* or *available for sale*, if there exists a ready market for liquidation. The distinction between classes determines whether gains and losses will affect revenues and expenses in a given period or whether the gains and losses will be excluded from revenues and expenses but included in the organization's change in net assets.

Bond investments, by contrast, can be carried at cost or fair-market value, depending on the investment's classification. If management intends on holding the investment until the bonds reach maturity (held-to-maturity classification), cost or amortized cost is used as the basis for valuation. Essentially, this requires the organization to carry the investment at cost through maturity and not adjust to fair-market value from one reporting period to the next. If the debt investment is classified as trading or available for sale, the valuation model is similar to that of an investment in equity securities. The Home Depot's investments, consisting primarily of high-grade debt securities, are recorded at fair value and are classified as available for sale. Therefore, unrealized gains and losses are recognized as a part of other comprehensive income and reported in stockholders' equity.

Income Taxes

The disclosure in note 1 states that The Home Depot uses the asset/liability approach when accounting for income taxes. As discussed in Chapter 3, the determination of expenses and revenues differs under GAAP versus the Internal Revenue Code (IRC). Many of these differences are temporary (or timing differences) and subsequently create deferred tax assets (future tax benefits) or deferred tax liabilities (future tax obligations). The asset and liability valuation will thus be a function of the income tax rates that are in effect when the temporary differences are recovered or settled. As a result, a company's deferred tax assets and liabilities can change over time as changes in income tax rates are enacted.

In The Home Depot's annual report, note 1 addresses income taxes in this way:

The company provides for federal, state and foreign income taxes currently payable, as well as for those deferred because of timing differences between reporting income and expenses for financial statement purposes versus tax purposes. Federal, state and foreign incentive tax credits are recorded as a reduction of income taxes. Deferred tax assets and liabilities are recognized for the future tax consequences attributable to differences between the financial statement carrying amounts of existing assets and liabilities and their respective tax bases. Deferred tax assets and liabilities are measured using enacted tax rates expected to apply to taxable income in the years in which those temporary differences are expected to be recovered or settled. The effect of a change in tax rates is recognized as income or expense in the period that includes the enactment date. The Company and its eligible subsidiaries file a consolidated U.S. federal income tax return. Non-U.S. subsidiaries, which are consolidated for financial reporting, are not eligible to be included in consolidated U.S. federal income tax returns, and separate provisions for income taxes have been determined for these entities. The Company intends to reinvest the unremitted earnings of its non-U.S. subsidiaries and postpone their remittance indefinitely. Accordingly, no provision for U.S. income taxes for non-U.S. subsidiaries was required for any year presented.

Depreciation and Amortization

The purpose of this note is to disclose a company's selected depreciation method and the estimated lives of its fixed assets. According to the note, The Home Depot uses a straight-line method to allocate depreciation cost for buildings, furniture, fixtures, and equipment. This means that a depreciable asset's cost will be allocated uniformly to its period of benefit. The Home Depot also selected a straight-line method to allocate (amortize) the cost of leasehold improvements over the life of the lease or the useful life of the improvement whichever is shorter. What these approaches do is create consistent depreciation and amortization expenses on earnings from one year to the next.

Advertising

Television and radio advertising, as well as media placement costs, benefit the period in which the advertising is seen. Therefore, these costs are initially capitalized but written off over the period of benefit. As a result, most capitalized costs move quickly from the balance sheet through the income statement.

According to The Home Depot notes:

Television and radio advertising production costs are amortized over the fiscal year in which the advertisements first appear. All media placement costs are expensed in the month the advertisement appears. Included in current assets are $20.2 million and $24.4 million at the end of fiscal 2000 and 1999, respectively, relating to prepayments of production costs for print and broadcast advertising.

Cost in Excess of the Fair Value of Net Assets Acquired

The purpose of this note is to disclose The Home Depot's amortization method and period of amortization. According to the note, The Home Depot amortizes the excess acquisition cost on a straight-line basis over 40 years. Historically, the amortization of goodwill has resulted in an annual charge against earnings for affected companies. But a recent accounting pronouncement (FAS No. 141) requires companies to no longer write off goodwill unless the asset becomes impaired (future benefits no longer exist). As a result, The Home Depot and other companies will no longer report a systematic write-down of goodwill. The Home Depot assesses whether intangible assets can be recovered by determining whether the amortization of the goodwill balance over its remaining useful life can be recovered through undiscounted future operating cash flows of the acquired operation.

Impairment of Long-lived Assets

All long-lived assets, including intangible assets, must be tested for impairment of value when certain conditions exist. The purpose of this test is to prevent the overstatement of an asset's recorded value. Some conditions that might require a company to consider an impairment test are:

- Significant decrease in the market value of an asset
- Significant change in how the asset is used
- Pattern of losses or a projection of continuing losses
- Significant adverse change in legal factors or in the business climate that affects the value of an asset

As a result, certain long-lived assets will be written down (and a loss taken to income) when the carrying value of an asset is not recoverable. When this occurs, a loss on impairment is reported in the income statement as a nonoperating activity under other gains and losses. The balance sheet would now report the asset at its adjusted fair market value. Neither occurrence is disclosed for The Home Depot, as any impairment recognized was either immaterial, and therefore not required disclosure, or did not occur in the respective reporting periods.

Stock Compensation

Companies are encouraged by Statement of Financial Accounting Standards No. 123 (FAS 123) to apply the fair-value approach when measuring stock compensation. Under this method, an option-pricing model (or some other option valuation technique) is utilized to determine the fair value of the option. The option's value is then compared to the market price of the stock and, if greater, compensation expense is reported by the company. Generally, compensation expense is spread out over a predetermined vesting (or service) period. Companies that choose to use the intrinsic value approach are required to disclose the impact of the fair value approach in the notes to the financial statements.

According to the note, The Home Depot accounts for stock-based compensation under the intrinsic value method. This requires The Home Depot to recognize compensation expense as the excess of the market price of the stock over the exercise price of the option at the grant date and disclose in a subsequent note the impact of the alternative fair value method.

Comprehensive Income

As discussed in Chapter 4, comprehensive income includes net income as well as other gains and losses that have traditionally been excluded from net income. These items are reported as other comprehensive income and as a separate component of stockholders' equity. For The Home Depot, comprehensive income includes net earnings adjusted for revenues, expenses, gains, and losses that are excluded from net earnings under generally accepted accounting principles. Foreign currency translation adjustments and unrealized gains and losses on available-for-sale investments are examples.

Foreign Currency Translation

All companies that operate foreign subsidiaries are required to consolidate balance sheet and income statement information. As a result, foreign-currency-denominated financial measures are combined with domestic currency financial measures. And because foreign revenues and expenses are earned and incurred throughout the reporting period, all balances are translated to U.S. dollars using an average translation rate. Balance sheet accounts are translated to U.S. dollars at the current exchange rate. This method of translation is known as the current rate method, and it requires that translation gains and losses be placed directly into a stockholders' equity account and not be pushed through the income statement.

For The Home Depot, foreign-currency-denominated assets and liabilities are translated into U.S. dollars at the current rate of exchange on the last day of the reporting period, revenues and expenses are translated at the average monthly exchange rates, and all other equity transactions are translated using the actual rate on the day of the transaction.

Use of Estimates

All financial statements include a statement regarding the use of estimates in financial reporting. Generally accepted accounting principles require management to better measure assets and liabilities at the balance sheet date, as well as report the proper amount of revenues and expenses. Estimation techniques are used to determine a fixed asset life and related residual value for depreciation purposes, percentage of accounts receivable collectible, mortality rates for organization retirees and the related pension and health-care benefits, and recognition of contingent liabilities. The Home Depot notes that it uses estimates in conformity with GAAP.

Subsequent Events

One note that does not appear in The Home Depot annual report (yet is often included by other companies) is the reporting of a subsequent event. A subsequent event is a material transaction or event that occurs after year-end but prior to the release of the financial statements. This might include a statement regarding a company's divestiture, a recent court decision affecting a previously accrued contingent liability, or a disaster affecting one of the organization's facilities.

6.3.2 Other Significant Note Disclosures

Following the summary of significant accounting policies, there are additional, more comprehensive notes to help improve the transparency of the financial statements. These notes may consist of a considerable number of pages in addition to the financial statements themselves. This is often where tables, schedules, and calculations of particular assets, liabilities, revenues, and expenses are illustrated on a comparative year-to-year basis.

Our discussion is limited to the notes found in The Home Depot's annual report. You are likely to encounter notes not covered in this book that are difficult to read and understand. When this occurs, we suggest you contact a professional accountant or contact the company's investor relations department.

Note 2: Long-term Debt

The purpose of this note is to enhance the quality of the debt information provided in the balance sheet. A balance sheet line item that identifies long-term debt of $1.545 billion is relevant but simply limited in use. Additional information regarding the type of debt, its related maturity structure, and its carrying value needs to be provided by management. Supplemental information found in note 2 allows users to better understand a company's liquidity and solvency position.

A careful review of The Home Depot's note disclosure suggests that commercial paper, senior notes, capital leases, and installment notes make up a significant portion of its long-term liabilities:

- *Commercial paper*: Unsecured notes sold in minimum denominations of $25,000 with original maturities of 30 to 270 days or longer
- *Senior notes*: Notes that specify which note holders will be paid first in the event of liquidation
- *Capital leases*: Rent agreements between two parties that are accounted for as if they emulate a purchase with long-term financing
- *Installment notes*: An obligation paid in installments rather than in a lump sum

Alongside this disclosure is information concerning the instrument's maturity, associated interest rate, and total valuation at the close of the fiscal year. For example, the $754 million commercial paper obligation has been classified as long term as the company intends, and has the ability to refinance the obligations on a long-term basis. Likewise, the $500 million, 6-percent senior notes will not be redeemed until September 2004.

The capital lease obligations and the installment notes payable each require periodic installment payments. Therefore, any current maturities of long-term debt, $4 million as of January 28, 2001, and $29 million as of January 30, 2000, are reported as short-term liabilities and affect the company's current liquidity.

Note 3: Income Taxes

Typical income tax note disclosures provide financial statement users with significant relevant information. The Home Depot's note disclosure is no exception. To illustrate, let's carefully review The Home Depot's income tax footnote. The income tax note has three important sections:

1. An identification of the current and deferred components of income tax expense
2. The reconciliation between the U.S. statutory income tax rate and the company's effective income tax rate

3. An identification of those events that give rise to and create changes in deferred tax assets and deferred tax liabilities from one period to the next

The note begins by identifying the components of income tax expense, as reported on the income statement. The $1.636 billion, reported as "income taxes" on the income statement, has two components: the amount that is currently payable and the amount that is deferred to future periods. The deferred component is the result of temporary or timing differences that resulted from differences reported on the income statement and the tax return. Within each component is the amount of income taxes payable (currently or in the future) to U.S. federal, or state, or foreign government agencies.

The next section provides the reconciliation between income taxes at the U.S. statutory rate (35 percent) for fiscal year 2000 ($1.476 billion = 35 percent * $4.217 billion of income before tax) and the reported income tax expense of $1.636 billion shown on the income statement. The income tax expense reported on the income statement compared to income before tax reported on the income statement yields an effective tax rate of 38.8 percent. The difference between the U.S. statutory rate and the effective tax rate is often the result of different tax jurisdictions and rate differentials between countries. Also, permanent differences (those differences that never reverse) create an imbalance between taxable income and GAAP income. Permanent differences will cause the effective tax rate to be lower or higher than the statutory rate.

Some examples of permanent differences include

- Nondeductible fines and penalties
- Interest received on state and municipal bonds
- Premiums for executive life insurance policies for which the company is not the designated beneficiary

The last section identifies those items that caused the net deferred tax liability (deferred tax assets minus deferred tax liabilities) to increase by $108 million in fiscal year 2000. According to the table, the net deferred tax liability increased from $87 million to $195 million during the current year. This was the result of an increase in deferred tax liabilities of $81 million (attributable to depreciation timing differences) and a decrease in deferred tax assets of $27 million (attributable to financial accounting accruals). The combined change of $108 million indicates that The Home Depot has a net tax disadvantage in the upcoming years as a result of reported timing differences, (i.e., the amount of cash due taxing authorities increased).

Note 4: Employee Stock Plans

As discussed in note 1 under stock compensation, The Home Depot provides various incentive compensation programs to selected employees. The purpose of a second, more comprehensive discussion on employee stock plans is to identify the programs, the number of shares available under these incentive agreements, vesting periods, and compensation expense that the company would have reported (pro forma) had the company utilized the fair-value approach.

According to note 4, the company provides incentive stock options, nonqualified stock options, stock appreciation rights, restricted stock, and deferred shares to selected associates, officers, and directors. A brief discussion of these instruments follows:

- *Incentive stock options.* Employee stock option plans under the Internal Revenue Code allow the recipient to pay no ordinary income tax on the difference between the market price of the stock and the option price on the date of exercise. All taxes are deferred until the acquired shares (from the options exercise) are subsequently sold. However, in the year of exercise the individual could be subject to alternative minimum tax on the difference between the market price of the stock on the date of exercise and the option price on the grant date.

Example: Assume a Home Depot employee exercises a stock option at $30 when the market price of the stock is $40. In other words, the employee purchases a $40 share of stock for only $30. The resulting $10 benefit under IRS rules remains untaxed until the stock is later sold. As you can see, incentive stock options allow for the income tax consequences for the individual to be deferred indefinitely. Such incentive programs offer great appeal to prospective executives. Companies, on the other hand, are not allowed a deduction for the difference between the option price and the market price on the date of exercise.

- *Nonqualified stock options.* Nonqualified stock options are the opposite of incentive stock options in terms of advantages and disadvantages. Nonqualified stock options under the IRC allow the company a tax deduction for the difference between the market price of the stock on the date of exercise and the option price. The recipient, however, is required to pay income tax on the difference between the market price of the stock on the date of exercise and the option price. The tax benefit in this case lies with the issuing corporation.

- *Stock appreciation rights (SAR).* Instruments that provide the same benefit as stock options but do not require the purchase of the stock (exercise of the option). An SAR allows the recipient to receive in cash the difference between the market price of the stock at the exercise date and the market price of the stock at the grant date. Therefore, if the market price is $45 at the exercise date and $20 at the grant date, the recipient will receive $25 for each stock appreciation right.

- *Restricted stock.* These are company shares that may be forfeited by the recipient should he/she terminate employment with the company before a specified period elapses from the date of grant or if the performance measures established at the time of the grant are not met.

- *Deferred shares or deferred stock units.* Instruments that grant a predetermined number of shares of stock to selected individuals after a specific vesting period elapses. A deferred stock unit requires no cash contribution by the recipient when granted.

The note proceeds to discuss the respective vesting periods of these instruments and the number of related shares. Although this is not unimportant information, the significance of this note lies in the closing paragraphs and related illustrations. Here, The Home Depot recalculates compensation expense and related earnings per share under the fair-value approach rather than under the intrinsic value method. The effects of the fair value approach on earnings and earnings per share are substantial. For fiscal year 2000, The Home Depot would have reported a reduction in earnings of $217 million, or 8.4 percent. On a per share basis, basic EPS would have fallen to $1.02 from $1.11.

The incentive to not report compensation expense tied to stock option plans (incentive and nonqualified) under the fair-value approach is quite apparent when one considers the number of stock options held by key executives of major corporations. Some studies have shown that reported earnings would have declined in excess of 35 percent if companies reported compensation expense under the fair value approach.[1]

---

[1] P. McConnell, "Employee Stock Option Disclosures: An Addendum," *Accounting Issues*, New York: Bear, Sterns, & Company, Inc., April 21, 1997.

Note 5: Leases

Recall from note 2, The Home Depot reported a $230 million capital lease obligation and referenced note 5. Many companies, however, attempt to structure their lease contracts so they can be accounted for as operating leases (as discussed in Chapter 3). If they are successful in classifying a lease as operating, no leased assets or lease liabilities will be reported in the balance sheet. This method of *off-balance-sheet* financing often avoids the recognition of a significant lease liability. The purpose of this note, therefore, is to enhance the quality of lease disclosure. This is accomplished by providing a schedule of future minimum lease payments under both capital and operating leases at the close of the year.

According to the footnote, The Home Depot has $7.485 billion of future minimum lease payments under operating leases and $710 million of future minimum lease payments under capital leases. Both of these amounts include interest expense over the lease term. If we eliminate the interest from the capital lease obligation, the result is the $230 million lease liability reported in note 2. All capital leases are reported on the balance sheet at their present value (excluding future interest expense).

Operating leases, by contrast, bypass the balance sheet but must be disclosed in the notes to the financial statements. This note disclosure provides two important benefits. First, it allows the user to better understand The Home Depot's unreported operating lease obligations and related maturity. For example, The Home Depot's ratio of operating lease payments to capital lease payments is greater than 10. The airline industry for example has an average ratio of operating lease payments to capital lease payments in excess of 80.

Minimum lease payments under operating lease agreements = $512 million
Minimum lease payments under capital lease agreements = $38 million

Typically, a proportion in excess of 10 to 1 indicates management's philosophy on leasing. However, you would also need to evaluate the number of locations that are owned (The Home Depot owns approximately 80 percent of the store locations) by the company to truly understand management's overall asset to debt management philosophy. Under operating leases, earnings will report an equal amount of rent expense from one period to the next, as well as prevent the recognition of lease liabilities in the balance sheet. Under capitalization guidelines, management would report a greater combined expense during the early years of the contract's life and a reduced combined expense during the contracts later years. The timing differentials are a result of two key components:

1. *Effective interest computed on the capitalized lease liability:* As time passes, the lease obligation falls, therefore reducing the related interest expense.
2. *Depreciation of the leased asset:* The capitalized cost of the leased asset is written off over its period of benefit, similar to that of a purchased asset.

Keep in mind, however, that the total reported expense under either approach is equal over the lease term. In both cases the lessor must recover interest and loss of asset value. The only difference between capitalization and noncapitalization is the timing of the expense recognition, and the balance sheet disclosure.

A second important benefit of a lease footnote is that it allows analysts to re-compute certain ratios under the assumption that all operating leases are classified as capital leases. Analysts would simply eliminate the interest from the operating leases future minimum lease payments and gain an estimate of a capitalized leased asset and lease liability amount. This information would be placed into the balance sheet to gain a clearer understanding of a company's current financial position. As an aside, many accountants believe that operating leases should simply be capitalized to avoid companies continually circumventing capitalization rules.

Note 6: Employee Benefit Plans

Employee benefit plans 401(k) or employee stock ownership plans (ESOPs) are additional examples of deferred compensation. Under these programs, companies contribute stock or cash to a special trust, created as a separate legal entity. Employees may also contribute cash (through company withholding) to this trust. The cash contributions by the employees are then used to invest in funds chosen by the employee (e.g., mutual funds, international funds or the company stock) to become part of the trust. Over time, the value of the funds can often fluctuate substantially.[2] When an employee exits the company, share ownership in ESOPs is liquidated and the proceeds are distributed in the form of cash. However, 401(k) funds typically stay with the plan until the former employee reaches retirement age or rolls them over into another plan.

Companies and employees alike have certain incentives to participate in these programs. Employees contribute to these funds with pretax dollars (within IRS guidelines) and defer the tax on this compensation until their cash receipt. The company gains a tax deduction for the market value of the contributed shares.

Note 7: Basic and Diluted Earning Per Share

Recall from Chapter 4 that the income statement must include a presentation of earnings per share and weighted average shares outstanding for each year presented. Unfortunately, a mere presentation of EPS and shares outstanding can lack substance for certain users. As a result, reconciling basic earnings per share and diluted earnings per share is required in the notes to the financial statements. The reconciliation has two steps:

1. *Hypothetical numerator adjustments to net earnings, assuming that certain "equity-related" instruments are converted into common stock.* For example, if convertible bonds exist and we assume that they are converted into common stock we must also assume that no interest would have been paid on these bonds during the year. Therefore, earnings (in the numerator of the EPS model) would have been higher because interest expense would be less than reported when the instrument is converted to stock. This "if-converted" principle assumes that conversion takes place at the beginning of the year (or the instrument's issue date if after the beginning of the year).
2. *Hypothetical denominator adjustments to weighted average shares outstanding, assuming that certain "equity-related" instruments are converted into common stock.* For example, if the same convertible bonds exist and we assume that they are converted into common stock, the number of shares outstanding in the denominator of the EPS model would be higher.

The placement of these effects into the EPS model will, in most cases, reduce earnings per share. Occasionally, equity-related instruments can increase earnings per share. When this results, the instruments are said to be antidilutive and therefore excluded from the calculation of diluted earnings per share. Disclosure of all antidilutive securities must be reported in the notes to the financial statements. The purpose of the disclosure is to alert the reader that these instruments are currently antidilutive but might become dilutive in the future.

The Home Depot's note 7 presents the reconciliation between basic and diluted earnings per share. As you can see, an adjustment to earnings (numerator adjustment) in fiscal years 1999

---

[2] As an example, Enron Corporation, an energy trading operation that recently filed for bankruptcy protection, had company shares trading as high as $90 but were recently valued at less than a dollar.

and 1998 is necessary as a result of The Home Depot's 3 percent notes payable. This indicates that the notes payable are equity-related instruments and would reduce earnings per share if converted. Under a hypothetical assumption that the notes are converted into common stock, the after-tax adjustment of net interest cost to earnings amounts to $17 million in 1999 and $23 million in 1998. No adjustment to fiscal year 2000 earnings is necessary because all convertible notes were converted into common stock during fiscal year 1999.

Note 7 also discloses the adjustment to weighted average shares outstanding, the denominator of the EPS model. Under the if-converted principle, the 3 percent notes would increase the denominator of the EPS model by 51 million shares in 1999 and 72 million shares in 1998. In addition, employee stock options would, if exercised, increase weighted average shares outstanding by 37 million, 47 million, and 42 million shares respectively for fiscal years 2000, 1999, and 1998. As a result, diluted earnings per share is .01 less than basic earnings per share in fiscal year 2000, .03 less in fiscal year 1999, and .02 less in fiscal year 1998. The increased reduction in earnings on a per share basis for fiscal years 1999, and 1998 is a direct result of the 3 percent convertible notes.

Note 8: Commitments and Contingencies

Many companies, including The Home Depot, agree to buy products weeks or months in advance. These "purchase commitments" help to ensure that a company's inventory will be sufficient to meet ongoing consumer demand. Purchase commitments are generally not accounted for because they represent unexecuted contracts but are disclosed in the notes to the financial statements. According to note 8, The Home Depot was contingently liable for approximately $442 million under outstanding letters of credit issued in connection with purchase commitments.

A second contingent liability discussed in note 8 involves the reporting of pending or threatened litigation. Often, these cases can include hundreds or even thousands of plaintiffs. The outcome of these cases, as one would expect, can seldom be predicted with any degree of certainly. Nonetheless, companies must evaluate the probability of the claims being asserted and the probability of an unfavorable outcome. If the loss is "probable" and "estimable," then the company should accrue for a loss contingency. Ordinarily, companies, including The Home Depot, state, "The litigation is not expected to materially affect the consolidated results of operations or financial position."

The contingent liability illustration in Figure 6.1 is extracted from Philip Morris Companies Inc.'s 2000 annual report. The entire note disclosure spans seven pages, with much of its discussion tobacco related.

Figure 6.1 Contingent Liability Note

Philip Morris Companies Inc.
2000 Annual Report

Note 15. Contingencies

Legal proceedings covering a wide range of matters are pending or threatened in various United States and foreign jurisdictions against the Company, its subsidiaries and affiliates, including PM Inc., PM International and their respective indemnities. Various types of claims are raised in these proceedings, including product liability, consumer protection, antitrust, tax, patent infringement, employment matters, claims for contribution and claims of competitors and distributors.

Overview of Tobacco-Related Litigation

Types and Number of Cases: Pending claims related to tobacco products generally fall within the following categories: smoking and health cases alleging personal injury brought on behalf of individual plaintiffs, (ii) smoking and health cases primarily alleging personal injury and purporting to be brought on behalf of a class of individual plaintiffs, including cases brought pursuant of a 1997 settlement agreement involving claims by flight attendants alleging injury from exposure to environmental tobacco smoke ("ETS") in aircraft cabins, (iii) health care cost recovery cases brought by governmental (both domestic and foreign) and non-governmental plaintiffs seeking reimbursement for health care expenditures allegedly caused by cigarette smoking and/or disgorgement of profits and (iv) other tobacco related litigation. Other tobacco-related litigation includes suits by former asbestos manufacturers seeking contribution or reimbursement for amounts expended in connection with the defense and payment of asbestos claims hat were allegedly caused in whole or in part by cigarette smoking and suits by foreign governments seeking to recover damages for taxes lost as a result of he allegedly illegal importation of cigarettes into their jurisdictions. *Damages claimed in some of the smoking and health class actions, health care cost recovery cases and other tobacco-related litigation range into the billions of dollars.*

Note 9: Acquisitions

Current disclosure rules require that business combinations accounted for as purchases be discussed in the notes to the financial statements. As a result, companies are required to disclose all material acquisitions that take place during the years presented, as well as provide a *pro forma* or *as if* footnote. The purpose of pro forma presentation is to create comparability between years. For example, let's assume that a business combination takes place during 1999. The consolidated financial statements of the acquiring company would now include the revenues and expenses of the acquired company but only from the acquisition date through the end of the fiscal year. As a result and assuming three years of comparative information (1998 to 2000), a loss of comparability becomes apparent. Fiscal year 2000 now includes full-year revenues and expenses from the acquired company, fiscal year 1999 includes partial year revenues and expenses from the acquired company, and fiscal year 1998 includes no revenues or expenses from the acquired companies.

To improve comparability, the reporting company would disclose three years of comparative information as if the acquisition had taken place on the first day of the earliest year presented. Therefore, the numbers reflect full-year results for all years presented.

A subsequent review of note 9 identifies three business acquisitions disclosed by The Home Depot:

1. Maintenance Warehouse, a wholly owned subsidiary of The Home Depot, acquired N-E Thing Supply Company during fiscal year 2000. The acquisition was accounted for as a purchase but no pro forma disclosures were necessary due to the immateriality of this acquisition.

2. The Home Depot acquired Apex Supply Company and Georgia Lighting in fiscal year 1999. Additionally, these acquisitions were accounted for as a purchase, but no pro forma disclosures were necessary due to the immateriality of these acquisitions.

3. During the first quarter of 1998, The Home Depot purchased, for $261 million, the remaining partnership in The Home Depot Canada. The acquisition was accounted for as a purchase and the excess of purchase price over the estimated fair value of the assets ($117 million) was recorded as goodwill. No pro forma presentation is necessary, as 1998 is the first year presented for comparative purposes.

Note 10: Quarterly Financial Data (unaudited)

The purpose of note 10 is to identify The Home Depot's quarterly results of operations. This presentation allows users to compare revenues from one quarter to the next, as well as quarterly revenues between years. Obviously, depending on a company's industry and product mix, revenues can be markedly different from one quarter to the next. Candy manufacturers, for example, see revenue spikes during special holidays such as Easter, Valentine's Day, and Halloween. For The Home Depot, however, revenues are generally uniform from one quarter to the next. Second-quarter revenues (May to July), are an exception, and appear to be more favorable. This result might be attributed to the late-spring, early-summer home-improvement period.

6.4 CONCLUDING REMARKS

Our preceding discussion illustrates that the extent of note disclosure can be significant and far-reaching. Many individuals and organizations have commented that financial reporting requirements are too stringent and lead to what has been commonly called *information overload*. The evidence of this contention can be seen by the increase in the length of annual reports. Some annual reports now exceed more than 100 pages, with the average number of pages of notes increasing from 9 to 17 pages. Yet most users would prefer more information to less information. This, in itself, has a way of reducing investment risk.

So why has disclosure become so substantial over the past decade or two? There are a number of reasons. First, the business environment is continuously changing and becoming more complex. An example of this is e-business. Second, the complexity of the elements within the financial statements that arise from lease contracts, pension programs, executive compensation agreements, and business combinations have made disclosure more detailed and difficult to comprehend. And finally, users demand information that is more and more disaggregated, and they require it on a timely basis.

Questions for Review

1. Where can the user of financial information find information on dividends declared and/or paid by a company?

2. In general, what items will cause a change in a company's retained earnings from one year to the next?

3. What is the difference between net income (earnings) and retained earnings?

4. What is the purpose of the notes accompanying the financial statements? Are they required to be presented?

5. What is the purpose of the summary of significant accounting policies footnote? What specific types of information are disclosed in this note, and how does this benefit the user of financial information?

6. As the chapter states, one significant note not included in the annual report of The Home Depot is the one describing subsequent events. What is a subsequent event, and why would this disclosure be of significant interest to users of financial information?

7. Note 5 in the annual report for The Home Depot contains information on activities characterized as off-balance-sheet financing. What is the effect of such arrangements on the financial statements of a company? How do financial analysts incorporate this information into their analysis?

8. Why is information on commitments and contingencies important to users of financial statements? What types of information would you expect to find in the contingent liability footnote?

Internet Exercises

1. Another important required footnote disclosure for a publicly held company is concerned with related party transactions. Search the Internet for a recent example of a publicly held company that discloses related party transactions. Summarize the contents of the disclosure. Why is this information useful to users of financial information?

2. Locate the notes to the financial statements for AT&T. In the first footnote to the financial statements, locate the basis for revenue recognition. Describe how AT&T recognizes revenue. How does this differ from the realization principle described in previous chapters? Why is this important?

CHAPTER **7**

Analysis of The Home Depot's Annual Report

CHAPTER OUTLINE

Steve Ray has just finished studying about Baker Electronics. Now, using the annual report, he plans to confirm Baker's corporate strategy. Steve will critically evaluated Baker's financial liquidity, profitability, and solvency. Steve will then decide whether Baker Electronics has the financial resources to continue as a leader in bringing quality electronic products to the forefront of the industry, based on his evaluation and interpretation of several financial and nonfinancial pieces of information. Thus far, Baker's success appears to be driven by the quality of engineering staff, resources dedicated to research and development, and support for creative engineering teams. Steve will look to the annual report to verify that impression.

LEARNING OBJECTIVES

1. Develop the skills to confidently evaluate a corporate annual report.
2. Use the resources that are readily available to recognize a corporate strategy.
3. Learn and practice systematic financial analysis tools and techniques.
4. Evaluate and interpret financial and nonfinancial measures in reference to corporate strategy.

7.1 INTRODUCTION

An informed consumer reaches for the corporate annual report for answers to many questions. Suppliers evaluate a customer's ability to pay for merchandise acquired using the annual report. Bankers seek information that supports a history of loan repayment. A customer wants to be assured that someone will stand behind the product. An investor needs to understand a company's potential for creating wealth. Employees want to know about a company's ability to offer the opportunity to earn a living. Financial reports, along with qualitative information found in the annual report, serve as the central information source used to answer these and many other questions about a company.

This chapter provides a framework and a systematic process, showing how to use the annual report as a tool to meet your information needs in company analysis. Developing an answer to a question is a dynamic process. The user must apply judgment and dedicate time and energy. No single measure or value will provide the necessary information to reach a decision. Only by combining financial and nonfinancial information can the informed consumer of financial reports arrive at a reasonable decision.

This is the longest chapter in the book. The reason is that we want to present one complete road map and a comprehensive example of how to evaluate and interpret the information found in the annual report. The early part of this chapter shows you how to identify different corporate strategies. The middle section illustrates a common set of financial measures and ratios. The last section glues together this and the earlier sections of this book in a comprehensive financial analysis. You can follow the framework presented in this book as a guide to your use of a company's annual report.

7.1.1 Strategy, Tools, and Interpretation

Effective and efficient use of the annual report is a three-step process. The first step is to gain a focus on the business environment and company's corporate strategy. A conclusion about a specific question/issue must be framed in the context of the company's future goals and objectives and how it plans to meet identified targets. Knowledge of the competitive environment and the company's corporate strategy forms the reference point for financial evaluation and interpretation.

The second step is financial analysis. This chapter covers the most common financial analysis tools and techniques. Previous chapters moved you into position to conduct financial analysis on the required financial statements and related notes. Your knowledge of GAAP and financial statements at this point places you in position to understand why certain measures and ratios are drawn from specific sections of the financial statements and what they mean.

The third step is interpretation. The business press and the Internet typically focus on a common set of financial measures drawn from financial statements. Only the informed consumer can reasonably interpret these ratios and critically consume the analysts' comments and opinions. This is where judgment, knowledge of corporate strategy, and the ability to look at the overall picture painted by qualitative and quantitative information becomes essential.

The business press and financial analysts all have a certain bias. Informed consumers must carefully read these opinions and comments. Completing your own analysis places you in a position to confirm or challenge others' comments and enables you to reach your own conclusion. In many situations, the information and insight provided by financial analysts will be in line with the company's corporate strategy—and on other occasions, it will not.

For example, a corporate growth strategy requires cash. A company must generate cash flows to support day-to-day operations and must be able to pay interest and principle on loans. If cash flow is not being generated from previous growth attempts, a continued growth strategy might not be possible. In addition, you will find that most of the information available in the business press and on the Internet is designed for the investing public. Depending on your needs, you might have to read and critique the information from a different vantage point. The methodology and framework provided in this chapter will enable you to consume annual report information to meet your needs.

7.1.2 A Real-world Case Study

One of the best ways to learn the analysis tools and techniques presented in this book is through a real-world case study illustration. Keep a pencil in hand and circle the numbers on the financial reports when they are referenced in the text and recompute the ratios. This is how to achieve a higher level of learning and greater takeaway when reading and studying this material. The Home Depot serves as an excellent company for this purpose and is thus the focus of this chapter. You will find that the information provided in The Home Depot's annual report and financial statements supports its strategic focus.

The targeted level of learning for this book is the ability to read, evaluate, and interpret the annual report. The best source for the annual report is the company's Web site. Related information is also widely available from Internet sites. For example, Quicken.com provides a great deal of information about a company. The lead page for a company on the Quicken.com Web site is presented in Figure 7.1. Notice the various types of company information on the left-hand side: one-click scorecard, evaluator, analyst ratings, and more. An informed consumer can focus on this, or any other Web site that offers company data, and critically evaluate the information.

Figure 7.1 Illustrative Company Information Available at Quicken.com. Clicking the tabs on the left-hand side provides valuable information about a company.

HOME DEPOT INC

Quote
Chart
Intraday
News
One-Click
Scorecard
Evaluator
Analyst Ratings
Research
Reports
Message Boards
Compare
Companies
Profile
Insider Trading
Fundamentals
Financial
Statements
SEC Filings

Enter symbol(s):

HD   Go

Don't know the symbol?
Tip: You can enter multiple stocks (ex: AOL INTU)

Add to My Portfolio
Printer-friendly Version
E-mail this Page to Your Friends

Additional Internet site content
intentionally removed by the authors.

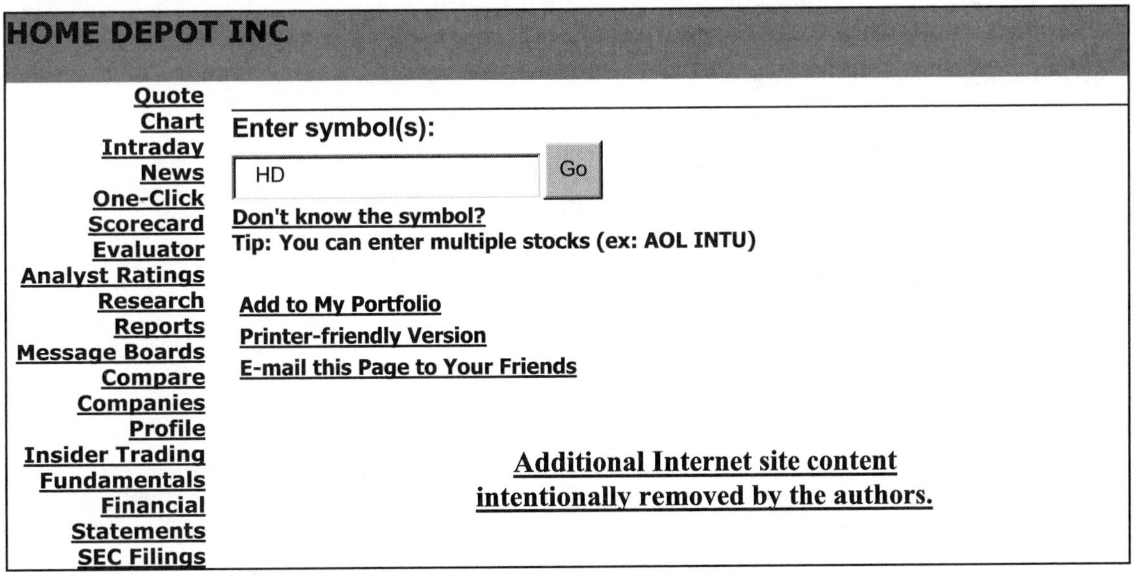

One comment is necessary before we begin. The topic of financial analysis is broad and complex. Books in excess of 800 pages are dedicated to this topic alone. Serious students of financial analysis would look to these books in preparation for a career as a financial analyst. This book has two less-ambitious goals:

- Provide a methodology and solid framework to understand and use the annual report as a business decision-making tool.

- Place you in position to further learn and study financial and nonfinancial tools and techniques.

7.2 CORPORATE STRATEGY FRAMEWORKS

A company sets its overall direction in what is labeled the corporate strategy. The corporate strategy is important because it serves as leadership's guide in directing financial and other corporate resources.

The annual report is an excellent tool for evaluating a company's corporate strategy. The report is designed to communicate (1) management's future strategy, (2) recent successes and failures, and (3) information regarding future cash flows and available resources. A clear vision of the corporate strategy is necessary to evaluate and interpret the current and future financial position and performance of a business. For many years the corporate annual report has served as an excellent source of information to learn about and evaluate corporate strategy, and this role will likely continue for many years to come.

A corporation will follow one of three general corporate strategy frameworks (see Figure 7.2): *growth*, *stability*, or *retrenchment*. The arrows in Figure 7.2 signal that corporate strategies tend to be a moving target. As industry and economic conditions change, so must the corporate strategy.

Figure 7.2 Corporate Strategies

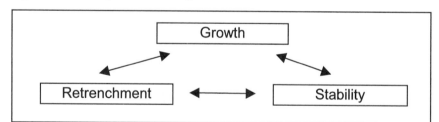

7.2.1 Growth Strategies

Most popular is a corporate growth strategy. A user can identify a corporate growth strategy when management announces a decision to increase sales and capital expenditures. Growth occurs when leadership strategically directs corporate financial resources in one or a combination of ways: horizontal growth, vertical growth, concentric growth, or conglomerate growth.

A *horizontal* corporate growth strategy is in action when a business works to increase profits in the same market segment (i.e., same product mix to similar customers). Walgreen's follows a horizontal corporate growth strategy. This company continues to open stand-alone stores in convenient locations to serve the retail customer with prescription drugs and common household products. The Home Depot clearly signals a horizontal corporate growth strategy. Robert Nardelli, The Home Depot's president and chief executive officer, places horizontal growth at center stage in The Home Depot 2000 annual report "president's message:"

> The approach is straightforward: Our growth will be driven by new stores, comparable sales increases in existing stores and through adjacent businesses. Our growth will be both productive and profitable…

A *vertical* corporate growth strategy is in action when leadership dedicates corporate financial resources to business operations previously controlled by suppliers or distributors. The way Henry Ford built the Model T at the turn of the century provides an excellent example of vertical integration. Car production began with iron ore entering the factory at one end and the automobile being driven out the other. Financial resources were dedicated to turning iron ore to steel, and producing and assembling parts into an automobile. The entire production process was owned and managed by Ford. The business research literature reports that backward, vertical integration into the value chain is more profitable than a forward integration into customer markets.

A *concentric* (related industry) corporate growth strategy is in action when a business dedicates corporate financial resources for expansion into related industries. The Home Depot is following a concentric corporate growth strategy by adding a product mix and selling to professional home improvement contractors, such as plumbers and electricians. In addition, The Home Depot reports in its annual report that it is working to gain a greater market share in supplying building maintenance contractors. The reason is that the home improvement professional market and building maintenance market segments combined have more than $200 billion in annual sales. The Home Depot has less then 10 percent of these market segments, and therefore views them as attractive growth opportunities.

A *conglomerate* (unrelated industry) corporate growth strategy is in action when a business dedicates corporate financial resources for expansion into different industries. General Electric follows a conglomerate corporate growth strategy, for example. The General Electric name is found in the financial services, jet engines, and medical equipment industries.

7.2.2 Stability Strategies

Some businesses follow a corporate stability strategy. A user can identify a corporate stability strategy by noticing a lack of announcements calling for change. Stability occurs in reasonably predictable industries in which change is slow and/or problems loom on the horizon. Three types of stability strategies are practiced: pause and proceed with caution, no change, or profit maximization. A corporate stability strategy may be the most difficult to identify. You will need to carefully read between the lines to pick-up on this strategy. The following paragraphs provide several signs and symptoms.

A *pause and proceed* with caution corporate stability strategy is essentially leadership's way of letting the business catch up and stabilize. America Online (AOL) had to follow a corporate stabilization strategy when it shifted its business model from a fee-for-time revenue stream to a flat-fee pricing structure. Growth was stronger than expected, and therefore leadership had to allow the infrastructure of the business time to catch up to market demand. In the early to middle 1990s, Dell Computer had to pause and allow its business time to build the infrastructure and personnel to support it current sales level. A pause and proceed with caution strategy is common following periods of rapid and continuous growth.

A *no change* stability strategy is when leadership decides to maintain its current course. Industry conditions and corporate resources are stable and there is simply no need to change when all is going well. A no change strategy is common among small businesses.

The informed consumer must keep a watchful eye for the *profit maximization* corporate stability strategy. This strategy is in place when leadership seeks short-term success at the risk of long-term decline. Oftentimes, leadership will manage reported earnings to show a profit, when in fact the business is in decline. When managed earnings are not possible, marginal performance will be blamed on poor economic conditions, government policy, or whatever excuse is available to point a finger. Chapter 8 covers several ways management goes about the profit maximization stability strategy and presents ways to spot this type of behavior. The Securities and Exchange Commission and the accounting profession are working hard to curtail management's abuse of FASB and SEC reporting guidelines.

7.2.3 Retrenchment Strategies

The final strategy is labeled a corporate retrenchment strategy. A retrenchment is exactly what logic tells us—the existing business strategy is not working. Financial analysis points to poor financial performance and perhaps a weak financial position. Required is a new business model that can bring life back to the company. Drastic action is necessary or business failure is imminent. A user can identify a corporate retrenchment strategy when numerous product lines are eliminated, plant layoffs are announced, or there is talk of general business closure. Corporate retrenchment strategies fall into three categories: corporate turnaround, captive, or last-resort.

A corporate *turnaround* strategy focuses management's attention on critical problems. The problems are typically identified in the business press, along with management's actions to correct the problems. At the time of this writing, Kmart announced the hiring of a new CEO to guide it through a turnaround retrenchment strategy. The new CEO's charge was to stabilize the current business environment and return Kmart to financial health. Ford Motor Company also announced a retrenchment strategy in January 2002. The company's work force worldwide was to be reduced by 35,000, and several car models would be dropped from Ford's line of automobiles. Many companies have experienced a turnaround retrenchment at one point or another in their history.

A *captive* corporate strategy positions the business to focus substantially all of its productive and financial resources to meet the needs of one customer. In return, the customer enters into a long-term contract to purchase a substantial amount of the supplier's production. One of two possible leadership decisions guide management to adopt this business model. On the one hand, this might be the only reasonable option for the business to remain a viable, functioning organization. On the other hand, this type of strategic focus is common to several industries. In the agriculture industry, for instance, farmers or ranchers often supply all of their products to one grocer. Certainly, this strategy carries unique risks.

Sale or bankruptcy/liquidation are *last-resort* corporate strategies. Each represents leadership's public acknowledgment that it is unable to sustain the business. An analysis and evaluation of the company's annual report is of little value at this point.

In summary, it is important to identify a company's corporate strategy before evaluating and making a business decision. Knowing a company's strategic focus helps the user put into perspective historical performance and future projections. The following chapters follow a logical building block sequence showing how to read, evaluate, and interpret the corporate annual report.

7.3 PROCESS TO IDENTIFY THE HOME DEPOT'S CORPORATE STRATEGY

The annual report, company press releases, and the general business press provide ample signs and signals of a company's corporate strategy. A review of The Home Depot's annual report for the years 1999 to 2001 provide sufficient evidence that this company is following horizontal and concentric growth strategies. The president's message in the 2001 annual report resonates this message with wording such as "launching new ventures," "expanding globally," "partnerships with suppliers," and more.

The next step is to find support for the corporate strategy in company press releases. The best source for press releases is the company's Web site. Press releases, along with financial statements, are typically located on the company's Web site under a tab labeled "Investor Relations" or something similar. An illustrative section of a press release in support of The Home Depot's horizontal growth strategy follows:

WORLD'S LARGEST HOME IMPROVEMENT RETAILER CELEBRATES 1,200TH-STORE MILESTONE, RETAILER ON TRACK TO OPEN 200 STORES THIS YEAR

> **Atlanta - May 31, 2001** - The Home Depot®, the world's leading home improvement center, is celebrating a new milestone this week—the opening of its 1,200th store, and, according to President and CEO Robert L. Nardelli, the retailer is on track to meet its goal of 200 new stores in 2001.

An illustrative press release in support of The Home Depot concentric growth strategy follows:

HOME DEPOT ANNOUNCES AGREEMENT TO ACQUIRE PLUMBING PRODUCT DISTRIBUTOR, YOUR "OTHER" WAREHOUSE

> **Atlanta - Oct 03, 2001** - The Home Depot, the world's leading home improvement retailer, has entered into a definitive agreement to purchase Your "Other" Warehouse, one of the country's premier plumbing distributors, with a focus on special order fulfillment. The cash transaction is expected to close in November. Terms of the transaction were not disclosed.

Ford Motor Company announced its retrenchment strategy with the following press release:

FORD MOTOR COMPANY ANNOUNCES REVITALIZATION PLAN, *January 11, 2002*

> North American restructuring actions outlined:

> "Our revitalization plan is based on executing the fundamentals of our business to build great products," said Chairman and Chief Executive Officer Bill Ford. "What we are outlining today is a comprehensive plan that builds for the future. It's going to take everyone in the extended Ford family – employees, suppliers and dealers – working together, over time, to make it work."

The final step in the process is to search the business press. Public relations professionals prepare the annual report and press releases. These communication vehicles are designed and written to convey information from the company's vantage point. The advantage of confirming your findings in the business press is that it provides an objective view regarding the validity of the corporate strategy. For instance, the March 19, 2001, issue of *Fortune* magazine, ran a full-length story on The Home Depot. This article confirmed and challenged The Home Depot's growth strategy. Throughout 2002, several business publications, such as the *Wall Street Journal* and *Business Week,* ran pieces on The Home Depot supporting and challenging the company's growth strategy. Each source contributes a piece to the analysis, and by reading different opinions a clear corporate strategy emerges.

7.4 FINANCIAL ANALYSIS

Financial analysis tools and techniques are useful for a variety of reasons. Creditors are most concerned about the risk of not being paid interest on a loan and the return of principle according to the contract terms. Investors turn to financial analysis for insight regarding the short-term and long-term profitability of the business. Employees, government officials, unions, and others turn to financial analysis to estimate the viability of the company for meeting individual and community needs. This section of the chapter has four purposes:

- It identifies where to seek-out the necessary information for financial analysis.
- It provides a framework to critically consume financial measures and ratios.
- It clarifies financial measures and ratio analysis limitations.
- It defines a common set of financial measures and ratios.

Once the corporate strategy is identified, you are ready to begin the analysis. Keep an eye open for stability in measures and always question whether the findings are consistent with the corporate strategy. Begin your inquiry with a study of the annual report and related financial statements that cover a reasonable period of time. Three to five years should be sufficient. Each annual report will include a recap of key financial and nonfinancial indicators for a range of 5 to 10 years. Look for consistency in the corporate strategy. A successful strategy of a well-run business is signaled by steady financial performance. If leadership communicates a particular strategy over time and financial performance is erratic, then this signals that problems might exist with the current strategy that will lead to greater trouble in the near future.

Note the word *signals* in the preceding paragraph. The essential benefit of financial analysis is that it will provide signs and signals of success and failure.

7.4.1 Sources of Information

The Internet and the local library are excellent sources for information. Press releases, the annual report, business articles, and analysts' reports and computed ratios are all readily available. The annual report and press releases can be accessed by clicking on an *investor relations* or a similarly identified button on a company's Web site. Certainly, the public relations department of a company will mail a hard copy of the annual report to anyone making an inquiry. The left-hand column in Table 7.1 identifies illustrative Web sites and the right-hand column identifies the type of information that is readily available.

Table 7.1 Illustrative Internet Sources for Company Information

Site	Type of Information
Quicken.com	Financial statements and nonfinancial information Selected ratios and three types of analyst reports
Reportgallary.com	Annual reports
Money.excite.com	Financial statements and nonfinancial information Selected ratios and three types of analyst reports
Hoovers.com	Financial statements and nonfinancial information Annual reports

Some sites charge for information and others do not. Analyst reports may cost in the range of $10 to $30. The user can typically access information by typing the ticker symbol or full name of the company. Look-up screens are available to help with the company ticker symbol. Given the market dynamics of the Internet world, the authors offer no assurance that these sites will be available upon production of the book.

7.4.2 Framework to Critically Consume Financial Measures and Ratios

Knowing how to evaluate measures and ratios is essential in financial analysis. Users encounter two types of information in financial analysis:

- Measures
  - Nonfinancial measures, such as the number of stores or employees
  - Financial measures, such as net income or operating cash flows
- Financial ratios (standardizing of measures)

Measures are whole unit values, such as a temperature, a pound, a gallon, or a dollar. To interpret a measure of performance, the user must have an established reference point or benchmark. For instance, 98.6 degrees is the normal body temperature for a person and a common benchmark used by health care professionals. A temperature above or below this point signals a medical condition that may or may not need treatment. Small deviations from normal, typically, are not a concern. But a temperature substantially above or below 98.6 degrees is a cause for concern. A physician must take age, gender, most recent physical activity, and more into consideration with temperature in the diagnosis process of a patient's medical situation.

The same is true for financial and nonfinancial measures. Analysts focus on measures, such as net sales, net assets, net income, and operating cash flows. Evaluation of these values is only possible when reference points to the respective measures are available. Analysts most typically use historical patterns when evaluating individual measures and interpreting overall financial performance, looking for stability and trends. In addition, the analyst must take corporate strategy, market conditions, industry dynamics, and more into consideration with financial and nonfinancial measures in arriving at a decision.

However, it is difficult to compare one company to another using financial and nonfinancial measures alone. Comparing companies of different size with whole dollar amounts does not provide meaningful insight. For example, a medium-size company might have profits of $10,000, and a larger company might have profits of $13,000. Certainly, the larger company is more profitable, but the relative difference of $3,000 is meaningless in rigorous financial analysis. Users of this information cannot determine which company is more profitable in relation to assets employed by the company. Consequently, users turn to financial ratios to complete their work.

A ratio is a means to standardize the measures found on financial statements. Measures must be standardized to enable comparison across time and companies of different size. *Standardization* means that measures are put into a ratio format. For instance, miles per hour (mph) is a standardized measure. Miles traveled are standardized by time. Standardizing by time is necessary for a person that travels 600 miles in 10 hours to know the average speed was 60 mph. A different person can travel the same 600 miles in 9 hours with an average speed of 67 mph (600/9). The two travelers can then compare their relative speeds of 60 mph to 67 mph. Two types of standardized ratios are computed for financial analysis.

Common-Sized Statements

First, financial statement values are put into a common size (standardized) format (Tables 7.2 and 7.3). The format of the balance sheet and income statement is identical to financial statements discussed previously in Chapters 3 and 4, except for the measures have been standardized in a ratio format. In Table 7.2 the balance sheet measures have been standardized by total assets. In Table 7.3 the income statement measures have been standardized by net sales.

A subtle, yet important, difference distinguishes the interpretation of the common-sized balance sheet and income statement values. Total assets serve to standardize the balance sheet. For example, for the year ending January 28, 2001, The Home Depot's balance sheet reports current assets at $7,777 million and total assets at $21,385 million. Current assets is put into a common size format by computing a ratio: $7,777 / $21,385 = 36.3 percent. Interpretation of the ratio goes as follows: Of The Home Depot's total assets, 36.3 percent consists of current assets. Another way to think about the 36.3 percent is this: For every one dollar The Home Depot reports in total assets, 36 cents consists of current assets.

The same thinking applies to the liability and equity side of the balance sheet. For the year ending January 28, 2001, The Home Depot's balance sheet reports long-term debt at $1,545 million and total liabilities and equity at $21,385 million. Long-term debt is converted to a common size format by computing a ratio: $1,545 / $21,385 = 7.2 percent. Interpretation of 7.2 is as follows: Of The Home Depot's total liabilities and stockholders' equity, 7.2 percent consists of long-term debt. Extending this concept, the user also knows that 7.2 percent of The Home Depot's total assets is financed by long-term debt. (Why? A common-sized balance sheet works for the liability and equity side of the balance sheet because of the balance sheet equation, where total assets equals total liabilities plus total equity.) The evaluation is this: For every one dollar of total assets, The Home Depot owes 7.2 cents of long-term debt.

The user is well served by a common-size balance sheet. Table 7.2 enables the comparison of balance sheet measures over time, on a relative basis, similar to the mph illustration. Note the percent of current assets to total assets. The percent is relatively steady, ranging from 37.4 to 36.4 percent. This signals that leadership is doing a good job controlling current assets as The Home Depot growth strategy continues. Looking further, it is apparent that inventory is a substantial component of current assets, from 30 to 32 percent for the reported period. Further support of management's abilities to manage inventory is that the ratio remains at approximately 31 percent over the three-year period. This is impressive, given that the number of stores grew from 761 at January 31, 1999 to 1,134 stores at January 28, 2001.

An easy way to monitor and read the information provided by a common-sized statement is to illustrate it in a graph. Figure 7.3 shows common-sized current assets, for example. The stability is readily apparent.

Figure 7.3 **Common-Sized Current Assets**

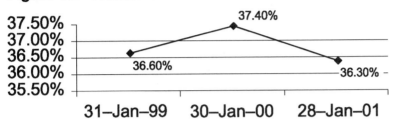

Net sales are used to standardize the income statement (see Table 7.3). For example, for the year ending January 28, 2001, The Home Depot's income statement reports cost of goods sold at $32,057 million and net sales at $45,738 million. Cost of goods sold is put into a common size format by computing a ratio: $32,057/$45,738 = 70.1 percent. Interpretation of 70.1 goes as follows: On average, each item sold to a customer cost The Home Depot 70.1 cents. The next row in Table 7.3 shows the gross profit ratio. Gross margin divided by net sales is in the range of 29 to 30 percent for the three years. Standardizing gross margin by net sales is often labeled the gross margin ratio (GMR). Again, the stability of this ratio for a company with a growth strategy shows management is doing a good job at controlling inventory costs. Evaluation of ratios is the subject of Section 7.4.4.

In summary, setting the balance sheet and income statement into common size formats provides useful insight. Informed consumers can evaluate specific ratios, interpret company performance across time, and benchmark this performance against different companies. The ability to complete a thorough evaluation is improved with a graphical presentation.

Combined Statement Ratios

The second type of financial ratio standardizes a financial statement measure on one statement or section of a statement to a measure on a different statement or section. For instance, a common ratio using measures from different statements is return on assets (ROA), computed as net income/total assets. For the year ending January 28, 2001, The Home Depot's income statement reports net earnings at $2,581 million and the balance sheet reports total assets at $21,385 million. To standardize these measures requires a ratio: $2,581/$21,385 = 12 percent. Interpretation of 12 percent goes as follows: For every dollar of total assets, The Home Depot is earning 12 cents. Similar to common size ratios, ratios computed across statements are computed over a period time for evaluation and interpretation. Figure 7.4 shows a steady ROA for The Home Depot.

Table 7.2 Common-Sized Balance Sheets

Consolidated Balance Sheets The Home Depot, Inc. and Subsidiaries	January 31, 1999	January 30, 2000	January 28, 2001
Assets	%	%	%
Current Assets			
Cash and cash equivalents	0.5	1.0	0.8
Short-term investments, including current maturities of long-term investments	0.0	0.0	
Receivables, net	3.5	3.4	3.9
Merchandise inventories	31.9	32.1	30.7
Other current assets	0.8	0.8	1.0
Total Current Assets	36.6	37.4	36.3
Property and Equipment, at cost			
Land	20.3	19.0	19.8
Buildings	27.9	28.3	28.8
Furniture, fixtures and equipment	13.1	13.3	13.5
Leasehold improvements	3.1	2.9	3.1
Construction in progress	4.0	4.6	4.8
Capital leases (notes 2 and 5)	1.5	1.4	1.2
	70.0	69.6	71.2
Less accumulated depreciation and amortization	9 .4	9.7	10.1
Net property and equipment	60.6	59.9	61.1
Long-term investments	0.1	0.1	0.1
Notes receivable	0.2	0.3	0.4
Cost in excess of the fair value of net assets	2.0	1.8	1.5
Other	0.5	0.5	0.6
Total Assets	100.0	100.0	100.0
Liabilities and Stockholders' Equity			
Current Liabilities:			
Accounts payable	11.8	11.7	9.2
Accrued salaries and related expenses	2.9	3.2	2.9
Sales taxes payable	1.3	1.6	1.4
Other accrued expenses	4.4	4.5	6.6
Income taxes payable	0.7	0.4	0.4
Current installments of long-term debt (notes 2 and 5)	0.1	0.2	0.0
Total Current Liabilities	21.2	21.4	20.5
Long-term debt, excluding current installments (notes 2 and 5)	11.6	4.4	7.2
Other long-term liabilities	1.5	1.4	1.1
Deferred income taxes (note 3)	0.6	0.5	0.9
Minority interest	0.1	0.1	0.1
Stockholders' Equity			
Common stock,	0.8	0.7	0.5
Paid-in capital	20.9	25.3	22.5
Retained earnings	43.6	46.5	47.5
Accumulated other comprehensive income	-0.5	-0.2	-0.3
	64.9	72.3	70.2
Less shares purchased for compensation plans (notes 4 and 6)	0.0	0.0	0.0
Total Stockholders' Equity	64.9	72.2	70.2
Total Liabilities and Stockholders' Equity	100.0	100.0	100.0

(Rounding effects are present)

Table 7.3 **Common-Sized Income Statements**

Consolidated Statements of Earnings The Home Depot, Inc. and Subsidiaries	Fiscal Year Ended		
	January 31, 1999	January 30, 2000	January 28, 2001
	%	%	%
Net sales	100.0	100.0	100.0
Cost of merchandise sold	71.5	70.3	70.1
Gross profit	28.5	29.7	29.9
Operating expenses:	0.0	0.0	0.0
Selling and store operating	17.6	17.7	18.6
Pre-opening	0.3	0.3	0.3
General and administrative	1.7	1.7	1.8
Total operating expenses	19.6	19.8	20.7
Operating income	8.8	9.9	9.2
Interest income (expense)			
Interest and investment income	0.1	0.1	0.1
Interest expense (note 2)	-0.2	-0.1	0.0
Interest, net	-0.1	0.0	0.1
Earnings before income taxes	8.8	9.9	9.2
Income taxes (note 3)	3.4	3.9	3.6
Net Earnings	5.3	6.0	5.6

(Rounding effects are present)

Figure 7.4 **The Home Depot Return on Assets (ROA)**

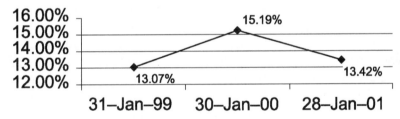

7.4.3 Financial Analysis Limitations

A critical consumer of financial statement information knows the limitations of the reporting process. Care must be taken in comparing measures and ratios. Watch for consistency regarding how the accounting rules were applied. The major area of concern is management's selection of inventory valuation method. If one business uses a first-in, first-out (FIFO) and the other uses a last-in, first-out (LIFO) inventory valuation method, financial statement measures and ratios are no longer comparable. The inventory measures must be adjusted for this difference for the comparison to be meaningful. Most often, the LIFO inventory value will be converted to a FIFO inventory value. The relevant information for converting LIFO inventory values to a FIFO inventory values found in the notes to the financial statements. Also, keep an eye open for change in depreciation method. This type of change makes difficult the comparison of a company's performance over a period of time. Turn to the notes to financial statements to identify inventory methods, changes in depreciation, or any type of change to the reporting process that affects comparability of performance.

Comparing companies on an industry basis is another concern. Some companies, such as The Home Depot, operate in clearly defined industry segments. In this case, comparing industry average to like competitors is a logical pursuit. However, other companies conduct business in many different industries. In this situation, the user must exercise caution. It is acceptable to compare firms across industries, but the user must be aware of how the industry was defined and how the specific ratios were computed.

Industry average details are readily available in the front pages of most industry average publications or on their respective Web sites. Industry average data points for this text were drawn from Dun & Bradstreet, Industry Norms and Key Business Ratios One Year Ending (2000), Retailing, Standard Industrial Code (SIC) No. 52 (building material, hardware, garden and supplies) and industry average assets over $50,000 million. This is The Home Depot's primary SIC cost classification.

Being aware of the issues and limitations mentioned in this section should improve financial analysis. The user of the annual report must know the basis of how accounting rules were applied and that financial and nonfinancial benchmarks represent reasonable comparisons. No single measure or benchmark provides adequate insight. Several measures and ratios must be evaluated in the context of benchmarks and the corporate strategy. Sound judgment is necessary to arrive at any conclusion.

7.4.4 Common Set of Financial Measures and Ratios

The title to this section is a bit misleading. No absolute authoritative body defines a common set of financial measures and ratios. More than 100 different ratios can readily be computed from annual report data. The measures and ratios selected for this book commonly are used in financial analysis. This set of measures and ratios provides a clear picture of a company's financial position and performance. In addition, the set encompasses those measures and ratios you will most likely encounter, regardless of individual needs, industry dynamics, or corporate strategy situation. The essential point is that knowledge, judgment, and common sense are necessary when using measures and ratios. The skills developed from reading this book can be readily extended to additional measures and ratios you encounter.

Knowing where to find measures and ratios and how to organize this information makes financial analysis a fun and rewarding pursuit. The financial statements serve as the central location for the majority of the data. The 5- to 10-year summary will include selective financial and nonfinancial measures and financial ratios. The notes to the financial statements will also have data points you may need for an evaluation and interpretation. Some information is reported in more than one location within the annual report. You will likely have to compute the common-sized ratios on your own. Some ratios are not provided in the annual report and must be computed as needed. The trick is to put the various sources of data points into a logical framework, the topic of the section to follow. Tables 7.4 to 7.8 recap the common financial measures and ratios by specific categories. The information captured in these measures and ratios serves the needs of most users in financial analysis. The concept and rationale behind each category is introduced in this section with these tables:

- Liquidity Measure and Ratios (Table 7.4)
- Profitability Measures and Ratios (Table 7.5)
- Activity Measures and Ratios (Table 7.6)
- Solvency Measures and Ratios (Table 7.7)
- Other Measures and Ratios (Table 7.8)

Liquidity Measure and Ratios (Table 7.4)

Liquidity refers to a company's ability to meet its current period obligations (i.e., can the business pay its suppliers and meet its short-term debt commitments?). One measure and four coverage ratios can be used to signal liquidity. Analysts estimate liquidity by evaluating *working capital* and operating cash flows. Working capital is defined as current assets less current liabilities. A business needs working capital to finance its inventory and accounts receivable and pay current liabilities. An adequate supply of working capital enables management to be proactive in taking advantage of purchase discounts and to better manage inventory and accounts receivable.

Three coverage ratios signal a company's ability to repay current liabilities. The *current ratio* is a popular measure of liquidity. Dividing current assets by current liabilities standardizes short-term resources to short-term amounts due. The word *current* means one year or less. A current ratio greater than one is a signal that the company has the cash or soon will have the cash to pay off its current liabilities. Analysts typically view a current ratio greater than one to be a good sign of liquidity.[1] However, a business can still have liquidity problems with a current ratio greater than one. The *quick ratio*, a more conservative measure of liquidity, eliminates from the current asset group those assets that are least liquid. At this point, the numerator is limited to cash, accounts receivable, and short-term investments. An additional measure of pure liquidity can be obtained by computing a *cash ratio.* Now, the numerator is limited to available cash only. A cash ratio signals the company's liquidity under the most stringent conditions.

An *operating cash flows ratio* signals a company's ability to generate the necessary cash flows to meet current and future obligations. Notice that the previous ratios considered resources on hand to meet current obligations. Each used current assets in the numerator. These ratios offer a limited view of liquidity because a business may have current assets accumulated, but lack the ability to generate cash in the future. The operating cash flows ratio changes the focus to operations. This ratio points to the ability of a company to generate future cash flows. The ability to generate cash is an important indicator of future liquidity. When a business has a negative operating cash flow, this ratio will become negative, simply due to the mechanics of a ratio. A negative result becomes meaningless for interpretive purposes, yet signals a concern.

Recognize that liquidity—and all ratios—are controlled, to some degree, by management. Let's use an illustration, and assume current assets equal $150 and current liabilities equal $100. Under this situation, working capital equals $50 ($150 - $100) and the current ratio equals 1.5 ($150/$100). How can management improve the current ratio? The current ratio can be improved by paying off, for example, $25 of accounts payable. Under this situation, working capital remains equals $50 ($125 - $75) and the current ratio improves to 1.67 ($125/$75). The ratio increased because the numerator changed by 17 percent [($150 - $125)/$150] and the denominator changed by a greater amount, 25 percent [($100 - $75)/$100].

This illustration shows the sensitivity of ratio analysis. Recognize that changes to the numerator and denominator impact ratios differently. Ratio values go up or down depending on the percentage change to the numerator and denominator. The advantage of using various liquidity coverage ratios is that they limit management's ability to control liquidity signs and signals.

---

[1] Palepu, K.G., Healy, P.M. and Bernard, V.L. *Business Analysis & Valuation Using Financial Statements* (Cincinnati, Ohio: South-Western College Publishing, 2000) pp. 9 to 15.

Table 7.4   **Liquidity Measure and Ratios**

Measure or Ratio	Measure or Ratio Computation	Unit of Measure	Measurement and Ratio Interpretation	Approximate Relationship to Corporate Strategy: Industry Average (IA) and Trend		
				Growth	Stability	Retrenchment
Working capital	Current assets - Current liabilities	Dollar amount	Amount of net current resources dedicated to running the business	Increasing and/or stable amount	Stable amount	Decreasing amount
Current ratio	Current assets / Current liabilities	Coverage	Indicates ability to pay short-term debt. For every $1 in current liabilities, the business holds x amount of current assets	Random above and below IA, stable or trending upward	Random above and below IA, stable	Below IA, trending downward
Quick (acid-test) ratio	(Cash + Accounts receivable + Short-term investments) / Current liabilities	Coverage	A refined view of liquidity; only cash, accounts receivable, and short-term investments are used as liquid assets	Random above and below IA, stable or trending upward	Random above and below IA, stable	Below IA, trending downward
Cash ratio	Cash / Currents liabilities	Coverage	A refined view of liquidity; only cash is assumed to be a liquid asset	Stable and/or trending upward	Stable	Variable and trending downward
Operating cash flows ratio	Net operating cash flows / Average current liabilities	Coverage	Cash generated from operations used to cover current liabilities	Stable and/or trending upward	Stable	Variable and trending downward

Profitability Measures and Ratios (Table 7.5)

Measuring and evaluating business profitability is a systematic process. Begin your study by looking first at *return on equity* ratio (ROE). ROE indicates how well management utilized shareholder resources. The logic behind this ratio is similar to placing money in the bank. Management must invest the corporation's assets wisely to generate an acceptable return to the shareholders. This return must be greater than what the shareholders can earn on other investments with similar risk. A high ROE indicates that management is successful at using shareholder resources to generate wealth, and a low ROE indicates that management's strategy may not be working as planned.

Next, profitability ratios can indicate where and how management generated a return for the investor. ROE is composed of two ratios: *return on assets* (ROA) and *financial leverage*. ROA identifies the return for each dollar of assets invested by management. A solidly performing company will have an ROA measure above the industry average, while a poorly performing company will have an ROA below the industry average. Financial leverage is a measure of the net assets of the company in relation to stockholders' equity. High levels of financial leverage suggest management has borrowed excessively to fund operations or to purchase assets. Wealth is generated for shareholders when management employs those assets and earns a higher rate of return than the cost to borrow the funds. Thus, ROE is driven by two factors: (1) ROA signals the performance of the assets and (2) financial leverage signals the relationship between equity and debt-financed assets used by management.

ROE = ROA x Financial leverage

= (Net income / Average net assets) x
  (Average total assets / Average shareholders' equity – Preferred stock)

= Net income / (Average shareholders' equity – Preferred stock)

The computation shows that management can improve ROE by improving operating performance as signaled by ROA, and/or increase the amount of financial leverage.

Focusing further on ROA may indicate how well leadership is managing the performance of the company. ROA can be divided into two components, a *return on sales ratio* (ROS) and an *asset turnover ratio*. ROS signals the net income for each sales dollar. The asset turnover ratio signals the sales dollar generated for each dollar of company assets. Thus, ROA is driven by management's success in controlling revenues and cost and the relationship between sales and assets employed.

ROA = ROS x Asset turnover

= (Net income / Net sales) x (Net sales / Total assets)

= Net income / Total assets

Several additional ratios can be used to evaluate the details behind ROS. These ratios will indicate where and how management is generating the ROS. This is where the common-sized income statement becomes a useful tool. All the pertinent performance measures are computed in an identifiable format, making for easy comparison.

The *gross profit margin ratio* signals average gross profit for each sales dollar (Gross Profit / Net sales). Figure 7.5 illustrates that The Home Depot generates on average gross profit of 29 cents from each sales dollar. This means that 29 cents from each sales dollar is available to cover business selling, general and administrative expenses, and the remaining income statement items. Evaluating whether this is good or poor performance is only possible by comparing it against an industry average and the company's key competitors. Figure 7.5 makes it easy to see that The Home Depot's gross profit margin ratio is consistently better than Lowe's Companies, Inc., yet Lowe's is moving ever closer to The Home Depot's at 29.9 percent.

The common-sized income statement also enables comparison of *selling, general and administration ratios* (SGA)(Table 7.3). A well-run business will carefully control expenses to maximize its long-term success. SGA ratios should remain stable or have a decreasing slope. A poorly run business, typically, cannot control selling, general, and administrative expenses. In this situation, the SGA ratios will likely bounce around and have an increasing slope. A review of The Home Depot's SGA ratios indicates selling and store operating expenses increased by 1 percent of sales in the most recent period, to 18.6 percent. The Home Depot's SGA ratios are evaluated in the next section.

Table 7.5 Profitability Measures and Ratios

Measure or Ratio	Measure or Ratio Computation	Unit of Measure	Measurement and Ratio Interpretation	Approximate Relationship to Corporate Strategy Industry Average (IA) and Trend		
				Growth	Stability	Retrenchment
Return on equity (ROE)	Net income / (Average shareholders' equity – Preferred stock)	Percent	Rate of return, based on the book value of shareholders' equity	Random above and below IA, stable or trending upward	Random above and below IA, stable	Random above and below IA, and trending downward
Return on assets (ROA)	Net income / Average total assets	Percent	Rate of return, based on the book value of assets	Random above and below IA, stable or trending upward	Random above and below IA, stable	Below IA, trending downward
Operating ROA	Operating income / Average total assets	Percent	Rate of return based on operating performance only	Stable or trending upward	Stable	Stable or trending downward
Financial leverage	Average total assets / Average shareholders' equity	Coverage ratio	Book value of assets employed by management for each dollar invested by shareholders	Stable or trending upward	Stable	Stable or trending downward
Return on sales (ROS)	Net income / Net sales	Percent	Net income generated by each dollar of sales	Random above and below IA, stable or trending upward	Random above and below IA, stable	Below IA, trending downward
Operating ROS	Operating income / Net sales	Percent	Operating profit from sales	Stable or trending upward	Stable	Stable or trending downward
Asset turnover	Net sales / Total assets	Coverage ratio	Number of times sales are greater than the company assets	Random above and below IA, stable or trending upward	Random above and below IA, stable	Below IA, trending downward
Gross profit margin	Gross profit / Net sales	Percent	For each one dollar in sales a percentage gross profit remains to cover operating and non-operating expenses	Random above and below IA, stable or trending upward	Random above and below IA, stable	Below IA, may be trending downward
Selling, general and admin.	Respective expense / Net sales	Percent	Expense analysis	Random above and below IA, stable or trending downward	Random above and below IA, stable	Below IA, trending upward
Net sales, net income, net operating cash flows	Same for each	Dollar amount	Graphed over time to identify performance trends in sales, earnings and operating cash flows	Stable and trending upward	Stable or random	Random and trending downward

Figure 7.5 Gross Profit Margin Ratios

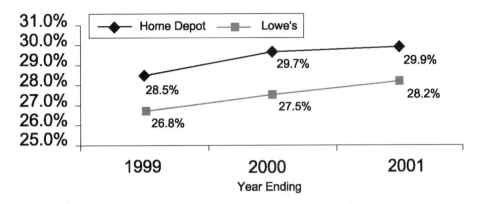

Two additional ratios focus users' attention on operating performance. *Operating ROA* signals performance regarding day-to-day operations. This is a clear indicator of asset utilization because income tax expense, interest revenue and expense, and other nonoperating activities are removed from the ratio. An *operating ROS* signals the company's profit level generated from sales activity alone. This is why the income statement is designed as it is. The operating ROS value standardizes the operating performance for comparison over time. The Home Depot's operating margins have been steady, ranging from 8.8 to 9.9 percent for the years presented, again drawn from Table 7.3.

Interpreting whole dollar measures over time completes the profitability analysis. The user should graph net sales over time, looking for a trend. Net income and net operating cash flows should also be on a separate graph. Smooth trend lines suggest to the user that the business is under control and management has a solid understanding of the business model. Random variability of earnings and operating cash flows suggests management does not have control of the business operations. For an illustration of smooth compared to random variability, see Figure 7.6. The Home Depot net operating cash flows compared to the Kmart Corporation. You will note stability and growth in The Home Depot and minimal growth in Kmart's measures.

Figure 7.6 Net Operating Cash Flows

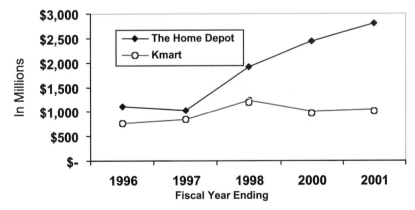

One final comment is necessary about profitability analysis. EBITDA, read *earnings before interest, taxes, depreciation and amortization,* is frequently reported by companies in press releases and by analysts. The intent of EBITDA is to proxy the amount of operating cash flows generated from day-to-day operations. Although this measure remains in the business press, the authors of this book do not recommend using it in the evaluation of a company's ability to generate operating cash flows or in any other form of analysis. Net operating cash flows reported on the SCF is a valuable cash flow measure.

Activity Measures and Ratios (Table 7.6)

Activity measures bring additional insight to the user. Liquidity and profitability ratios provide signals regarding management's successes and failures. Lacking in these ratios is an indicator helping to explain management's performance. Activity ratios point the user in this direction. Activity ratios focus the users' attention to the efficiency and effectiveness of leadership in managing working capital, a key business resource.

Table 7.6 Activity Measures and Ratios

Measure or Ratio	Measure or Ratio Computation	Unit of Measure	Measurement and Ratio Interpretation	Approximate Relationship to Corporate Strategy Industry Average (IA) and Trend		
				Growth	Stability	Retrenchment
Inventory turnover	Cost of goods sold / Average inventory	Times	Measures the number of times that average inventory of finished goods was turned over or sold during a period	Random above and below IA	Random above and below IA, stable	Below IA, trending downward
Days in inventory	365 / Inventory turnover	Days	Measures the number of days worth of inventory that a company has on hand at any given time	Random above and below IA	Random above and below IA, stable	Above IA, trending upward
Accounts receivable turnover	Annual credit sales/Average accounts receivable	Times	Measures how many times that average accounts receivable were collected during a period	Random above and below IA	Random above and below IA, stable	Below IA, trending downward
Average collection period	365 / Accounts receivable turnover	Days	Indicates average length of time in days that a company must wait to collect a credit sale	Random above and below IA	Random above and below IA, stable	Above IA, trending upward
Net working capital turnover	Net sales / Average net working capital	Times	Measures how effectively the net working capital is used to generate sales	Random above and below IA	Random above and below IA, stable	Below IA, trending downward or random

Inventory and accounts receivable typically consume a substantial amount of working capital. *Inventory turnover* measures how quickly inventory is consumed in operations through the business. A well-run business will have high inventory turns. A poorly run business will have low inventory turns. For instance, assume two competitors sell 100 dishwashers, each costing $100, for a cost of goods sold of $10,000. A well-run business may hold, on average, an inventory of 10 dishwashers, for an average inventory value of $1,000, and turn the inventory 10 times per year ($10,000/$1,000). A poorly run business may hold, on average, an inventory of 25 dishwashers, for an average inventory value of $2,500, and turn it 4 times a year ($10,000/$2,500). It is certainly more costly to hold an average inventory of $2,500 compared to $1,000 because of the cost of money for the difference of $1,500. The business press would report this in saying the well-run business ties up $1,000 in working capital and the poorly run business ties up $2,500 in working capital for the same resource.

The inventory turnover measure is often referenced in *days*. This is simply computed by dividing the days in a year by the number of turns. For the well-run business illustration, it turns the inventory every 36 days (365/10). For the poorly run business illustration, it turns the inventory every 91 days (365/4). Holding a minimum amount of inventory and turning it more quickly suggests that management carefully controls this resource and commits a minimum amount of working capital to inventory. Typically, this will lead to substantial cost savings and increase profitability. The reverse is true with less turnover and increased days of inventory outstanding.

A similar analysis applies to *accounts receivable*. Accounts receivable turnover measures how often average accounts receivable turn over in the form of credit sales. A well-run business will turn receivables often to increase cash flows. *Average collection period* measures the amount of time it takes to collect an average accounts receivable. It is computed by dividing the number of days in the year by the number of turns. Note that average collection period is measured in days, while accounts receivable turnover is measured as a frequency.

As an example, assume two competitors have $400,000 in credit sales for the current year. A well-run business may hold an average accounts receivable balance of $50,000, and turn the receivables eight times per year ($400,000/$50,000). A poorly run business may hold an average accounts receivable balance of $80,000, and turn it five times a year ($400,000/$80,000). For the well-run business, accounts receivable turn every 46 days (365/8). For the poorly run business, accounts receivable turn every 73 days (365/5). Holding a minimum amount of accounts receivable and turning it more quickly suggests management carefully controls this resource, and invests a minimum amount of working capital in accounts receivable. Typically, this will lead to substantial cost savings and increase profitability. The reverse is true with lower accounts receivable turn and increased days.

The last activity ratio, net *working capital turnover*, helps to measure management's ability to generate sales for each dollar invested in working capital. Management must control working capital for a business to be successful. If this measure widely fluctuates or is below the industry average, then this signals a mismanagement of working capital.

Solvency Measures and Ratios (Table 7.7)

Solvency is a fundamental business concept. A business is considered solvent when it generates a sufficient stream of cash flows to support day-to-day operations, and satisfies interest and principle payments on debt. When the business press identifies a company as insolvent, this means the company is unable to meet the cash flow demands of day-to-day operations and debt repayment obligations. If a business is insolvent, then it must be liquidated or reorganized. Liquidation means the business ceases to exist and the assets are sold. Reorganization means the business will undergo a restructuring under the protection of the courts. The advantage of court protection is that it prohibits creditors from seeking immediate repayment of outstanding claims.

Table 7.7 Solvency Measures and Ratios

Measure or Ratio	Measure or Ratio Computation	Unit of Measure	Measurement and Ratio Interpretation	Approximate Relationship to Corporate Strategy: Industry Average (IA) Trend		
				Growth	Stability	Retrenchment
Net financing cash flows	Taken from statement of cash flow	Dollar amount	Graphed over time to identify increasing or decreasing amounts	Trending upward	Stable or random	Trending upward
Debt to total assets	Total liabilities / Total assets	Percent	Percent of business financed by creditors	Management decision	Stable, trending downward, management decision	Unable to predict
Debt to equity	Total liabilities / Shareholders' equity	Percent	Percent of business financed by creditors for each dollar of equity	Management decision	Stable, trending downward, management decision	Trending upward
Long-term debt to equity	Long-term liabilities / Shareholders' equity	Percent	Percent of business financed by creditor long-term debt for each dollar of equity	Management decision	Stable, management decision	Trending upward
Net investing cash flows	Taken from statement of cash flow	Dollar amount	Graphed over time to identify reinvestments into the business	Trending upward	Stable or random	Trending downward
Interest coverage (Income statement)	(Profit before taxes + interest charges) / Interest charges	Coverage ratio	The number of times earnings plus other expenditures were above (below) interest expense	Trending upward	Stable or trending upward	Trending downward
Interest coverage (Statement of cash flows)	(Net operating cash flows + Interest paid) / Interest paid	Coverage ratio	The number of times net operating cash flows plus interest paid is above (below) interest paid	Similar pattern to interest coverage (income statement)	Similar pattern to interest coverage (income statement)	Similar pattern to interest coverage (income statement)

Ratios are required to see how financing activity impacted business solvency. Business solvency is evaluated with two different sets of ratios. The first set of ratios considers the relationship between a company's debt and assets and debt and equity. The *debt to total asset ratio* signals the percent of assets financed with debt (i.e., leverage). A high debt-to-asset ratio indicates that the company is financed substantially through debt sources. A low debt-to-asset ratio indicates that the company has been substantially financed through equity sources or day-to-day operations.

The *debt to equity ratio* signals the percent of the business financed by external debt holders compared to shareholders. The ratio reads, for every dollar invested by equity holders, *x* amount is financed externally. Notice that the numerator includes short-term and long-term debt. Long-term debt is the amount of debt that must be repaid beyond the current year. The *long-term debt-to-equity ratio* provides a refined view of the total debt to the shareholders' equity ratio. If this ratio is high relative to industry average, this means that management is leveraging external debt in an effort to generate more wealth for the shareholders.

Determining the relationship between business debt and equity is a leadership decision. There is no one optimal relationship. If the business environment is stable and management can predict operating cash flows with a degree of certainty, leadership is more likely to increase the debt structure near to the level that operating cash flows can support. The reason is that interest expense is tax deductible, and this makes it easier to increase shareholder wealth by borrowing money at a rate lower than the amount earned by investments into the business. For instance, if management can earn 15 percent on an infrastructure investment where the interest cost runs 8 percent, it can increase the wealth of the shareholders by 7 percent. However, if the business environment is unstable and management cannot predict operating cash flows with a degree of certainty, management is more likely to keep the debt structure conservative to prevent increased risk of insolvency. In this situation, more equity will be used to finance the business. The advantage of equity is that it does not demand a cash flow in the way of principle and interest payment.

A graph of *net investing cash flows* signals the company's overall investment pattern. Although not purely a solvency measure, it does signal what management has done with its cash. If management is generating cash inflows through financing activities, then the user should see an investing activity pattern as well. To see a cash inflow form operating and financing activities with no corresponding investments, suggests that management is using the cash inflows for some other purpose. Certainly the user would want to investigate carefully what the company is doing with its excess cash flows.

A second set of ratios helps to evaluate a company's ability to pay interest. The *interest coverage ratio* signals the degree of risk faced by the debt holder. This traditional ratio, drawn from the income statement, shows how much greater earnings are than the company's required interest payments. If this measure is one or less than one, for any significant period of time, then the business is likely facing insolvency. The interest coverage ratio drawn from the SCF offers a similar view. An industry average ratio was not readily available at the time this book was written. However, measuring coverage on a pure operating cash flow basis removes the effects of accrual accounting. Logic tells us that the two coverage ratios should run parallel over time. If they do not, additional research should be done.

Other Measures and Ratios (Table 7.8)

Common in the business press are ratios that summarize overall business performance. *Earnings per share (EPS)* is a widely discussed measure for publicly traded organizations. EPS signals the earnings for each share of common stock. Basic EPS is computed as net earnings minus preferred stock dividends divided by the weighted average common shares outstanding. This is a straightforward computation reported at the bottom of the income statement.

Table 7.8 Other Measures and Ratios

Measure or Ratio	Measure or Ratio Computation	Unit of Measure	Measurement and Ratio Interpretation	Approximate Relationship to Corporate Strategy: Industry Average (IA) Trend		
				Growth	Stability	Retrenchment
Earnings per share (EPS)	(Net earnings - Preferred stock dividends) / Weighted average # of common shares	Dollars per share	Net earnings generated for each share of common stock, basic and diluted	Random above and below IA	Random above and below IA, stable	Below IA, trending downward
Price to earnings (PE)	Market price per share / EPS	Dollar amount	The number of times the open market selling price per share is above the EPS	Random above IA	Random above and below IA, stable	Below IA, trending downward
Dividend pay-out	Annual dividends per share / EPS	Percent	Percentage of profit that is paid out as a dividend	Management decision	Management decision	Management decision

Diluted EPS is a much more complex measure to compute (as shown in Chapter 4). A company will finance the business with many different types of debt and equity instruments. For example, preferred stock is a financing instrument that falls between a pure debt instrument and a pure common stock instrument. Many times these instruments will include the option to convert to common stock. Diluted EPS considers the impact of all such instruments on earnings per share. This is why diluted EPS is always less than basic EPS. If there is a significant difference between basic and diluted EPS this indicates a complex financial structure and the potential for future shareholder dilution.

The *price to earning (P/E) ratio* links the market value of a stock to reported earnings. The market price for a stock is widely distributed. EPS signals the earnings for one share of stock. Dividing market price per share by EPS signals the market's perception of how successful the company will be in the future. A high P/E ratio is one indicator that the open market feels management can create significant long-term shareholder wealth. A low P/E ratio indicates that the open market is less certain of management's ability to generate future wealth for the shareholder.

The *dividend payout ratio* is applicable when a company pays dividends. This ratio indicates the percentage amount of earnings returned to the shareholder. For example, a company that pays a $1 dividend and has a basic EPS of $4 is returning 25 percent ($1/$4) of the earnings to the shareholder.

Next, we show how to step through an analysis of The Home Depot. The case study demonstration is designed to show how to organize, manage, and draw a logical conclusion from your analysis. We want to emphasize the importance of this last statement. The current and future financial reporting process will be scrutinized and criticized in the business press. In some situations this is justified and in others it is not. Much of the criticism comes from investors that blindly relied on someone else's analysis and opinions. Your analysis can support or challenge the opinions of the professional analyst. GAAP provides a solid framework for reporting and financial analysis. The informed consumer can use this framework to gain a solid understanding of a company's financial position and potential for long-term success.

No longer will you rely on the opinions and comments of professional analysts as the sole authority. A careful evaluation of each measure and ratio will enable you to make informed decisions regarding a company's liquidity, profitability, and solvency. The user's judgment must be framed within the organization's corporate strategy.

7.5 THE HOME DEPOT EVALUATION

Many users turn to the annual report for answers to a wide range of questions. Suppliers want to build a relationship with financially sound customers, bankers and creditors are concerned about the risk of a loan default, customers look to purchase necessary supplies from a reliable company. For these reasons and more, the annual report serves as a central repository of information.

This section illustrates a systematic framework showing how to use the annual report and related financial statements to evaluate and interpret The Home Depot's (1) current financial health and performance and (2) ability to grow as identified by its corporate strategy. We selected The Home Depot because it is visible in most communities, is a well-managed company, and follows sound reporting practices both in complying with the letter of the law and the spirit of the law.

Recall that sound financial analysis can only begin if one understands a company's corporate strategy. The president's message in the annual report typically outlines the strategy and offers clues as to how management will implement its corporate strategy. Bob Nardelli, president and CEO of The Home Depot, discusses strategy in his February 19, 2001, letter to the stockholders. He states that growth is going to occur by (1) opening approximately 200 new stores and (2) generating greater profits from each store.

Additional illustrative phrases include:

- We continue to be a great growth company…
- Our growth will be driven by new stores, comparable sales increases in existing stores…
- Our growth will be both productive and profitable…
- We will continue to be innovative and more productive in existing stores…

Whether the CEO's declared strategic initiatives make sense can be substantiated by external sources. The business press is an excellent place to find support for or conflicting views regarding the company's corporate strategy. Generally, two to three quality business publications will suffice in gaining a cross-section of opinions. This is necessary to offset the editorial bias of one publication over another. In addition, you should read and study three to five analyst reports. Again, a cross-section of analyst reports reduces the bias of a single analyst.

The Home Depot's growth strategy is soundly supported in the business press and by analysts. On February 6, 2002, the business press reported The Home Depot opened 17 new stores in 12 states, adding 3,000 new associates. On January 14, 2002, the business press reported that The Home Depot would consolidate its Mid-south Division and Southern Division, effective immediately. This change is designed to leverage operating efficiencies. In March 2002 The Home Depot purchased four stores in Mexico and reported plans to open two new stores. These reports and several throughout this and previous years provide ample evidence that The Home Depot continues to open new stores and focuses on improving store profitability in support of its growth strategy.

Analyst reports support The Home Depot's growth strategy. Common themes throughout the reports are that The Home Depot is liquid and profitable, and that management has conservatively balanced long-term debt to equity. In addition, the reports suggest that The Home Depot has the necessary resources to sustain a growth strategy.

Interestingly, some analysts do not recommend The Home Depot as a stock to purchase. They find the company to be liquid, financially sound, and profitable, and the current market price clearly reflects its success. This fact is reflected in a P/E ratio substantially above industry average. Thus, for an investor looking for substantial growth in market value, this may not be a stock to purchase. Alternatively, this is a good sign for someone looking for a sound investment in a stable company. This is a good signal for a supplier, banker, employee, or customer looking to build a long-term relationship with a business partner.

Armed with qualitative information, the next step is to complete a financial analysis of The Home Depot. To complete this work, the user must first evaluate each measure and ratio, and then interpret the combined signs and signals according to each respective category. This work is completed in a step-by-step fashion in Tables 7.9 to 7.13. Each table concludes with an interpretation of financial performance in reference to The Home Depot's horizontal and concentric growth strategy.

Table 7.9 Liquidity Analysis

Measure or Ratio	Ratio Computation	Fiscal Year Ending		
		January 31, 1999	January 30, 2000	January 28, 2001
Working capital	Current assets – Current liabilities	$ 2,076	$ 2,734	$ 3,392
Evaluation: Working capital shows an increasing trend.				
Current ratio	Current assets / Current liabilities	1.73	1.75	1.77
Evaluation: For every $1 in current liabilities, The Home Depot holds approximately $1.75 of current assets. The upward trend indicates an improving current ratio and slightly less than the industry average, reported at 1.9 for the most recent year.				
Quick (acid-test) ratio	(Cash + Accounts receivable + Short-term investments) / Current liabilities	.19	.21	.23
Evaluation: For every $1 in current liabilities, The Home Depot holds approximately $.23 in liquid assets for the most recent period. This amount is very near the industry average of .3 and the upward trend indicates an improving quick ratio.				
Cash ratio	Cash / Currents liabilities	.02	.05	.04
Evaluation: For every $1 in current liabilities, The Home Depot had an immediate cash reserve of approximately $.04, for the most recent period. A particular trend is not identifiable. This signals that The Home Depot relies on a continuous turn over of accounts receivable and inventory, and day-to-day operations to meet its recurring liquidity requirements.				
Operating cash flows ratio	Net operating cash flows / Average current liabilities	.72	.75	.70

Evaluation: For every $1 in current liabilities, The Home Depot generates approximately $.70 in operating cash flows. A stable trend is identifiable. This signals that the net operating cash flows generated from stores provides a substantial source of liquidity for The Home Depot. Combining this insight with the net working capital turnover ratio found in the activity category provides reasonable evidence that the company will generate sufficient cash flows to remain liquid.

Liquidity Interpretation:
- The decline between the current ratio and quick ratio indicates that much of The Home Depot's liquidity is tied to its inventory levels. The stability of both coverage ratios and proximity to industry average for the current ratio indicates inventory is carefully controlled and managed.
- Turning to the common-sized balance sheet shows inventory is stable at approximately 31 percent for the years presented, another sign of good control, especially under a growth strategy.
- The low and stable cash ratio indicates that management carefully manages this valuable resource. This is supported by the stable percent of current liabilities at 21 percent indicated on the common-sized balance sheet.
- The operating cash flow ratio signals The Home Depot stores generate cash to meet the demands of a growth strategy. The historical pattern suggests that this trend will continue into the future.

Conclusion: Currently, The Home Depot appears liquid. The evidence of liquidity demonstrated by the substantial operating cash flows indicates that The Home Depot will be able to re-invest and continue to grow.

Table 7.10 Profitability Analysis

Measure or Ratio	Ratio Computation	Fiscal Year Ending		
		January 31, 1999	January 30, 2000	January 28, 2001
Return on equity (ROE)	Net income / (Average shareholder's equity – Preferred stock)	20.38%	22.01%	18.88%

Evaluation: For every $1 of shareholder equity book value, The Home Depot is returning in the range of 19 to 22 cents. The recent decline ROE to 18.88 percent for the year ending January 28, 2001, is a concern. The reported industry average is 9.8 percent. Although The Home Depot's ROE is above industry average, the most recent decline signals a critical eye must be cast to seek for explanations of why this occurred and look for a management response in the annual report and business press.

Recall that ROE = ROA x financial leverage. An analysis of each will provide signals as to why ROE declined.

Return on assets (ROA)	Net income / Average total assets	13.07%	15.19%	13.42%
Operating ROA	Operating income / Average total assets	21.62%	24.93%	21.79%

Evaluation: For every $1 of assets, The Home Depot's ROA ranges from 12 to 15 cents. The recent decline to 13.42% for the year ending January 28, 2001, is one contributing factor to the decline in ROE. The reported industry average is 2.9%. The common-sized income statement will help explain why ROA declined.

Recall ROA = ROS x asset turnover

The operating ROA also declined. A similar decline to ROA signals that the user must carry the analysis further into the operating section of the income statement to explain why ROA declined. The advantage of an operating ROA is that it shows business performance specifically, and the measure is not confounded by interest, taxes, and other business events outside of day-to-day operations. If in fact ROA is moving in one direction and operating ROA is moving in a different direction, then it would signal a careful analysis of nonoperating revenues and expenses. The common-sized income statement provides the necessary information for this analysis.

Financial leverage	Average total assets / Average shareholder's equity	1.54	1.45	1.41
Evaluation: Financial leverage has been reasonably steady for the years presented. This signals that management is consistent in managing the relationship of assets financed with debt and equity. The Home Depot holds at the end of January 28, 2001, $1.41 of assets for each $1 of shareholders' equity. Due to the stability of financial leverage, it does not explain why ROE declined.				
Return on sales (ROS)	Net income / Net sales	5.34%	6.04%	5.64%
Operating ROS	Operating Income / Net sales	8.84%	9.91%	9.16%
Evaluation: Both measures are relatively stable, but declined in the most recent year. The decline follows a similar pattern to ROA. The industry average is approximately 1.7% for the most recent period. Drilling further into the operating section of the common-sized income statement will help explain the decline. Similar to ROA, if the two ROS measures move in different directions, then the user must carefully analyze the operating and nonoperating sections of the common-sized income statement.				
Asset turnover	Net sales / Total assets	2.24	2.25	2.14
Evaluation: Asset turnover is relatively steady. The small changes explain little for the user in terms of why ROA declined. The industry averages for the most recent period is slightly over 2.00. The stability and proximity to industry average provides further evidence that leadership is doing well at managing resources.				
Gross profit margin	Gross profit / Net sales	28.48%	29.69%	29.91%
Evaluation: The Home Depot continues to improve the gross profit margin. In the most recent years $1 of sales generated 30 cents of gross profit. The trend is shown on Table 7.3 and graphed earlier in this chapter. The 30 cents is used to cover operating and nonoperating expenses, and the remainder is profit. The industry average is very near 30 percent. This movement improves ROS.				
Selling, general and admin.	Respective expense / Net sales	19.35%	19.49%	20.44%
Evaluation: The selling, general, and administrative expenses as a component of sales increased by approximately 1 percent. That 1 percent decreased profits before tax by approximately $460 million. This is a sign that the overhead cost structure of The Home Depot is increasing in relationship to each dollar of sales. This appears logical because the product mix of each store continues to grow as part of the sales growth strategy. This explains why ROS declined. It also explains why the Mid-south and Southern Divisions were consolidated as announced January 14, 2002. The president's messages are now logical. In the annual report and business press, Bob Nardelli stresses growth through new stores and to make each store more profitable. The Home Depot leadership recognizes the need to control operating expenses at the corporate and store level because of the impact on ROE.				
Net sales		$ 30,319	$ 38,434	$ 45,738
Net income		$ 1,614	$ 2,320	$ 2,581
Net operating cash flows		$ 1,917	$ 2,446	$ 2,796
Evaluation: The Home Depot's growth in sales is reflected in the growth in net income and net operating cash flows. Encouraging is that net operating cash flows is slightly greater than net income. The primary reason for this is that depreciation expense on the income statement is a noncash expense. The steady and consistent measures suggest that The Home Depot leadership is carefully managing its growth.				

Profitability Interpretation:
- The Home Depot's gross profit margin signals product costs remain under control.
- The selling, general, and administrative ratio signals an increase in the most recent year. Management appears to be responding.
- Remaining successful requires proactive leadership. A dip in The Home Depot's profitability reflects the competitive dynamics of this industry. When this occurs, look for leadership's response. The Home Depot quickly responded to the early signal of operating efficiency concerns when it noticed selling, general, and operating expenses increase in relationship to sales dollars. The MD&A section highlights that operating expenses have increased.
- With this insight, the user should find in the business press reports addressing how The Home Depot is working to manage its operating cost structure as it continues with its growth strategy.

Conclusion: The Home Depot remains profitable. Managing growth is a challenge for large and small businesses. The common-sized income statement points to where leadership is successful and where to direct its attention. The evidence suggests The Home Depot will be profitable in the future and continue to generate positive operating cash flows. Look for improved performance in the future, especially ROS. If this occurs, ROA improves, driving an improved ROE.

Table 7.11 Activity Analysis

Measure or Ratio	Ratio Computation	Fiscal Year Ending		
		January 31, 1999	January 30, 2000	January 28, 2001
Inventory turnover	Cost of goods sold / Average inventory	5.48	5.53	5.32
Days in inventory	365 / Inventory turnover	67	66	69

Evaluation: The Home Depot turns its inventory in the range of 5 to 6 times a year. The industry average is approximately 4.4. Converting The Home Depot's turnover to a day measure shows that the inventory turned, on average, every 69 days in the most recent year. This signals that management is doing a fine job at controlling the inventory levels as the business grows. This finding is consistent with the profitability results. To remain profitable, the company must vigilantly manage inventory.

As The Home Depot continues to grow, a sign of good leadership will be to maintain the inventory turns at or above industry average. In doing so, this contributes to the success in generating positive operating cash flows. If inventory turnover begins to decline, this is an early sign of management control concerns.

Accounts receivable turnover	Annual credit sales/Average accounts receivable	59	73	64
Average collection period	365 / Accounts receivable turnover	6	5	6

Evaluation: Accounts receivable are not a major component of The Home Depot's business model. However, it may be important to other businesses, and therefore we demonstrate the analysis.

The Home Depot turns receivables in the range of 60 to 73 times a year. Converting this to a day measure, the accounts receivable turn, on average, every 6 days in the most recent year. The most recent reported industry average is 16.8 days.

High turns and short days is a sign of good accounts receivable management. The success at controlling accounts receivable impacts net operating cash flows. Increasing turnover generates operating cash flows, and a decreasing turnover decreases net operating cash flows.

Net working capital turnover	Net sales / Average working capital	15	16	15
Evaluation: Appears stable for the years presented and substantially above industry average, reported at 8 times earnings.				
Activity Interpretation: • The activity measures provide further evidence that leadership has control of key business operating components. The measures are above industry average and stable throughout. • Activity findings support and explain why the company is successful.				
Conclusion: The activity ratios provide further evidence that management focuses attention on these key attributes for success. The Home Depot appears well managed from this view, providing further evidence that it will continue to generate positive cash flows in the future.				

Table 7.12 Solvency Analysis

Measure or Ratio	Ratio Computation	Fiscal Year Ending		
		January 31, 1999	January 30, 2000	January 28, 2001
Net financing cash flows	Taken from SCF	$ 248 million	$ 281 million	$ 737 million
Evaluation: Trending upward, as expected for a business with a growth strategy. The following ratios signal the relationships among asset, debt, and equity accounts. Only by studying the relationships can the user estimate the solvency of a business. When you see financing cash inflow, look to determine what the company did with the cash. When you see financing cash outflow, look to determine the type of debt extinguished or particular distribution, such as to pay dividends.				
Debt to total assets	Total liabilities / Total assets	35.09%	27.75%	29.84%
Evaluation: For every $1 of assets, debt holders carry 30 cents in the most recent period. Management is controlling the overall liability structure in relationship to assets and improving the solvency of The Home Depot.				
Debt to equity	Total liabilities / Shareholders' equity	54.06%	38.41%	42.53%
Evaluation: For every $1 of equity, debt holders carry 43 cents in the most recent period. Management is controlling the overall liability structure in relationship to equity and improving the solvency of Home Depot. A useful industry average is not available. This ratio is defined differently throughout the industrywide databases that compile industry average.				
Long-term debt to capital structure	Long-term debt / Shareholders' equity	17.92%	6.08%	10.30%
Evaluation: For every $1 of equity, long-term debt holders carry 10 cents in the most recent period. Management is controlling the overall long-term structure in relationship to equity and maintaining the solvency of The Home Depot. A useful industry average is not available. This ratio is defined differently throughout the databases compiling industry average.				
Net investing cash flows	Taken from SCF	($2.271)	($2.622)	($3.530)
Evaluation: The Home Depot continues to invest in itself. Noteworthy is the investing cash outflows is greater than the financing inflows. This pattern provides further evidence that the company is generating sufficient cash flows to grow from within, financing growth through profits. It also explains why the debt ratios have declined in most recent years.				
Interest coverage (Income statement)	(Profit before taxes + Interest expense) / Interest expense	56.70	91.78	199.81
Interest coverage (SCF)	(Net operating cash flows + Interest paid) / Interest paid	54.25	95.08	175.75

Evaluation: The interest coverage ratios (income statement and SCF) provide a consistent signal. The respective debt ratios indicate that The Home Depot carries a low level of debt. Therefore, the interest payments are low relative to its earnings. The most recent interest coverage (income statement) ratio reads that for every $1 of interest charge, The Home Depot earned $199.81.

Solvency Interpretation: The Home Depot appears to be very solvent. This explains why in the MD&A, last paragraph of the liquidity and capital resource section of the most recent annual report reads as follows:

> "Management believes that its current cash position, internally generated funds, funds available from the $1 billion commercial paper program and the ability to obtain alternate sources of financing should enable the Company to complete its capital expenditure programs."

Conclusion: The Home Depot's solvency position supports its growth strategy. The company has available the resources to grow and respond to competitive pressures. The Home Depot's current solvency position also signals leadership's careful attention to controlled growth. This company has been growing for many years, and yet remains very solvent. When uncontrolled growth occurs in a company, the solvency ratios will typically signal a weak position. Thus, one conclusion beyond the solvency issue is that The Home Depot appears to have a leadership base that understands how to grow successfully into the future.

Table 7.13 Other Analysis

Measure or Ratio	Ratio Computation	Fiscal Year Ending		
		January 31, 1999	January 30, 2000	January 28, 2001
Earnings per share (EPS) Basic Diluted	(Net Earnings - Preferred stock dividends) / Weighted Average # of common shares	Basic $.73 Diluted $.71	$1.03 $1.00	$1.11 $1.10

Evaluation: Earning per share continues to improve. For the most recent year, The Home Depot earned $1.11 for each weighted share of common stock outstanding. The value changes very little, if dilution occurs. The annual report 10-year summary shows that EPS has improved for 10 consecutive years. This is another sign of a well-run business.

The Dun & Bradstreet report does not provide an industry average for EPS. Dow Jones & Company (2000) reports an EPS of .37 for the retail (specialty) industry. The Home Depot is part of this SIC grouping and appears to be substantially outperforming this industry average.

Price to earnings (P/E)	Market price per share / EPS	44	57	57

Evaluation: The Home Depot's P/E continues to grow. In the most recent period, for each $1 of EPS, the stock sold for $57. The Home Depot's high P/E is both good and bad. This signals that many investors recognize The Home Depot as a solid investment, thus a lower risk justifies a higher market price. Analysts do not like a stock with a high P/E ratio because its growth potential is limited. For this reason, some analysts do not recommend its purchase. The market has adjusted the price to the risk. However, as a supplier, creditor, or employee, this is another signal that The Home Depot is a company to partner with. The analysis points to the quality of the company, and an open market price consistent with this finding.

Dividend pay out	Annual dividends per share / EPS	10%	11%	14%

Evaluation: The Home Depot continues to return a portion of the wealth to it shareholders in dividends. In the most recent period, the company paid out 14 cents for each dollar earned per share.

Other Interpretation: The market response to The Home Depot is consistent with the qualitative and quantitative information presented in the business press and annual report.

Conclusion: The Home Depot appears to be an attractive investment. However, this fact is recognized by the open market price and P/E ratio. For this reason you will find mixed analyst reports, some recommending and others not recommending the purchase of The Home Depot stock. What is consistent is that most analysts view The Home Depot as a well-run business.

7.6 CONCLUDING REMARKS

The foregoing analysis appears to support The Home Depot's growth strategy (i.e., the numbers support their initiatives). Liquidity analysis points to the company's ability to meet its short-term obligations and generate the necessary cash flows to sustain future growth. Profitability analysis seems to project consistent earnings as well. The only identifiable weakness pertained to its recent control of selling, general, and administrative costs. Because of this, the business press will certainly monitor The Home Depot's progress in controlling operating costs while continuing to grow. In addition, quarterly earnings announcements will likely include a discussion regarding management's progress in this area. The reason for this is that success or failure in this area impacts ROE.

Solvency analysis signals that The Home Depot has available the necessary resources to continue its growth strategy. The low amount of debt after several years of growth signals that management understands market demands and can continue on its current path. Other analysis indicates that the market views The Home Depot as a sound investment.

In conclusion, the annual report provides an abundant amount of information. The framework presented in this chapter serves as a basis for evaluation and analysis of any company. The MD&A section provides a historical performance review and may include a discussion about management's future projections. The 5- to10-year summary of financial and operating results highlights financial and nonfinancial performance indicators. A user can take the many pieces of information and add it to the framework presented in this book to serve their individual needs. The advantage of using the framework is that it helps the user to organize the many diverse measures and ratios into a focused, systematic evaluation and interpretation of a company's financial position and performance.

You are now in position to expand your understanding of any company using the annual report. Chapters 1 to 6 developed a foundation of knowledge about the annual report and financial analysis. Chapter 7 showed how to organize the annual report's nonfinancial and financial information into a meaningful framework The Home Depot case study provides a real-world example of how to evaluate and interpret the annual report in a systematic framework.

Chapter 8 shows how to read "between" the lines of an annual report. Presented will be the most common tools and techniques used by leadership to control the measures and ratios presented in the annual report. In addition, we will explain and demonstrate a common reporting practice, labeled pro forma reporting. Last, we highlight the latest developments in the call for supplementary information and the changes forthcoming to the annual report in light of the public's call for greater transparency in financial reporting.

Questions for Review

1. How can the user of an annual report identify a corporate growth strategy? A corporate stability strategy? A corporate retrenchment strategy?

2. In analyzing financial information, ratios and relative measures are most useful. Why? What are common-sized statements? Why do common-sized statements provide useful insight for users of financial information?

3. Describe at least two limitations of the financial reporting process that may significantly impact the financial analysis process.

4. Define *liquidity*. What specific classes of users of financial information would be interested in a company's liquidity? Why? List some common liquidity ratios. When computing these ratios, what comparisons should be made in order to make the information useful?

5. Define *profitability*. What specific classes of users of financial information would be interested in a company's profitability? Why? List some common profitability ratios. When computing these ratios, what comparisons should be made in order to make the information useful?

6. Define *activity*. What specific classes of users of financial information would be interested in a company's activity (efficiency and effectiveness in operations)? Why? List some common activity ratios. When computing these ratios, what comparisons should be made in order to make the information useful?

7. Define *solvency*. What specific classes of users of financial information would be interested in a company's solvency? Why? List some common solvency ratios. When computing these ratios, what comparisons should be made in order to make the information useful?

8. What information is contained in a company's EPS, PE ratio, and dividend payout ratio? How do financial analysts use these ratios?

Internet Exercises

1. Locate the most recent annual report of The Home Depot and one of its competitors (e.g., Lowe's or any SIC code 5211 company) on the Internet. Perform a financial analysis similar to the one in the chapter for each company.

2. Use information obtained from the Internet to determine the corporate strategies of Wal-Mart, Target, and Kmart.

CHAPTER **8**

Emerging Issues in Financial Reporting

CHAPTER OUTLINE

Steve Ray understands that the annual report and the financial reporting process are designed to measure and communicate complex economic events. Management and accounting teams make an abundance of financial estimates and decisions to complete this task. When evaluating Baker Electronics' annual report, Steve critically read and identified how management estimates and reporting decisions impacted the bottom line. Most importantly, upon reading this chapter he was able to raise questions about issues that have not been fully disclosed in the corporate annual report.

LEARNING OBJECTIVES

1. Understand different earnings management techniques.
2. Learn how to critically read pro forma financial information.
3. Consider the FASB and SEC's responses to the consumer's changing information needs.

8.1 INTRODUCTION

Financial reporting is not an exact science. Management and accounting teams make estimates regarding:

- the life of a fixed asset
- warranty returns
- bad debt expense
- revenue recognition

These and many other complex economic events demand careful analysis of how best to capture and measure transactions.

Accordingly, the accounting profession's Concept Statements, GAAP, and SEC guidelines are designed to offer flexibility in the reporting process. It simply is not plausible for accounting rules to be so rigid that all events are reported exactly the same way. Unfortunately, many companies have taken advantage of the flexibility built into the reporting process; thus, the informed consumer must read between the lines of an annual report.

Chapter 8 addresses three topics that pertain to the informed consumer's need to read between the lines. The first topic is earnings management. Earnings management is not a new phenomenon in financial reporting, but recently has been addressed by the financial media. Next, we discuss pro forma reporting. Pro forma reporting originally was intended to provide predictive value to investors and other users of financial information. Unfortunately, management has abused this means of communication. Last, we consider the FASB and SEC's response to the public's call for improved financial and nonfinancial information. Accountants and the SEC began working to improve information to the user long before the Enron debacle and the public outcry to improve financial reporting and auditing practices. Combining all three issues should help the consumer read between the lines of the annual report.

8.2 EARNINGS MANAGEMENT

8.2.1 Earnings Management Defined

Earnings management generally takes two forms. Legitimate business decisions, such as adding a product line, selling a division, or decreasing expenditures are all part of management's efforts to control company earnings. Shareholders empower management to make decisions that, in the final analysis, generate earnings and enhance shareholder wealth.

Problems occur when management circumvents generally accepted accounting principles (GAAP) in an effort to influence reported earnings. This is known as *abusive earnings_management*. GAAP is designed to conservatively measure earnings. However, the flexibility built into accounting rules to improve the value of information supplied to the user can be manipulated to manage and smooth earnings.

Leadership can employ a variety of techniques to manage and smooth earnings. To a large extent, revenues, expenses, and other accounting measures are managed to produce targeted numbers. Some companies simply falsify the accounting records to meet earnings expectations. Others do not report all of their legal liabilities.

But let's remember that managed earnings by leadership is not a new topic. Numerous cases have been identified and discussed in the business press. In the early 1930s, Ivar Krueger controlled two-thirds of the world's match market. To keep his business going during the Depression, he used 400 off-the-book vehicles, scamming bankers about the true value of his business ventures.[1] "Manipulating Profits: How It's Done," was a lead story in *Fortune* in 1984.[2] The article recounts managed-earnings techniques at the time. In the 1990s, entire books were written on this topic, alone. Arthur Levitt, former SEC chairman, dedicated a substantial amount of his time and energy in this position to earnings management concerns. The Enron debacle, as well as other high-profile cases, has simply brought to light the extent of abusive earnings management. The concern is that the practice of managed earning contributes to destabilizing the stock markets and undermining the fabric of capitalism. A careful study of earnings management techniques will allow you to better analyze financial information provided within corporate annual reports.

8.2.2 Managing Revenues

Simply stated, revenue should be recognized when it is earned. This concept is abused by managers who record revenue when it is beneficial to the bottom line. Here are some common techniques.

Vendor Financing

Vendor financing occurs when a company loans money to a customer to purchase goods from the company. The result is an increase in sales revenue on the income statement and an increase in notes receivable on the balance sheet. The increase in revenue improves earnings and the related ratios that have operating income and net income in the computation.

An informed user can look to the balance sheet and the notes to the financial statements to recognize vendor financing. A common-sized balance sheet might point to a percentage increase in notes receivable in regard to total assets. Also, check for a percentage increase in notes receivable from one year to the next. An increase in one or both raises the question of why. Such a change may or may not be fully disclosed in the notes to the financial statements.

Industry-specific knowledge might also help identify a vendor financing arrangement. The technique is common to some industries such as telecommunications. For example, in early 2000, Motorola loaned more than $2 billion via vendor financing to Telsim, a Turkish telecommunications company. Subsequent to the financing, Telsim defaulted on the principle and interest payments, forcing Motorola to write off the receivable and recognize a loss. The problem this creates in financial analysis is that decisions made about a company based on the current period revenues and earnings are immediately distorted. At the time the financial statements are released, the $2 billion vendor financing might not be disclosed. Only when the loan is subsequently written off in a following period does the consumer of the information realize that revenues were overstated in the prior period. This example points out that a careful read and study of specific industry practices should direct the user's attention to vendor financing revenue concerns.

Booking a Sale Before It Is Time

A sure way to increase revenue is to record sales into the accounting records before they are earned. There are several ways to accomplish this. One approach involves *stuffing the sales channel.* Under this approach, managers ship inventory to customers and record the associated revenue. What is not disclosed is the related option to return the goods without cause beyond year-end. Recording this type of sale is a violation of GAAP.

---

[1] Ellen Florian, "Schemers and Scams: A Brief History of Bad Business" *Fortune* (March 18, 2002) p. 62.
[2] F. S. Worthy, "Manipulating Profits: How it's Done" *Fortune* (June 25, 1984) pp. 50-54.

Another technique is to record a sale and leave the delivery date open for the customer. Retailers may do this by recording layaway goods as a sale. Manufactures may do this for a customer that claims it is unable to take delivery due to space or capacity constraints, for example. A seller may take a liberal interpretation on this issue by identifying and segregating the inventory in its own store or warehouse and then booking the sale. According to GAAP, booking these types of economic event as a sale is a violation. A sale cannot be recorded until the customer takes legal ownership of the goods.

Not reducing sales for promised rebates is another common technique to increase revenues. To move inventory at the close of a quarter or year, a company may generate sales by offering substantial rebate opportunities. Revenues are recognized for the full value of the sale, with no deduction for the associated rebate.

Revenue can also be increased by shipping and recording as a sale goods delivered on consignment. According to GAAP, however, consigned goods represent a sale only when they are sold. Some companies violate this rule and simply record consigned goods as revenue.

Companies in the service business also manage revenues. Software support and maintenance contracts, engineering updates, equipment maintenance contracts, and others may call for a long-term agreement between the service provider and customer. To increase revenue, a service provider may record as revenue the entire or a substantial portion of the contract the first year. The rationale is that this is when the majority of the work is performed, "so they say," and thus earned. According to GAAP, only when revenue is earned should it be recorded into the accounting records. Certainly, this is a judgment call that only someone close to the business is capable of making. It is very difficult for the user of financial statements to identify this practice of managed revenues. Again, knowledge about industry specific practices should help recognize this approach to managing revenues.

Internet retailers and advertising agencies commonly book gross sales to manage revenues. For example, how much should an Internet retailer of airline tickets recognize as sales? Under the gross approach, revenues collected and the cost of the ticket are recorded separately. This method creates an appearance of a high-revenue business. Another method is to simply book the net amount (selling price less cost of ticket) for the ticket revenue. This approach gives the appearance of a much smaller business, in terms of revenue. You can identify the method employed by analyzing the cost of goods section of the income statement. The business that uses the gross method will report cost of goods sold, and the business that uses the net method will have no cost of goods sold.

The informed consumer can identify earnings management techniques by carefully tracking accrual-based earnings against operating cash flows and through industry awareness. A single revenue-based earnings management event is difficult to identify. However, over time this type of behavior will produce a trend where reported earnings are higher than operating cash flows. Another sign may be a steady reported earnings pattern and random operating cash flows. These are signals that the earnings reports require further review. The reasons may or may not be attributable to managed revenues.

An additional clue may come from common industry practices. Vendor financing is a common practice in the telecommunications industry. Many Internet retailers and advertising agencies use the gross method of recording revenue. Businesses that sell long-term service contracts will likely record as much revenue as possible the first year of the contract.

8.2.3 Managing Expenses

Managers control earnings by selecting the amount and time period an expense is reported on the income statement. Using techniques known as *cookie jars, nonrecurring charges*, and/or taking the *big bath* are common.

Cookie Jars

Balance sheet cookie jars are used to manage earnings. This is a technique where managers selectively record or fail to record certain expenses on the income statement, using an offsetting balance sheet account (cookie jar) to absorb the impact on earnings. Management employs the cookie jar concept by using one or more expense categories, such as bad debt expense, inventory write-downs, warranty expenses, sales returns, depreciation, and others.

Let's see how bad debt expense works with a cookie jar. Each period management evaluates accounts receivable for a projected amount that will not be collectible; for example, 2 percent of credit sales. The estimated expense amount is recorded as bad debt expense on the income statement and the allowance for doubtful account is adjusted accordingly.[3] Managed earnings occurs (1) when in periods management needs to bump earning upward, the amount recorded as bad debt expense is reduced, for example, to 1.25 percent of credit sales, resulting in a lower bad debt expense or (2) when in periods management needs to bump earnings down, the amount recorded as bad debt expense is increased, for example, to 3 percent of credit sales, resulting in a higher bad debt expense. The cookie jar, the allowance for doubtful accounts, simply floats up and down to accommodate the desired expense accrual. The user fails to see the allowance account because companies typically report *net accounts receivable* on the balance sheet. Net accounts receivable are computed by taking gross accounts receivables less the allowance for doubtful account estimate. Rarely will a company report in the notes to financial statements its justification for changes to the allowance account. This leaves open the allowance for a doubtful-accounts cookie jar for executives to manage earnings.

Product warranties and related expenses are another area often abused. Each period a business estimates the amount of warranty expense. The estimated expense is typically based on the goods sold for the period. When management needs to improve earnings, the amount of warranty expense decreases. When management wants to reduce earnings, warranty expense increases. The cookie jar, a short-term liability account labeled *estimated liability for future warranty obligations* floats up and down to accommodate managed earnings decisions. Because the amount is small compared to other balance sheet and income statement accounts, it is typically not a separate line item on the financial statements and is often merged with *other short-term liabilities* and *other expense* categories. The user typically has no information to estimate the extent that earnings were managed with warranty expense.

Two additional concepts are related to the use of cookie jars. First cookie jars are often composed of relatively small balance sheet accounts. Second, managing a single expense account typically is not enough to appreciably move earnings up or down. Managers can influence earnings, however, by manipulating several small expense accounts in the same direction. Unfortunately for the user, managers' decisions via cookie jars are very difficult to identify.

Nonrecurring Charges and the Big Bath

The use of nonrecurring charges is simply an extension of the cookie jar concept. It is common for businesses to close plants, reposition operating units, reduce labor counts, outsource noncore business functions, and more. These types of business decisions fall under the restructuring

---

[3] The allowance for a doubtful account, a balance sheet account, increases to accommodate the bad debt expense. (The allowance for doubtful accounts is a contra asset account that reduces gross receivables reported on the balance sheet.)

umbrella of GAAP. When this occurs, GAAP requires the business to estimate the current and future restructuring cost to fully measure the change in business model in the period occurred. The FASB intentionally designed GAAP guidelines for managers to conservatively represent the financial outcome of the restructuring decision. The entire amount is recorded as an expense in the current period as a nonrecurring charge (also labeled a restructuring charge). *A restructuring reserve* account is established as a liability on the balance sheet to offset the actual cash payments for restructuring the business, which may occur over one or more subsequent accounting periods. Oftentimes, these restructuring reserves are underestimated to enhance current period earnings. When they occur again and again, year after year, the SEC calls these *reoccurring*, nonrecurring charges an abuse of GAAP.

A user can identify the habitual abuse of nonrecurring charges when substantial restructuring charges occur every year. The user needs to ask why and request information regarding the legitimacy of the restructuring charge.

A *big bath* occurs when overstated restructuring charges hit the income statement in the current year. Management uses the restructuring charge to establish a restructuring reserve cookie jar on the balance sheet by overestimating the current period restructuring expense, thus reducing earnings in excess for the current period. By doing this, the restructuring reserve cookie jar can be used in future periods to reduce expenses, thus inflating income. Because stockholders cannot estimate the restructuring charge, they simply respond to a restructuring activity as a signal that management is being proactive in moving toward a more efficient and effective operating business, and they assume that earnings will improve in the future.

Cisco Systems executives' behavior provides an excellent illustration of a big bath.[4]

> Cisco Systems, one of the most respected companies in technology, has been known to talk out of both sides of its router. Last May the networking firm announced that it would take a $2.25 billion inventory write-off in the third quarter. Chief Financial Officer Larry Carter told analysts during a conference call that the company would "scrap and destroy" most of the inventory. Although it implied a major management misstep, the write-off would allow Cisco to improve its profit margins in future quarters by removing the deadweight from its books. And as a one-time event, most analysts saw it as healthy purging. Two quarters later, Cisco posted a net loss of $268 million on a 32 percent drop in sales. What was less obvious appeared in a from Cisco's 10-Q:

> If one happened to find that note and could understand it and its context one would know that the company sold $290 million worth of inventory it previously categorized as useless. It's like bringing $290 million back from the dead and it saved Cisco the dread of having to report a net loss of half a billion dollars. While not honorable, at least Cisco was fairly straightforward in reporting the recycling of written-of inventory.

8.2.4 Off-Balance-Sheet Financing

Off-balance-sheet financing is defined as debt obligations that are not recorded on the balance sheet. Although off-balance-sheet activities do not technically alter earnings, they do affect the ratios that use debt in the numerator or denominator. Examples of off-balance-sheet financing include:

---

[4] David Raymond, "Where We Go From Here: Bull (crap) Market: In The Loss-Is-Profit World Of Voodoo Accounting, Fancy Footnotes Can Fool Investors" *Forbes* (March 25, 2002) p. 59.

- Operating leases
- Limited partnerships (joint ventures)
- Pension obligations
- Receivables that have been factored (sold)

An operating lease is one that requires a monthly or quarterly payment to the leasing company. The lease is identified as off-balance-sheet financing because the leased asset and related lease liability are not recorded on the balance sheet. Yet, the company is obligated to pay a fixed amount each period for a specified term.

A limited partnership (joint venture) is another arrangement that can create a substantial liability for a company. The business press may identify this arrangement as an off-balance-sheet partnership. It is a popular tool for many companies to isolate and control risk.

Here is how it works. Assume a trucking company wants to purchase a new fleet of refrigerated transportation units. The new refrigerated units are necessary for entering a new market segment. The financing of the new refrigeration units would go through a new business entity where the company owns less than 50 percent. By owning less than 50 percent, the company avoids consolidation of the new business into its financial statements. The portion of the new company not owned by the trucking company is sold to outside investors. The trucking company would then lease the new refrigeration units from the new business entity that was established to finance the trucks. The trucking company benefits from the full use of the trucks and satisfies the lease obligation through revenues of the new business venture. In theory, this is a legitimate business transaction. The risk of the new business venture is shared by outside parties, and the trucking company benefits from new resources (the refrigerated units).

Recently, management and its associated legal counsel have abused GAAP and the partnership arrangement by creating off-balance-sheet financing. What has evolved is a special purpose entity (SPE), similar to the 900-plus used by the Enron Corporation. The partnership agreements have evolved to the point where the company is fully obligated for the loan established to purchase the trucks, yet because of the partnership arrangement the loan amount is not reflected as a debt obligation for the company.

Pension obligations also create off-balance-sheet debt. This occurs when a company provides a defined benefit retirement plan to its current or past employees. Under this plan, a company guarantees a specific retirement benefit to each of its employees. Because of certain smoothing techniques allowed under GAAP, pension expense and the related obligation may fail to keep pace with the projected benefit obligation and the related plan assets. As a result, the reported pension obligation may not represent the full amount due to current and past employees.

Factored accounts receivable also create a potential obligation. For example, a company might sell its accounts receivable to raise cash. This is a legitimate business practice. If the receivables are sold with recourse and are not collected by the purchasing company, the company must reimburse the purchasing company for the amount not collected. Terms and conditions for this potential liability are spelled out in the factoring agreement. Thus, by selling low-quality accounts receivable with a recourse agreement, managers create a potential off-balance-sheet debt obligation. This information may or may not be disclosed in the financial statement notes.

8.2.5 Other Earnings Management Techniques

Auditors often find errors and irregularities regarding how a business records transactions into the accounting records. An error is defined as a legitimate mistake, while an irregularity is defined as an intentional act to misclassify a transaction. For example, a construction company's policy might be to capitalize all long-lived equipment purchases more than $10,000. All purchases less then $10,000 would therefore be expensed in the period. The auditor might find, however, that all purchases greater than $1,000 have been capitalized. The impact of this error or irregularity is that earnings are overstated in the current period but will be understated in future periods.

When the auditor discovers an error or irregularity, the materiality of the event must be addressed. Materiality is defined such that the reporting as it stands can affect a user's decision. Table 8.1 identifies four possible auditor responses:

Table 8.1 Decision Tree Response

| | Material | |
	Yes	*No*
Error	Adjust	No adjustment
Irregularity	Adjust	Adjust

When an accounting error or irregularity is identified as material, the company must adjust the accounting records and thus earnings. When an error is not material, no adjustment is made to the accounting records. When an immaterial irregularity occurs, an adjustment is necessary. The accounting literature is very clear on these issues. Ambiguity surfaces when the auditor and leadership must classify a misclassification as an error or irregularity, and determine the materiality of the event. Notice that no adjustment is necessary for an immaterial error.

A problem surfaces when the auditor discovers several immaterial errors, those that do not influence a user's decision as a standalone item. The profession's view is as follows: Immaterial errors too small to affect a user's decision are not worth the time and cost to change. Most would agree with this view as long as the immaterial errors are isolated. Managed earnings take place when several errors are deemed immaterial and push earnings in the same direction, according to a management plan. This is where the auditor must exercise judgment.

8.2.6 Earnings Management Concluding Remarks

Earnings management is not a new game for executives, and will likely continue in the future. The business press has provided numerous cases where managers have abused GAAP and SEC reporting guidelines. The practice dates back to before the Great Depression. For instance, in the early 1900s individual states adopted blue sky regulations to prevent companies from selling worthless securities. Stock analysts and investors reward such behavior by pushing up stock values for companies that meet or exceed earnings estimates and punish stocks that fail to meet estimates. History tells the informed consumer that regardless of the reporting guidelines issued by the accounting profession and the SEC, management will look to manage future earnings.

The informed consumer has available three tools to identify earnings management. First, your knowledge about the annual report and the ability to identify these signs and signals of earnings management:

- Profits grow faster than operating cash flows.
- Growth in accounts payable outpaces growth in accounts receivable on a percentage basis.
- Growth in accounts receivable outpaces growth in sales on a percentage basis.
- Growth in inventory is more than the growth in sales on a whole dollar and/or percentage basis.

- The percent of allowance for doubtful accounts in relationship to gross receivables fluctuates from year to year with no change in the customer base.
- Gross margin dollars and percentages increase/decrease widely.
- Change in executives, auditor, and/or legal counsel occur.

Second, brokerage houses such as Merrill Lynch have opted to move toward GAAP-based analytical standards. This means that analysts will analyze GAAP-based financial statements and related notes and not pro forma statements. Having professional analysts carefully review historical financial statements should provide better reports to the informed user to critically read, study, and evaluate. Third, for the interested reader, entire books are dedicated to the subject of earnings management.

8.3 PRO FORMA REPORTING

8.3.1 Pro Forma Reporting Defined

At the opposite ends of reporting integrity are the original objectives of pro forma reporting and the actual practice of pro forma reporting. *Pro forma* is a Latin word meaning according to form; as a matter of form. Pro forma financial information is a recasting of the most recent quarter's financial performance and financial position, assuming a change to the recent business model.

The intent of the SEC was to place a tool in management's hands to illustrate what the business's financial position and performance would appear to be, assuming certain transactions had or had not occurred in the most recent period. That is, pro forma reporting offers management a tool to communicate hypothetical earnings and financial position under a new business model—for example, the effect of a merger or acquisition that occurred shortly before or after year end.

Assume a company completes a substantial acquisition in mid-January 2003, this being the first month of the first quarter of the new calendar year. SEC regulations require the company to issue a pro forma statement for the fourth quarter of 2002 reflecting this acquisition. The reason is that this type of information should help the analyst and investor project future performance, much better than GAAP financial statements would provide. Why? Information and details about the acquisition are likely to impact future income and cash flow performance results. That insight would not be transparent in the GAAP financial statements.

SEC regulations § 210.11-01 to 210.11-03 provide the framework and guidance to pro forma reporting. According to regulations § 210.11-02(a):

> Pro forma financial information should provide investors with information about the continuing impact of a particular transaction by showing how it might have affected historical financial statements if the transaction had been consummated at an earlier time. Such statements should assist investors in analyzing the future prospects of the registrant because they illustrate the possible scope of the change in the registrant's historical financial position and results of operations caused by the transaction.

Survey results provide evidence that corporate America has followed the intent of pro forma reporting:

> According to NIRI's (National Investor Relations Institute) analysis, the vast majority of the companies prominently reporting pro forma numbers "provided a clear disclosed path or reconciliation for pro forma and GAAP measures." More than

75% provided a narrative in the news release describing how their results differed from GAAP, as well as both sets of numbers in the financial statements. A smaller number either presented just the narrative or the financial results. But in either case, from NIRI's vantage point, enough information was given that a reader could get from point A to point B.[5]

The business press, however, has documented widespread abuse of pro forma reporting. Pro forma reporting guidelines primarily point to its use in business merger and acquisition activities. However, managers appear to be taking a liberal interpretation of regulations § 210.11-01(a) (b), the SEC's last condition for which a company should use pro forma reporting:

> Consummation of other events or transactions has occurred or is probable for which disclosure of pro forma financial information would be material to investors.

Andy Serwer provides a clear illustration of how the game is played.[6] Pro formas are used to show the performance of a company for the previous quarter, with nonrecurring economic events removed. Shortly after the quarter ends, a company press release will identify a pro forma earnings statement with nonrecurring items removed (subsequent illustrations show how the word *nonrecurring* is liberally interpreted by management). Therefore, management uses pro forma information to guide analyst thinking before GAAP financials are available. GAAP financial reports are due 45 days (soon to be 30 days under the recently adopted Sarbanes-Oxley Act) after the last day in the respective quarter. Under this reporting model, the auditor and GAAP reports are completely removed from the pro forma game. By the time GAAP earnings are released, the company has diverted attention to the future and not to the historically based financial reports. Companies release pro forma information prior to GAAP statements because of the predictable response by analysts (meeting or beating earnings will move forward a stock's value, and the reverse is also true).

As a result, the game of pro forma reporting is widely practiced. It is a tool to manage analyst behavior and thus a company's stock value. Interestingly, logic would suggest that an intelligent analyst must be fully aware of the game, and read a pro forma press release with a substantial degree of skepticism. Practice, however, does not support this logic. What appears to occur is that pro forma numbers offer the first glimpse of information about the previous quarter's results. In an attempt to gain first-mover advantage, analysts and investors appear to be more than willing to make investment decisions based on pro forma statements. Competition blurs the judgment of an otherwise intelligent analyst and investor.

8.3.2 Illustrations

The following excerpts illustrate the treatment of pro forma reporting in the current business press:

> Companies such as Broadcom now have the leeway to present pro forma results rooted nowhere near reality. In the company's 2001 third-quarter results, the chipmaker excluded such items as acquisition-related expenses, some payroll tax, goodwill impairment, loss on minority equity investments, related income tax effects, and certain nonrecurring charges. No doubt investors didn't mind missing the

---

[5] Phyllis Plitch, "Companies in Many Sectors Give Earnings a Pro Forma Makeover" *Wall Street Journal* (01/22/2002) p, A4.

[6] Andy Serwer, "Dirty Rotten Numbers" *Fortune* (February 18, 2002) pp. 74-84.

information. The company reported a pro forma loss of 13 cents per share. Had they not excluded all those charges, they would have lost $6.36 per share or $1.6 billion.[7]

According to John May of SmartStockInvestor.com, an Internet investment site, the companies that make up the Nasdaq 100 index together reported $19.1 billion of profits in pro forma earnings announcements for the first three quarters of last year. Mr. May points out that those same companies reported to the Securities and Exchange Commission (SEC) a total loss for the same period of $82.3 billion.

The difference, $100 billion give or take, is due to the fact that, whereas the SEC numbers are audited and comply with American generally accepted accounting principles (GAAP), pro forma numbers are neither audited nor subject to any rules at all. Companies strip out the things they do not like and keep in the items that look pleasing.[8]

For the first three quarters of 2001, three Nasdaq giants—Cisco, Dell, and Intel— reported combined pro forma earnings of $4.4 billion. What were real GAAP earnings to the SEC? A $1.4 billion combined loss.[9]

Yahoo! Inc., one of the first to emphasize pro forma, in January 1999, presented results 35 percent better than GAAP by excluding a variety of costs of buying Internet companies. In its latest set of results (press release), issued on April 11, Yahoo excluded yet more items, such as payroll taxes on stock options. Data center operator Exodus Communications Inc., in its version of pro forma, also excludes some acquisition costs, but apparently not options taxes. …

In a Mar. 27 press release, software company Xcare.net Inc. reported revenues before subtracting the cost of warrants to buy Xcare shares that it gave to a customer. The value of the warrants was given lower down in the release, but the headline numbers boosted the company's apparent sales by 69 percent and cut its losses by 40 percent. Xcare Chief Financial Officer Gary T. Scherping says he wasn't trying to fool anybody. "I could probably have come up with another three things that I could have excluded had I wanted to play those games ... that other people regularly do," he says.[10]

In the same article Network Associates, Inc. conveniently dropped a loss-making 80 percent-owned subsidiary, McAfee.com Corp., in working out its pro forma results, which show only half the loss reached under GAAP (see Table 8.2). Network's pro forma sliced losses in half, with a GAAP loss of $47.4 million and a pro forma loss of $24.3 million.

The future role of pro forma reporting in business evaluation and interpretation is unresolved. Originally, the SEC intended pro forma reporting to serve as a tool to aid analysts in company evaluation. Recent abuses of this tool have brought into question its use and application.

---

[7] Raymond, p. 59.

[8] Out, by $100 Billion —How Pro-Forma Accounting Boosts Profits. The Economist Newspaper Limited (February 23, 2002).

[9] Serwer, pp. 74-84.

[10] David Henry, "The Numbers Game: Companies Use Every Trick To Pump Earnings And Fool Investors. The Latest Abuse: Pro forma" *Business Week* (May 14, 2001) pp. 100–110.

Table 8.2 Network Associates, Inc., Use of Pro Forma

(in millions)	Consolidated GAAP	Pro Forma
GROSS PROFIT	$136.4	$127.0
Less: R&D, sales, marketing, administrative expenses	-178.8	-168.1
Less: Amortization of intangibles and stock charge	-17.5	0
OPERATING LOSS	59.9	41.1
Plus: Net interest income, minority stakes, tax benefits	+12.5	+16.7**
NET LOSS	$ 47.4	$ 24.3
PER SHARE LOSS	35 cents	17 cents

* Excludes results of 80%-owned McAfee.com
** Omits interest paid on convertible debt
Source: Apr. 19 company earnings announcement, David Henry, "The Numbers Game: Companies Use Every Trick To Pump Earnings And Fool Investors. The Latest Abuse: Pro forma" Business Week (May 14, 2001) pp. 100–110.

On December 4, 2001, the SEC provided the following information tips for investors using pro forma financial statements:

Investors should always take the critical step of reading the financial statements of the companies they've invested in, or intend to invest in, because financial statements contain important corporate financial information that may not be readily apparent from news releases. Recently, some companies have put out press releases using so-called "pro forma" financial information to highlight what they claim are important portions of their actual financial reports.

Investors should know that "pro forma" financial information is not prepared in accordance with the standards applied to financial statements filed with the SEC. In other words, some of the numbers announced by companies in their "pro forma" financial information may be based on assumptions or principles that are not recognized as appropriate for SEC filings, and that an accompanying news release doesn't discuss or otherwise explain. While they aren't illegal—and in some cases can be helpful in focusing attention on critical portions of financial statements—"pro forma" financials have limitations, might create a confusing or misleading impression, and should be viewed with appropriate and healthy skepticism.

The federal securities laws require most publicly held companies to file with the SEC financial statements prepared under a set of accounting conventions called "Generally Accepted Accounting Principles," or "GAAP," that are accurate, truthful and complete. When a company prepares its financial statements using GAAP, investors can more consistently track the company's financial results from year to year and compare its performance with other companies.

In contrast, "pro forma" financial results aren't prepared using GAAP, and they may not convey a true and accurate picture of a company's financial well-being. They often highlight only positive information. And because "pro forma" information doesn't have to follow established accounting rules, it can be very difficult to compare a company's "pro forma" financial information to prior periods or to other companies.

Here are a few things to keep in mind when you see pro forma financial information.

- **What is the company assuming?** "Pro forma" financial results can be misleading, particularly if they change a loss to a profit or hide a significant fact. For example, they may assume that a proposed transaction that benefits the company has actually occurred. Or they may fail to account for costs or charges. Be sure to look behind the numbers, and find out what assumptions the numbers are based on.

- **What is the company *not* saying?** Be particularly wary when you see "pro forma" financial results that only address one component of a company's financial results—for example, earnings before interest, taxes, depreciation, and amortization (which is often abbreviated "EBITDA"). These kinds of statements can be misleading unless the company clearly describes what transactions are omitted and how the numbers might compare to other periods.

- **How do the "pro forma" results compare with GAAP-based financials?** Because "pro forma" information comes from selective editing of financial information compiled in accordance with GAAP, "pro forma" financial results can raise a serious risk of misleading investors—even if they do not change a loss to a profit. Look for a clear, comprehensible explanation of how "pro forma" results differ from financial statements prepared under GAAP rules, and make sure you understand any differences before investing on the basis of "pro forma" results.

- **Are you reading "pro forma" results or a summary of GAAP-based financials?** Remember that there is a big difference between "pro forma" financial information and a summary of a financial statement that has been prepared in accordance with GAAP. When financial statements have been prepared in compliance with regular accounting rules, a summary of that information can be quite useful, giving you the overall picture of a company's financial position without the mass of details contained in the full financial statements. It is always best, however, to compare any summary financial presentation you read with the full GAAP-based financial statements.

- **Read before you invest;** understand before you commit. Remember that "pro forma" financial information you see in a press release wasn't prepared according to normal accounting conventions, and make sure you have the full story before investing.[11]

With all the negative press surrounding pro forma reporting and the above SEC guidance, it is logical to question whether its practice will continue. In the authors' opinion, the answer is yes. Competition and stock evaluation are intense business issues among companies and analysts. Information about a company's performance can be used to improve the analyst's competitive position and stock evaluation. A pro forma report provides the first glimpse of the most recent period's performance, and was designed by the SEC for this very purpose. What must change is

---

[11] Investor Alert, "Pro Forma" Financial Information Tips For Investors," www.sec.gov/investor/pubs/proforma12-4.htm.

the abuse of this communication tool by management. For many years the accounting profession and the SEC have had in place voluntary supplementary disclosure rules to enhance the interpretation of pro forma and financial statements. In the future, we are likely to see the SEC strengthen the rules governing pro forma reporting.

8.4 IMPROVING FINANCIAL DISCLOSURE

For several years, the accounting profession and the SEC have recognized the need to improve quantitative and qualitative disclosures. As a result, the FASB and the SEC have responded with changes or proposed changes to existing disclosure rules. These changes or proposed changes are discussed in the following sections.

8.4.1 FAS No. 131

Evaluating the performance of a company engaged in many different industries and offering many different product lines is difficult. In response to this problem, the FASB adopted Financial Accounting Standard (FAS) Number 131: Segment Disclosures and Related Information.[12] FAS No. 131 established the way public companies disclose segment information and how they choose the information using the *management approach*. Under the management approach, companies must identify which segments to report on based on how management, the chief operating decision maker, organized the company. Accordingly, a company's organizational structure will determine which *operating segments* to provide disclosure. FAS No. 131 defines an operating segment as a component of business:

- That engages in activities from which it may earn revenues and incur expenses (including revenues and expenses relating to transactions with other components of the same business).
- Whose operating results are regularly reviewed by the enterprise's 'chief operating decision maker' to make decisions about resources to be allocated to the segment and assess its performance, and
- For which discrete financial information is available (FAS No. 131, ¶ 18).

The management approach not only dictates how to identify operating segments, but also which financial data about these operating segments warrant disclosure. The information to be disclosed under FAS No. 131 is the same information management uses to evaluate performance and make decisions.

Thus, if a company organizes its segments based on geographic sales regions, separate information regarding those geographic regions will require disclosure. Alternatively, if the company's structure distinguishes its segments based on product lines, segment information about each product segment will require disclosure. FAS No. 131 allows aggregation of operating segments possessing similar economic characteristics in certain situations.

Once operating segments have been identified, those segments whose revenue, profit (loss), or identifiable assets constitute at least 10 percent of the company's revenue, profit (loss), or identifiable assets, respectively, are considered reportable, and they require segment disclosure. Also, because FAS No. 131 requires segment disclosure for 75 percent of the company's consolidated revenue, additional segments not meeting the aforementioned criteria should be added until segments making up 75 percent of consolidated revenue are represented in segment disclosure.

---

[12] "Disclosures about Segments of an Enterprise and Related Information." *Statement of financial Accounting Standards No. 131* (Norwalk, CT: FASB, 1997).

The identification of segments based on the management approach has resulted in increased disclosure. Early comparisons of financial report disclosures for 1996 and 1999 revealed that 59 percent of the leading U.S. firms have increased the number of segments for which revenue, profit (loss), and/or asset information was provided.[13] Wal-Mart Stores, Inc. serves as an example of a company that continues to increase segment disclosure. It now reports discrete information on Wal-Mart Stores, SAM'S Club, International, and other operating segments.

Table 8.3 Segment Reporting Illustration

Geographic Segment Information (consolidated)
This table presents data by geographic region. Revenues and operating profit shown below are classified according to their country of origin (including exports from such areas). Revenues classified under the caption "United States" include royalty and licensing income from non-U.S. sources.

Revenues For the years ended December 31								
	Total Revenues			Inter-Segment Revenues			External Revenues		
(In millions)	2001	2000	1999	2001	2000	1999	2001	2000	1999
United States	$89,876	$90,981	$78,970	$3,877	$3,518	$2,690	$85,999	$87,463	$76,280
Europe	23,878	24,144	22,919	2,009	1,212	1,0 81	21,869	22,932	21,838
Pacific Basin,	11,447	12,9 21	7,879	1,258	1,218	924	10,189	11,703	6,955
Other (a)	8,963	8,754	7,365	1,107	999	808	7,856	7,755	6,557
Inter-company eliminations	(8,251)	(6,947)	(5,503)	(8,251)	(6,947)	(5,503)	—	—	—
Total	$125,913	$129,853	$ 111,630	$—	$ —	$ —	$125,913	$129,853	$ 111,630

	Segment operating profit (b)			Assets			Long-lived assets (c)		
	For the years ended December 31			At December 31			At December 31		
(In millions)	2001	2000	1999	2001	2000	1999	2001	2000	1999
United States	$18,055	$15,455	$ 13,391	$315,179	$277,818	$264,129	$18,593	$19,180	$21, 612
Europe	1,297	2,062	1,886	93,963	80,282	83,358	6,176	5,870	6,101
Pacific Basin	1,857	1,75 4	1,0 92	41,385	42,281	28,214	1,888	1,9 3 6	2,017
Other (a)	1,210	1,4 0 6	9 0 9	44,683	36,804	29,687	15,519	13,076	11,329
Inter-company eliminations	(8)	9	11	(187)	(179)	(188)	(36)	(47)	(37)
Total	$22,411	$20,686	$17,289	$437,006	$405,200	$495,023	$42,140	$40,015	$41, 022

a) Includes the Americas other than the United States and operations that cannot meaningfully be associated with specific geographic areas (for example, commercial aircraft leased by GE Capital Aviation Services).
b) Excludes GECS income taxes of $1,380 million, $1,912 million and $1,653 million in 2001, 2000 and 1999, respectively, which are included in the measure of segment profit reported on page 51.
c) Property, plant and equipment (including equipment leased to others).

General Electric most recently set a new standard for responsible segment reporting. In the 2001 annual report, several useful segment reports are provided. Table 8.3 is an illustrative component of General Electric's MD&A. This segment report is categorized by geographic location. For each segment of business, total revenues are recapped and the user can determine revenues generated from inter-segment and externally. Profits, total assets, and long-lived assets

---

[13] Companies used in research consisted of the top 25 rated firms based on Fortune 500 ranking for the year 2000 based on fiscal year ended on or before January 31, 2000. Firms discarded from the population are Citigroup, State Farm Insurance Companies, and TIAA-CREF. Citigroup was discarded because several business combinations have occurred since 1996, altering the organization structural inordinately that the comparative value is null. State Farm and TIAA-CREF were discarded because they are not a publicly traded companies.

are also provided for the informed consumer to study and evaluate. What is immediately apparent about GE is that a substantial amount of its revenues, profits, and asset structure resides in the United States.

The accounting profession views this improvement to financial reporting as part of an ongoing process. Routinely, issues are addressed and changes are made to authoritative accounting guidelines. In March 2002, the FASB announced a study to evaluate additional disclosure and reporting issues to improve financial reports and the reporting process:[14]

> The Financial Accounting Foundation (FAF), the body that oversees, appoints members, and funds the activities of the Financial Accounting Standards Board (FASB), announced today that it will strengthen its commitment to a strong, transparent, and rigorous system of financial accounting standards for America's capital markets. As part of that commitment, the FAF will issue for public comment a set of proposed changes to help achieve that objective.

8.4.2 SEC Proposed Legislation: "Supplemental Financial Information"

In 1999, the Securities and Exchange Commission's proposed legislation, "Supplemental Financial Information," was released with a comment deadline of April 2000. The proposed regulation is in response to an increase in the number of cases of what the SEC terms *abusive earnings management* by public companies. Earnings management can be accomplished in a number of ways. According to Lynn Turner, chief accountant, SEC, "Premature revenue recognition, accruals of future losses and general reserves or cushions, use of unsupportable depreciable lives, and misapplication of the concept of materiality have all been the focus of SEC staff reviews and comments." Each of these areas can be managed so that a company's loss (gain) or expense (revenue) recognition is delayed or accelerated. The practice is believed to be a direct result of the importance placed on companies being able to meet their projected earnings estimates. Proposed regulation "Supplementary Financial Information" is designed to improve the transparency or clarity of financial information by requiring companies to disaggregate information and/or provide more detailed information in several key areas.

The SEC has identified a number of company actions that have contributed to financial information becoming less transparent:

- A company's failure to comply with disclosure rules for changes in accrued liabilities
- Grouping dissimilar items into an aggregated classification
- Recurring "nonrecurring" charges
- Inadequate disclosure of changes in estimates
- Inconsistent application of SEC required disclosures of valuation and loss accruals
- Insufficient information about expected useful lives, changes in lives, and salvage values of long-lived assets

Table 8.4 illustrates the area of concern and provides some reasons as to why this may contribute to abusive earnings management. Although increased disclosure of changes in loss accrual accounts, valuation adjustments, and so on will enhance the quality of financial reporting, it is the authors' opinion that the disclosure of the *underlying accounting assumptions* that were made by management will be most meaningful.

---

[14] NEWS RELEASE 03/14/02, Financial Accounting Foundation Considers Changes to Streamline FASB Process; Emphasizes Need for Independent Accounting Standard Setter , Norwalk, CT, March 14, 2002

Table 8.4 Abusive Earnings Management Problems and Effects

Problem	*Effect*
A company's failure to comply with disclosure rules for changes in accrued liabilities	May involve a company's accrual for environmental remediation costs. Adjustments to accruals can increase or decrease net income. Information that explains these changes will help the investor understand better the company's present and future obligation.
Grouping dissimilar items into an aggregated classification	Occasionally, companies will combine or aggregate information to conceal something unfavorable. This practice adds to a loss of transparency.
Recurring "nonrecurring" charges	Nonrecurring charges are expenses recognized on an infrequent basis. Users often can ignore these one-time charges when predicting the future performance of the company. But when the events reoccur, they are no longer unique to one operating period. Nonrecurring items may include restructuring charges, merger expenses, and write-downs for asset impairment.
Inadequate disclosure of changes in estimates	Companies might change estimates of bad-debt losses or product returns. When companies change an estimate, it influences net income. Companies must disclose why these changes were made so that investors can understand the effects of the change on current and future performance.
Inconsistent application of SEC required disclosures of valuation and loss accruals	This might relate to a valuation adjustment for a future income tax benefit. Companies that possess future income tax benefits need to evaluate the benefit periodically. If all or a portion of the future tax benefit appears unlikely, the asset must be revalued. Lack of consistent application in the valuation adjustment process will cause periodic over/understatement of net income.
Insufficient information about expected useful lives, changes in lives, and salvage values of long-lived assets	Estimated lives of depreciable long-lived assets such as buildings or equipment can be modified when new information becomes available. When this occurs, more or less depreciation expense is recognized in the statement of income. Asset life expectancy, subsequent changes, as well as company rationale for the changes, needs to be thoroughly disclosed.

The SEC is also in position to penalize companies that are found to be in violation of the proposed regulation "Supplementary Financial Information." According to the Commission:

> The Division of Enforcement has stepped up its activity in investigating cases involving financial fraud, in particular inappropriate earnings management. The Division has created the Financial Fraud Task Force under the able leadership of Charles Niemeier. This Task Force is focusing on companies, their management and auditors when the financial statements reflect inappropriate earnings management or other financial reporting or disclosure practices that are not in compliance with Generally Accepted Accounting Principles (GAAP). Too often these abusive

practices result in investors losing millions and billions of dollars. As recent cases have shown, the Commission has been willing to use all the remedies available to it, including fines, officer and director bars, professional bars, and working with other law enforcement agencies to bring criminal changes in these areas.[15]

Recent SEC press releases and federal legislative activities indicate that many of the supplementary financial information proposals will be adopted. A SEC press release dated February 22, 2002, identified three areas where it will work to improve financial reporting.[16] First, the extent and timing of disclosure information will likely improve. Simply, the press release calls for explicit reporting of how leadership computes allowances and valuations. Second, greater emphasis is being given to requiring companies to post information on the Internet Web site, when it is released to the SEC. Third, auditor oversight, including who is to conduct the audit and under what organization structure, is open to debate.

The president of the United States, George W. Bush, issued guidance to the SEC regarding changes to financial reporting.[17] His proposals emphasize better information to investors, corporate accountability, and a call for the development of a stronger, more independent audit system. The president's report emphasized that the SEC accomplish these changes within its existing structure.

8.4.3 Accelerated Periodic Filings and the Sarbanes-Oxley Act of 2002

On July 30, 2002, President Bush signed into law the Sarbanes-Oxley Act. The Act, as well as recently adopted amendments by the SEC to accelerate periodic filings, improves financial reporting and disclosures. These developments also improve the audit profession's involvement with client companies. The following is an overview of some changes that affect both audit firms and reporting companies.

- Changes in corporate filing deadlines will be phased in over the next three years. SEC Annual Report 10-K filing deadlines will remain at 90 days for the first year, 75 days for the second year and 60 days for the third years. The quarterly report (Form 10-Q) deadline is 45 days for the first year, 40 days for year two, and thirty-five days for years thereafter. These rules are effective for fiscal years ending on or after December 15, 2003.

- The CEO and CFO of each reporting company must prepare a statement to "certify the appropriateness of the financial statements and disclosures contained in the annual and quarterly reports." This requires the principle executive and financial officers each to certify that they have reviewed the report, know of no material misstatement, are responsible for establishing and maintaining "disclosure controls and procedures", and that any deficiencies in the design or operation of internal controls were disclosed to the audit committee of the board of directors and the company's auditors. These rules apply to reports filed after August 29, 2002.

- A new "Public Accounting Oversight Board" will be appointed and overseen by the SEC. The Board is charged with the oversight of audits and auditors of publicly held

---

[15] Remarks to the 39th Annual Corporate Counsel Institute by Lynn E. Turner, Chief Accountant, U.S. Securities & Exchange Commission, Northwestern University School of Law, Evanston, Ill., October 12, 2000

[16] SEC Announces Financial Disclosure and Auditor Oversight Roundtables, SEC press release, February 22, 2002.

[17] Specifics on the President's Ten-Point Plan, White House, President George W. Bush, 03/07/2002.

companies. The Board also has the authority to issue or adopt standards that improve audit quality. Funding is provided through a "registration" fee and an "annual" fee assessed to each registered public accounting firm.

- The lead partner and audit review partner must be rotated every five years.
- Audit services may not be provided to client companies whose top official was employed by the firm and worked on the company's audit during the preceding year.
- All audit or review work papers must be retained for a period of at least five years.

A more detailed description of these new rules can be found on the SEC web site.

8.5 CONCLUDING REMARKS

The strength of the U.S. economy depends on a financial reporting network that provides reliable and relevant information to the informed consumer. For decades the corporate annual report has provided employees, investor, bankers, analysts, and others valuable financial and nonfinancial information. Today, Corporate America is being called on to provide a more complete explanation of its business operations through the annual report. Users need this information to make sound business decisions in an environment where functioning operations are diverse, economic events are complex, and business units reach across national borders.

The content, transparency, and distribution of the annual report will likely change. Remaining will be the corporate annual report as the central repository for company information for the investor, employee, government, supplier and consumer seeking information about a company.

The topics developed in this and the previous chapters justify the central theme of this book. Education is the key. Understanding the annual report places you in position to be an informed user of financial and nonfinancial company information. The informed consumer will be able to critically consume, evaluate, and interpret annual report information and make sound business decisions.

Questions for Review

1. The informed reader of financial statements understands that certain numbers are the results of estimates made by management and the accounting team. Give two examples of estimates made by management that affect the financial statements.

2. Often management and the accounting team exercise informed judgments as to where and when an event or transaction will be recorded in the financial statements. Give two examples of how management's judgments may impact the information recorded in the financial statements.

3. Define earnings management. Give an example of legitimate earnings management. Give an example of abusive earnings management. What motivation exists for earnings management?

4. How does vendor financing distort the financial picture of a company? What are some ways an informed user can determine whether the company is engaged in vendor financing?

5. GAAP says that revenue should be recognized when it is earned and collectibility is reasonably assured. Which of the following practices of Saucer TV, a satellite provider, may be questionable, and why?

- Saucer requires customers to commit to a two-year contract in order to receive free satellite equipment. Substantial penalties are assessed for early cancellation. Saucer recognizes revenue on a monthly basis on these contracts when customers are billed for the coming month's services.

- Saucer TV offers customers an optional two-year service contract on the dish equipment. The amount received is recorded immediately as revenue upon receipt.

- To increase sales, Saucer TV offered free premium channels for the first six months with the two-year commitment. Saucer records the full price of the premium services as revenue in the year of sale.

6. What is meant by the *big bath*? Why do analysts often respond favorably to corporate announcements regarding write-offs and restructuring?

7. Distinguish between an error and an irregularity. Give examples of each. Upon detection, what course of action does each require? Why?

8. Explain how pro forma reporting has been used to manage analysts' behavior and in turn stock prices.

Internet Exercises

1. Locate at least two articles from the professional literature on "earnings management." Summarize the importance of the information contained in these articles to users of financial information.

2. Locate the SEC Alerts concerning "pro-forma earnings" on the Internet. Summarize what you find and describe why this information is important to users of financial information.

APPENDIX **A**

Regulatory Environment of Financial Reporting

APPENDIX OUTLINE

Steve Ray's reliance upon the information provided in Baker Electronics' annual report is based on the regulatory environment that surrounds financial reporting. The SEC and the FASB continue to monitor corporate reporting practices. Having a general knowledge about these organizations and the processes underway improves Steve's ability to critically evaluate financial reports. Without this knowledge he would not be an informed consumer. His trust in the annual report is bolstered when he reads the following press release:

PROGRAM TO MONITOR ANNUAL REPORTS OF FORTUNE 500 COMPANIES
SEC NEWS DIGEST Issue 2001-245 December 21, 2001

Our Corporation Finance Division has determined to monitor the annual reports filed by all Fortune 500 companies that file periodic reports with the Commission in 2002 as part of its process of reviewing financial and nonfinancial disclosures made by public companies. Through this process, the Division will focus on disclosure that appears to be critical to an understanding of each company's financial position and results, but which, at least on its face, seems to conflict significantly with generally accepted accounting principles or Commission rules, or to be materially deficient in explanation or clarity. Where problems are identified, the division will select the filing for expedited review.

The Securities and Exchange Commission (SEC) and the Financial Accounting Standards Board (FASB) regulate much of what appears in the corporate annual report. Other organizations participate in the regulatory process but are more advisory in nature. These organizations will be discussed briefly at the close of this chapter.

LEARNING OBJECTIVES

1. Discuss the role that the SEC plays in financial reporting.
2. Explain the purpose of SEC Forms S-1, 10-K, 10-Q and 8-K.
3. Discuss the authority of the SEC Division of Enforcement.
4. Describe the purpose of the FASB plays in financial reporting.
5. Understand the purpose of the AICPA and the ASB.

A.1 SECURITIES AND EXCHANGE COMMISSION (SEC)

The primary mission of the U.S. Securities and Exchange Commission (SEC) is to protect investors and maintain the integrity of the securities markets. Their authority originates from the Federal Securities Acts of 1933 and 1934. The Securities Act of 1933 regulates the initial sale of securities by requiring companies to file registration statements and a prospectus with the SEC prior to the offering of the shares. The prospectus is then released to the public for their review. This process is part of what the SEC terms *protective disclosure*. The Securities Act of 1934, also known as the Continuous Disclosure Act, created the Securities and Exchange Commission and gave it the authority to administer federal securities laws and prescribe accounting principles and reporting practices.

Two significant SEC regulations pertain to the preparation of financial statements and their related disclosures:

1. *Regulation S-X* regulates the form and content of financial disclosures, financial statements and the notes accompanying the financial statements
2. *Regulation S-K* regulates the nonfinancial information contained in annual reports such as management's discussion and analysis of financial information.

Other means of communicating with reporting companies include *Financial Reporting Releases* (FRRs) that pertain to the preparation of and disclosure within financial statements, *Accounting and Auditing Enforcement Releases* (AAERs) that summarize enforcement actions against accountants, and Staff Accounting Bulletins (SABs) that SEC staff prepare to help clarify technical issues.

The SEC was also empowered to oversee the securities markets and control brokers and dealers. The passage of both securities acts was part of the government's initiative to better protect investors and help prevent accounting and reporting abuses. Many people felt that at the time there was too much flexibility in financial reporting, which contributed to the reporting inconsistencies. This weakness was thought to be a major contributor to the collapse of the stock market in 1929.

A.1.1 Reporting Requirements

All publicly traded companies are required to file certain reports under the SEC's integrated disclosure system. First, companies are required to complete *Form S-1* when registering their securities for the first time. Form S-1 includes the following:

- History and description of the business
- Description of properties
- Information about directors and executive officers
- Information about the securities being registered

After operating for a year as a public entity, companies are then required to file *Form 10-K*, also known as the annual report to the SEC. This report is much more inclusive than the annual report that is sent to the shareholders. It provides a comprehensive review of the company's business. It includes the following:

- Updated information that might be different than that included in the original registration statement
- A complete set of financial statements
- Description of the business and any changes that might have taken place
- Legal proceedings
- Management discussion and analysis of the company's financial position and results of operations
- Voting matters submitted to shareholders in the fourth quarter of the year
- Change of auditor or disagreements with auditors
- Business backgrounds of all directors, executive officers, and control persons
- Executive compensation
- Security ownership of certain beneficial owners and management[1]

Much of this information is due within 90 days of the company's year-end, but will soon become 60 days under new SEC reporting requirements (as discussed in Chapter 8).

Form 10-Q is filed on a quarterly basis with the SEC but is not required at the close of the fourth quarter. The annual report filed with the SEC takes the place of the fourth-quarter report. Each of the first three quarterly reports includes unaudited financial information and any significant information that the regulators should be made aware of by the company. Form 10-Q must be filed within 45 days of the close of the quarter and will soon become 35 days.

Form 8-K is filed when an event takes place that warrants the immediate attention of the SEC. Such events would include any of the following:

- Change in auditor
- Change in control of company
- Petition for bankruptcy
- Resignation of directors
- Acquisition or disposition of a significant amount of assets that is not customary during the normal operations of the firm
- Fiscal year change

Form 8-K, often referred to as the *current report*, must be filed within 5 to 15 days (the SEC is considering shortening this time period) of the event's occurrence so that regulators and investors can be apprised of the matter as soon as possible. Companies are allowed to file Form 8-K whenever they believe a significant event has occurred, even though it might not be one of the items just shown.

Each of the aforementioned reports must now be electronically filed with the SEC. This electronic reporting is part of the SEC's *Electronic Data Gathering, Analysis and Retrieval (EDGAR)* system. According to the SEC:

---

[1] Brownlee, Ferris, Hawkins, *Corporate Financial Reporting*, Fourth Edition, (McGraw-Hill Irwin), 2001, pp. 16-17.

The Electronic Data Gathering, Analysis, and Retrieval system performs automated collection, validation, indexing, acceptance, and forwarding of submissions by companies and others who are required by law to file forms with the U.S. Securities and Exchange Commission (SEC). Its primary purpose is to increase the efficiency and fairness of the securities market for the benefit of investors, corporations, and the economy by accelerating the receipt, acceptance, dissemination, and analysis of time-sensitive corporate information filed with the agency.

The EDGAR system, which took many years to develop, was fully implemented in 1996. *Regulation S-T* governs the electronic reporting requirements. Though the system is fully operative, there are some SEC forms not yet filed electronically.[2]

A.1.2 Enforcement Issues

The SEC Division of Enforcement possesses the authority to investigate any violation of federal securities laws. The Division of Enforcement was created in August 1972 to consolidate enforcement activities that previously had been handled by the various operating divisions at the SEC's headquarters in Washington. The SEC's enforcement staff is required to conduct investigations into possible violations of the federal securities laws, and prosecute its civil suits in the federal courts as well as its administrative proceedings.[3] Any violations of federal security laws can be reported directly to the Division of Enforcement via the SEC Web site. If a violation appears to be present, the SEC's Division of Enforcement has the right to subpoena company records and require testimony under oath. The SEC has the authority to bring civil charges against a corporation but only the Department of Justice has the authority to bring criminal charges.

A.2 FINANCIAL ACCOUNTING STANDARDS BOARD (FASB)

The responsibility for the issuance of accounting rules is considerable for a number of reasons. First, the research that precedes the issuance of a rule is substantial and oftentimes covers a lengthy period of time. For instance, the accounting rule that requires the measurement of derivative financial instruments was in the developmental stage for more than 10 years. Even at this time, the rule is controversial and quite complex. Second, the economic impact of a new accounting pronouncement on a company can be extraordinary. In 1992, for instance, a new rule on the accounting for post-retirement benefits other than pensions required General Motors to accrue a $20 billion liability. The accrual caused the simultaneous recognition of a current year expense in the same amount and required General Motors to report a 1992 loss that approximated $21 billion. As you would expect, many companies were opposed to the new accounting standard and lobbied heavily against its release. Nonetheless, the regulatory bodies chose to protect the interests of investors and help maintain the integrity of the financial statements.

As mentioned earlier, the SEC, under the Securities Act of 1934 was given the authority to prescribe accounting rules and reporting practices. Yet rather than exercise this authority, the Commission's policy has been to rely on the private sector for this function to the extent that the

[2] www.sec.gov
[3] www.sec.gov

private sector demonstrates ability to fulfill the responsibility in the public interest. Although this policy might sound a bit unusual, the SEC remains active in the standard-setting environment and monitors the impact that currently prescribed standards have on business reporting. As controversial issues arise, they work closely with the profession in an attempt to help resolve the problems.

A number of predecessor organizations were responsible for accounting and reporting practices prior to the creation of the Financial Accounting Standards Board (FASB). The Committee on Accounting Procedures (CAP) was the first private-sector organization that issued accounting rules. CAP established standards or accounting rules during the years 1939 to 1959. Although successful in issuing 51 accounting rules, CAP was often criticized for issuing accounting pronouncements that lacked authoritative substance. Others found fault with the group because only practicing accountants were committee members. Many users demanded a wider representation in the development of accounting rules and a full-time commitment on the part of each member.

The Accounting Principles Board (APB) replaced the CAP in 1959 and issued accounting rules for the next 14 years. The Board issued 31 *opinions* during its term, with each rule backed by an authoritative body. The American Institute of Certified Public Accountants (AICPA) required all companies to follow the standards or disclose the reasons for departure in the notes to the financial statements.

But as the years passed, the Accounting Principles Board was criticized just as CAP had been. First, independence questions arose among the membership. Companies and not the Board itself employed APB members, at the time. Yet because of their position as a board member, they had the authority to influence accounting rules that might affect their firm. Another criticism dealt with the structure of the Board. Each of the largest public accounting firms at the time was automatically awarded a member seat. This caused the Board's vote to carry a significant influence of the "Big Eight" firms. The most glaring criticism, however, revolved around the APB's response time to emerging problems. As the business environment became more complex, the profession demanded more timely and proactive initiatives on the part of the APB. The APB failed to meet this demand so the Financial Accounting Standards Board (FASB) was organized in 1973 to replace the APB.

The FASB is responsible for establishing the current standards of financial accounting and reporting. The standards or pronouncements that the FASB issues, *Statements of Financial Accounting Standards (SFASs),* are officially recognized as authoritative by the Securities and Exchange Commission (Financial Reporting Release No. 1, Section 101) and the American Institute of Certified Public Accountants (Rule 203, Rules of Conduct, as amended May 1973 and May 1979).

The Financial Accounting Standards Board has been successful for many reasons:

- *Broad representation.* All members are no longer required to be CPAs, as was once the case with the APB.
- *Autonomy.* The FASB is not a committee of the AICPA. It is a stand-alone entity that reports to the Financial Accounting Foundation that is not supported by any public funding.
- *Full-time, compensated membership.* FASB members are appointed for five-year, staggered terms and are well compensated.
- *Small membership.* The Board has 7 members, much smaller than the 18-member Accounting Principles Board.
- *Independence.* The Board members are required to sever all ties with their previous employer.

A.2.1 Mission of the FASB

According to the FASB Web site (www.fasb.org), its mission is to establish and improve standards of financial accounting and reporting. To accomplish its mission, the FASB promises to

- *Continually improve the usefulness of financial reporting* by focusing on the primary characteristics of relevance and reliability and on the qualities of comparability and consistency.
- *Keep standards current* to reflect changes in methods of doing business and changes in the economic environment.
- *Promptly address any significant areas of deficiency in financial reporting* that might be improved through the standard-setting process.
- *Promote the international comparability of accounting standards* concurrent with improving the quality of financial reporting.
- *Improve the common understanding* of the nature and purposes of information contained in financial reports.

Since its inception, the FASB has developed a number of accounting concept statements to help in the prescription of new accounting rules. These concept statements, while not GAAP, comprise the "conceptual framework of accounting" and oftentimes provide a frame of reference to help resolve controversial accounting issues. According to the Board, the framework helps to establish reasonable bounds for judgment in preparing financial information and to increase understanding of, and confidence in, financial information on the part of users of financial reports. It also helps the public to understand the nature and limitations of information supplied by financial reporting. As the Board and its related staff operate on a day-by-day basis, it promises the following:

- To be objective in its decision making and to ensure, insofar as possible, the neutrality of information resulting from its standards
- To weigh carefully the views of its constituents in developing concepts and standards
- To issue new standards only when the expected benefits exceed the perceived costs
- To bring about needed changes in ways that minimize disruption to the continuity of reporting practice
- To review the effects of past decisions and interpret, amend, or replace standards in a timely fashion when such action is indicated

The FASB has always followed a due process that precludes placing any particular interest above the interests of the many who rely on financial information. The Board believes that this broad public interest is best served by developing neutral standards that result in accounting for similar transactions and circumstances similarly and for different transactions and circumstances differently.

A.2.2 New Topics and the FASB's Agenda

As one would expect, the FASB reviews many requests for action on various financial accounting and reporting topics. Requests can be received from individual companies, industry representatives, trade associations, and the SEC. The auditing profession, as well, plays an active role in helping to uncover emerging issues in financial reporting. As a consequence, the Board may open new lines of research or revisit an already existing pronouncement.

When addressing emerging issues, the Board must be sensitive to those projects that are most urgent since they continue to operate under significant resource constraints. This continuous review process can change the Board's technical agenda at any time. To aid in the decision-making process, the FASB has developed a list of factors to which it refers in evaluating proposed topics:

- *Pervasiveness of the problem.* The extent to which an issue is troublesome to users, preparers, auditors, or others; the extent to which there is diversity of practice; and the likely duration of the problem (i.e., is it transitory, or will it persist?).
- *Alternative solutions.* The extent to which one or more alternative solutions that will improve financial reporting in terms of relevance, reliability, and comparability are likely to be developed.
- *Technical feasibility.* The extent to which a technically sound solution can be developed, or whether the project under consideration should await completion of other projects.
- *Practical consequences.* The extent to which an improved accounting solution is likely to be acceptable generally, and the extent to which addressing a particular subject (or not addressing it) might cause others to act (e.g., the SEC or Congress).

A.2.3 Due Process of Standard Setting

The FASB follows a due process of standard setting that allows users ample opportunity to review and respond to the issues before the Board. This includes research inquires, mailings, and public hearings, a process that can span one or more years. Table A.1 illustrates the FASB's standard-setting process.

Table A.1 Standard-Setting Process

Problem Identification	Problem is identified by the Emerging Issues Task Force (EITF).
Creation of Task Force	A group of experts is established to oversee the project.
Research Stage	The FASB technical staff conducts the research.
Release of Discussion Memorandum	Document is released that identifies problem along with alternative solutions.
Public Response	Public hearings are held to discuss the issue and comment letters received.
Review of Comments	The FASB and EITF review the alternatives.
Release of Exposure Draft (ED)	A draft of the proposed rule is released for review.
Exposure Period	Minimum of thirty (30) days is required for public review.
Review of Comments	The FASB and EITF review the comments.
Issuance of Standard	The FASB votes on the standard and issues a statement or defeats the proposed rule. If defeated, it is sent back for subsequent revision.

As can be seen from this illustration, some exposure drafts might not result in the issuance of a standard. Only seven FASB members are allowed to vote on the proposed standard. Occasionally, a proposed rule will be defeated or will not pass unanimously. At least five of the seven Board members must approve the proposal for the standard to become effective. Once approved by the FASB, the rule becomes a generally accepted accounting principle (GAAP) and becomes binding in practice. There have been occasions where a vote is not taken and the exposure draft is tabled for further development. The many comment letters received from the accounting and business community can influence this decision.

The due process of standard setting ensures that the views of many different user groups are taken into consideration. Obviously, users and preparers will not always be in agreement on the resulting standard.

A.3 AMERICAN INSTITUTE OF CERTIFIED PUBLIC ACCOUNTANTS (AICPA)

One other organization that plays a prominent role in the accounting and reporting environment is the American Institute of Certified Public Accountants (AICPA). The American Institute of Certified Public Accountants is the national, professional organization for all Certified Public Accountants. Its mission is to provide members with the resources, information, and leadership that enable them to provide valuable services that benefit the public as well as employers and clients. In fulfilling its mission, the AICPA works with state CPA organizations and gives priority to those areas where public reliance on CPA skills is most significant.

To achieve its mission, the Institute promises to do the following:

- Serve as the national representative of CPAs before governments, regulatory bodies and other organizations in protecting and promoting members' interests.

- Seek the highest possible level of uniform certification and licensing standards and promotes and protect the CPA designation.

- Promote public awareness and confidence in the integrity, objectivity, competence, and professionalism of CPAs and monitor the needs and views of CPAs.

- Encourage highly qualified individuals to become CPAs and support the development of outstanding academic programs.

- Establish professional standards, including audit standards; assist members in continually improving their professional conduct, performance and expertise; and monitor such performance to enforce current standards and requirements.[4]

A.4 AUDITING STANDARDS BOARD

Public accounting firms follow specific standards when they perform an audit of a client company. These auditing standards are issued by the Auditing Standards Board (ASB) and are designed to prevent the incidence and to increase the detection of financial fraud and accounting irregularities. According to the ASB, its purpose is to develop and communicate performance and reporting standards and practical guidance that enable the public auditing profession to

---

[4] www.aicpa.org/mssion

provide high-quality objective attestation services at a reasonable cost and in the best interests of the profession and the beneficiaries of those services, with the ultimate purpose of serving the public interest. More specifically, its charge is to do the following:

1. *Develop auditing, attestation, and related quality control standards that inspire the public trust.* These standards require independence and objectivity, promote a high level of performance, and contribute to a common understanding of the level of assurance provided, thereby enhancing the value of services to management, users, and the public. The high standards by which the auditing profession discharges its responsibilities serve to distinguish it from others in the assurance role.

2. *Improve existing attest services.* Auditors continue to audit financial statements, and they also provide services on the effectiveness of control systems over financial reporting, compliance, and operations; on the output, integrity, and security of databases; and on compliance with industry benchmarks and regulatory requirements. By continually improving standards and guidance to address technological change and other issues of concern to its constituencies, the ASB maintains and adapts existing services that are responsive to the public interest. The ASB also develops performance and reporting standards to enable new assurance services that should be accommodated in the audit/attest model for which the ASB is responsible.

3. *Take a leadership role in the development of international auditing standards.* The globalization of capital markets and cross-border transactions will necessitate development of and adherence to international standards to serve international constituencies. The ASB encourages the eventual convergence of U.S. and international audit and attest standards.

4. *Respond timely to the need for guidance and communicate it clearly to the profession and to users.* The ASB actively seeks the input of users and practitioners to identify priorities and elicit feedback in the development of standards and practice guidance. It continually strives to clarify standards and related guidance so that it is meaningful both to practitioners and to user constituencies. It enhances the dissemination and accessibility of standards and guidance.

A.5 CONCLUDING REMARKS

As illustrated throughout this chapter, the accounting and reporting of financial information is an important and strictly regulated process. The important point to remember is that without regulatory oversight the capital markets would operate inefficiently, and investors could not rely on management-prepared performance reports. The SEC, FASB, AICPA, and ASB work together to provide the bond that makes today's financial reporting environment arguably the best in the world.

Questions for Review

1. Which organizations are primarily responsible for monitoring financial information and disclosures in an annual report of a publicly held company?
2. Briefly describe the process of *protective disclosure*. What is the purpose of this process?
3. Differentiate between an S-1, 10-K, and 8-K in terms of the information content of each.
4. Why would the information contained in an 8-K be of particular interest and value to an investor?

5. How is the enforcement of the federal securities laws carried out? Differentiate between the processes of bringing civil versus criminal charges against a corporation.
6. Describe the respective roles of public-sector (SEC) and private-sector (FASB) organizations in the accounting rule-making process.
7. The AICPA also plays a prominent role in financial accounting and reporting. What is the nature of this organization, its membership, and its mission?
8. Describe the role of independent auditors (and public accounting firms) in establishing the credibility of the financial statements and the related disclosures in the annual report. What organization establishes the standards by which a financial statement audit is conducted?

Internet Exercises

1. Locate and identify accounting issues that are of current interest to the FASB on its Web site (http://www.fasb.org). Locate any one exposure draft and briefly summarize its contents.

2. Search the Web and locate one current example of a publicly held company under investigation or sanctioned by the SEC. Also find one example of a public accounting firm involved in an SEC action.

APPENDIX **B**

The Building Blocks of Financial Reporting

APPENDIX OUTLINE

This appendix covers the fundamental framework of accounting theory. Steve has gained a solid understanding of financial statements by reading this book, but this appendix explains the thinking behind the numbers and current form of financial reports. Knowledge of basic accounting theory enables Steve—and you—to better understand and interpret the content and limitations of financial accounting and reporting.

APPENDIX OBJECTIVES

1. Understand the need for a theoretical accounting framework.

2. Identify the objectives of financial reporting —SFAC No. 1.

3. Recognize the qualitative characteristics of accounting information—SFAC No. 2.

4. Appreciate the "objectives of financial reporting by non-business organizations— SFAC No. 4.

5. Grasp financial statement recognition and measurement issue—SFAC No. 5.

6. Know the elements of financial statements — SFAC No. 6.

7. Be familiar with using cash flow information and present value in accounting measurements—SFAC No. 7.

B.1 INTRODUCTION

In 1973, when the Financial Accounting Standards Board (FASB) first came into existence, board members recognized the need for a framework to structure financial accounting rules and standards. There was no broadly accepted framework for standard setting. Accounting standards were set in reaction to the current economic climate alone. The FASB created the *Statements of Financial Accounting Concepts* (SFAC) to:

> *...serve the public interest by setting the objectives, qualitative characteristics, and other concepts that guide selection of economic events to be recognized and measured for financial reporting and their display in financial statements or related means of communicating information to those who are interested.* [1]

The SFAC represent a descriptive theoretical framework. This means the concept statements are designed to help the FASB set accounting standards that ensure financial reporting information meets the needs of the general public, and not one user group over another. The advantage of a descriptive framework to the user is that it enables comparison and contrasts of business performance over time and across industries.

A careful read of the SFAC will improve your ability to evaluate and interpret the annual report. Knowledge of basic accounting theory enables you to better understand the content and limitations of financial accounting and reporting. In addition, as new financial reporting issues emerge, you will understand why the FASB responds in one way over another. For instance, the concept statements specifically address the issue of reliability. This means that when the FASB is in the process of setting a new accounting standard to capture a business transaction (economic event) it will establish the guideline such that the information is reliable in financial analysis. The conceptual framework also focuses the FASB's thinking to establish accounting guidelines that consistently measure economic events. Consistency in measurement is very important for benchmarking performance over time.

B.2 THE CONCEPTUAL FRAMEWORK

The conceptual framework is logical and easy to follow. Table B.1 lists the concept statements by number and title. Note, the numbering sequence is correct in Table B.1. SFAC No. 3 was originally written in 1980. SFAC No. 6 replaced No. 3 in 1985.

Table B.1 Statements of Financial Accounting Concepts

Concept Number	Concept Title
No. 1	Objectives of Financial Reporting by Business Enterprises
No. 2	Qualitative Characteristics of Accounting Information
No.4	Objectives of Financial Reporting by Nonbusiness Organizations
No.5	Recognition and Measurement in Financial Statements of Business Enterprises
No. 6	Elements of Financial Statements (a replacement of Concept Statement No. 3)
No.7	Using cash flow information and present value in accounting measurements

[1] Financial Accounting Standards Board, Statements of Financial Accounting Concepts: Accounting Standards 2001/02 edition. John Wiley & Sons, Inc, New York. 2001, page iv.

B.2.1 SFAC No. 1: Objectives of Financial Reporting by Business Enterprises

This statement establishes the objectives of *general purpose* external financial reporting for the business enterprises. The term general purpose means *financial reporting* should be designed to meet the needs of all industries, and not one specific industry segment. The term financial reporting includes *financial statements* and *other financial reports* that convey useful information. Other financial reporting tools are, for example, the corporate annual report, prospectus, and SEC fillings. The reader should take away from this section that useful information is gathered from financial statements and other quantitative and qualitative information sources spread throughout the annual report.

SFAC No. 1 identifies three objectives of financial reporting:

1. Financial reporting should provide information that is useful to present and potential investors and creditors and other users in making rational investment, credit, and similar decisions.[2]
2. Financial reporting should provide information to help present and potential investors and creditors and other users in assessing the amount, timing and uncertainty of prospective cash receipts from dividends or interest and the proceeds form the sale redemption, or maturity of securities or loans.[3]
3. Financial reporting should provide information about the economic resources of an enterprise, the claims to those resources (obligations of the enterprises to transfer resources to other entities and owner's equity), and the effects of transactions, events, and circumstances that change resources and claims to those resources.[4]

SFAC No. 1 also addresses two other issues. First, it delineates financial reporting limitations. Essentially, financial reports capture information based on estimates of economic events. To the user of the annual report, this means that financial reports are not exact measures, but management's approximation of financial performance and position. For example, depreciation expense is a common estimate. Bad debt expense is also an estimate. Abuse by management of accounting estimates is the basis of most earnings management games.

Second, SFAC No. 1 puts financial reporting into perspective for the user. Financial reports are analogous to looking out the review mirror at the parent company and its subsidiaries, all combined. Financial reports are retrospective. They provide information regarding what has occurred, a historical view, measured in a monetary unit (dollar, yen, euro). In addition, the reports measure the individual business enterprise. When a business enterprise combines the parent company and several subsidiaries into one set of financial statements, it files consolidated financial reports. For example, Enron titled the balance sheet *Enron Corp. and Subsidiaries Consolidated Balance Sheet*. This means the parent and the many subsidiaries are combined in the financial statement presentation.

B.2.2 SFAC No. 2: Qualitative Characteristics of Accounting Information

This section frames for the user the characteristics of financial information. You will find the FASB, through SFAC No. 2, carefully defines accounting information. The FASB looks to the characteristics of information that make it useful in decision making. The outcome is that a user has access to value-added general-purpose financial reports. The characteristics can be viewed as a hierarchy of qualities, as shown in Table B.2.

---

[2] *FASB Statement of Financial Accounting Concepts No. 1,* par. 34.
[3] *FASB Statement of Financial Accounting Concepts No. 1,* par. 37.
[4] *FASB Statement of Financial Accounting Concepts No. 1,* par. 40.

Table B.2 A Hierarchy of Accounting Qualities

Users of accounting information:	Decision makers and their characteristics
Pervasive constraint:	Benefits must be greater than costs
Threshold for recognition:	Materiality

• User-specific qualities	Understandability Decision Usefulness

• Primary decision-specific qualities:	Relevance • Predictive value • Feedback value • Timeliness	Reliability • Verifiability • Neutrality • Representational faithfulness
• Secondary and interactive qualities	Comparability and Consistency	

User-Specific Qualities

The first order in the hierarchy of qualitative characteristics is *understandability* and *decision usefulness*. Understandability is defined as information that enables users to perceive its significance. Decision usefulness is a broad statement that can be interpreted differently by the many different users of financial reports. Thus, the next order in the hierarchy defines the primary qualities of decision usefulness.

Primary Decision-Specific Qualities

Characteristics of decision usefulness are *relevance* and *reliability*. Accounting information is considered relevant when it serves as a base for predicting the future, provides feedback regarding what occurred in the business and is timely. Accounting information is considered reliable when it can be verified by others, is neutral (unbiased) in presentation and is representational faithful.

Secondary and Interactive Qualities

Secondary qualitative characteristics mean the accounting information is *comparable* and *consistent*. Comparability helps the user to identify similarities in and difference between two sets of economic phenomena. Consistency provides a uniform basis and application of accounting standards from period to period.

Threshold For Recognition

The issue of *materiality* is also addressed in SFAC No. 2. The user is likely to frequently encounter the issue of materiality in the business press and/or financial reports. Materiality is defined as:

> the magnitude of an omission or misstatement of accounting information that, in the light of surrounding circumstances, makes it probable that the judgment of a reasonable person relying on the information would have been changed or influenced by the omission or misstatement.

Other Topics

SFAC No. 2 also defines two additional issues not specifically identified in the hierarchy:

1. *Completeness*: Information of everything material that is necessary for faithful representation of the relevant phenomena.
2. *Conservatism*: A prudent reaction to uncertainty is to try to ensure that uncertainty and risks inherent in business situations are adequately considered. In practice, conservatism means reporting lower income and asset levels.

B.2.3 SFAC No. 4: Objectives of Financial Reporting by Nonbusiness Organizations

The FASB recognizes that nonbusiness organizations must also provide useful financial reports and financial statements. SFAC No. 4 builds on SFAC No. 1. The key difference is that SFAC No. 4 considers the needs of the nonbusiness organization financial report user. Generally, users of these reports are interested in knowing how efficiently and effectively the resources were used by the nonbusiness and if the organization is sustainable into the future. SFAC No. 4 fully addresses these issue. Beyond that, SFAC No. 1 and No. 4 are very similar.

B.4.4 SFAC No. 5: Recognition and Measurement in Financial Statements of Business Enterprises

This section clarifies the focus of financial statements. SFAC No. 5 focuses on three important financial statement issues. Note the specific reference to financial statements, and not financial reporting in general. First, SFAC No. 5 defines the meaning of a full set of financial statements. Second, SFAC No. 5 defines information that should be recognized in financial statements. Third, SFAC No. 5 identifies measurement attributes that are important to the recognition concept.

A Full Set of Financial Statements

SFAC No. 5 begins by defining a full set of financial statements to include the following:

- Financial position at the end of the period (Chapter 3 of this text)
- Earnings (net income) for the period (Chapter 4 of this text)
- Comprehensive income (total nonowner changes in equity) for the period (Chapter 4 of this text)
- Cash flows during the period (Chapter 5 of this text)
- Investment by and distribution to owners during the period (Chapter 6 of this text)

Information Recognition

Recognition, the second key area addressed by SFAC No. 5, is the process of formally recording or incorporating an item into the financial statements of an entity as an asset, liability, revenue, expense, or the like.[5] The FASB uses the recognition principle to determine (1) what economic event is recorded, (2) when the economic event is recorded, and (3) how much is recorded (measurement) in the financial statements. For example when long-term software service contracts entered the business world, the FASB used SFAC No. 5's definition of recognition, along with SFAC No. 2, to establish guidelines to estimate when and how much to report in the financial statements.

[5] *FASB Statement of Financial Accounting Concepts No. 5*, par. 58

The FASB uses the following guidelines to determine the recognition of economic events:

- The transaction meets the definition of a financial statement element (asset, liability, revenue, or expense, identified in the next section).
- The economic event can be measured.
- The information regarding the economic events is relevant.
- The information regarding the economic events is reliable.

Measurement

Recognize as the user of financial information that not all items are measured the same. SFAC No. 5 focuses the Board's thinking on measurement with the following:

Items (assets and liabilities) currently reported in the financial statement are measured by different attributes, depending on the nature of the asset and liability and the relevance and reliability of the attribute measured.[6]

Five different attributes to measurement are used in applying GAAP. Each is used in specific situations. Table B.3 summarizes the measurement attributes and provides a brief example. The balance sheet and income statement chapters provided expanded coverage on measurement with further examples.

Table B.3 GAAP Measurement Attributes

Method	*Applied Examples in Evaluation*
Historical cost: Amount in accounting records is the cost of the asset. This is the most common method of measurement employed in financial statements.	The cost of equipment for production
Current replacement cost: Amount in accounting records is the cost to replace the asset.	Inventory items that are outdated and have been restated under the LCM rule
Current exit value: Amount in accounting records is the liquidation value.	Certain securities
Expected exit value: Amount in accounting records is future expected cash receipt.	Short-term accounts receivable
Present value of expected cash flow: Amount in accounting records is future expected cash receipts or payments, discounted to their present value.	Long-term accounts receivable or long-term lease liabilities

Realization of revenue is an important issue regarding income statement measurement. Revenue should be recognized when the amount and timing of the revenue are reasonably determined and when the revenue has been substantially earned. Revenue is realized when a cash exchange occurs. For example, the sale of supplies to a customer on credit terms is recognized in the accounting records when the sale occurs. Realization occurs when the customer pays off the accounts receivable balance and cash flows into the business.

---

[6] *FASB Statement of Financial Accounting Concepts No. 5*, par. 66.

B.2.5 SFAC No. 6: Elements of Financial Statements (a replacement for SFAC No. 3)

This section explains the make-up of financial statements and shows how an accounting system works. Specifically, it identifies and defines financial statement elements. Next, SFAC No. 6 articulates the role of accrual accounting as a tool to meet the objectives of financial reporting. Knowing the basics of how an accounting system works represents a tool that helps the user critically analyze revenue, expense, and cash flow measures.

Financial Statement Elements

Financial statement elements are identified below and fully explained in the text:

- *Assets* are what the business owns.
- *Liabilities* are what the business owes.
- *Equity* is assets less liabilities.
- *Revenues* are sales from daily operations.
- *Expenses* are the consumption of resources necessary to generate revenue.
- *Gain/losses* are increases/decreases in equity from peripheral or incidental transaction.
- *Net income* is the change in equity.
- *Comprehensive income* is the change in equity not reported through the income statement.
- *Investments by owners* are dollars, assets, or services contributed to the business in exchange for stock.
- *Distributions to owners* are dollars, assets, or services distributed to the shareholders.

Accrual Accounting

SFAC No. 6 articulates the role of accrual accounting as a tool to meet the objectives of financial reporting. Accrual accounting is the mechanical technique used to recognize and measure business transactions. The output of an accrual accounting system is a reasonable estimate of financial performance and financial position of a business. This is why GAAP requires a business to use accrual accounting. The user needs a valid measure of economic performance, which a pure cash flow measure system does not capture.

An accrual accounting system records transactions into the accounting records when they occur. That is, an accrual basis of accounting measures revenues and expenses, as well as cash receipts and cash payments when they occur. Let's look at a few examples:

- *Example A*: The Home Depot sells $25,000 of lumber to a builder. The sale terms are such that the builder will pay The Home Depot $25,000 in 30 days. Using accrual accounting, The Home Depot would increase accounts receivable and *recognize* a sale of $25,000 in the accounting records. Notice, no cash flow has been received at this point yet the transaction is recorded into the accounting records. When the contractor pays The Home Depot, The Home Depot *realizes* $25,000 of cash inflow and records into the accounting records an increase of $25,000 in cash and a decrease of $25,000 in the accounts receivable balance.
- *Example B*: The Home Depot purchases on credit terms $500,000 of lumber from a supplier. In this case, The Home Depot's inventory account increases and accounts payable increases. Notice again that no cash flow has occurred at this point yet the transaction is recorded into the accounting records. When The Home Depot pays the supplier, the cash account will decrease by $500,000 and the accounts payable account will decrease by $500,000.

- *Example C*: Extending Example A, assume The Home Depot had a cost for the lumber sold to the builder of $19,000. Using accrual accounting, The Home Depot would decrease the inventory account by $19,000 and increase the cost of goods sold account at the time of the sale. Again, this is a transaction recorded into the accounting records that did not involve cash flow. Cash flowed out of The Home Depot for inventory when it paid the supplier, as illustrated in Example B.

- *Example D*: The Home Depot prepays an insurance bill for $24,000. The insurance is for a period of 24 months (or $1,000 per month). When the bill is paid, the cash account decreases and an account on the balance sheet labeled prepaid insurance increases. When the first year of coverage has expired, the accountant at The Home Depot will increase the insurance expense by $12,000 and decrease the prepaid insurance by $12,000 for the months that the insurance policy protected The Home Depot (12 months/24months or $12,000).

The take away for the informed consumer regarding accrual accounting is that all measurable economic events (transactions) are recorded into the accounting system and reported in the financial statement of a business. Some economic events include cash flows; others do not. The end result is that the business and those interested in its activities have useful measures of the business's financial position and financial performance.

A distinct advantage of accrual accounting for the user is that it matches revenue to expenses. The *matching principle* essentially says that costs are recognized as an expense in the time period the resources were used to generate revenue. This principle is both straightforward and difficult to apply. On the one hand, expensing the utility bill in the respective period is a simple process. An accrual to the utility expense is recorded when the bill arrives in the mail. This is a typical transaction accrued in the accounting records. Expensing a portion of a long-term maintenance contract on industrial equipment, on the other hand, requires a careful estimate in matching the use of the equipment to the period the equipment generated revenue. As business transactions continue to grow in complexity, matching revenues to expenses becomes more of a challenge.

B.2.6 SFAC No. 7: Using Cash Flow Information and Present Value in Accounting Measurements

SFAC No. 7 provides guidance to improve the quality of expected cash flow measures (measuring today the value of cash that is expected to flow into the business in the future). Notice that SFAC No. 7's focus is on measurement and not recognition, as discussed in SFAC No. 5. The statement applies to initial measurement of assets and liabilities, *fresh-start measurements*,[7] and amortization techniques of future cash flows. A user can more critically consume asset and liability measures found in the annual report when the cash measurement perspective is clear.

Essentially, SFAC No. 7 centers on how to apply the discounted cash flow approach to measurement. Discounting cash flows means taking into consideration the time value of money. For instance, a dollar received two years from today is worth less than a dollar received today. The traditional approach to discounting a sale with long-term financing, for example, is to reduce the value of expected cash flow by an interest rate that includes a

---

[7] Measuring a new carrying amount of an asset or liability on the balance sheet following initial recognition of the asset or liability on the balance sheet.

risk-free component plus a risk-adjustment factor for a specified period-of-time. This approach assumes that one interest rate, increased to adjust for risk, reflects all cash flow uncertainly with respect to this transaction.

SFAC No. 7 requires a more explicit application of discounting cash flows, labeled the *expected cash flow approach*, when incorporating uncertainly of cash flows into the measurement of an asset or liability. This approach requires expected cash flows to be weighted for the possible range of flows for the respective period as a means to incorporate risk into the measurement of future cash flows. Next, the weighted cash flows are discounted at a risk-free weight. The logic behind using SFAC No. 7 needs careful attention. SFAC No. 7 proscribes that the risk of cash flows should be measured by weighting each period cash flows, whereas the traditional approach assumes that one interest rate, adjusted for uncertainty, captures the risk associated with a transaction.

Let's look at an example comparing the traditional and expected cash flow approaches. The example centers on the measurement of an asset sale. Assume the asset has a fixed contract cash flow of $5,000, four years from today. The risk-free rate (interest rate) is 6 percent, with a 4 percent risk adjustment factor for a total interest rate of 10 percent. In addition, management estimates the possible fixed contract cash flow range of payments due to unforeseen risks and their respective probabilities are $2,000 (10 percent), $3,000 (10 percent), $4,000 (30 percent), and $5,000 (50 percent). The traditional and expected discounting methods are presented as follows:

Traditional cash flow discounting approach (prior to SFAC No. 7)

$ 5,000 x (factor: PV of 1, @ 10%, 4 years out)
$ 5,000 x (.683) = $ 3,415
This would be interpreted to mean that the fixed contract of $5,000 to be paid four years from today would be estimated in today's dollars at $ 3,415.

Expected cash flow discounting approach (SFAC No. 7)

Cash flow possibilities	Estimated probability	Expected cash flow
$2,000	10%	$ 200
$3,000	10%	300
$4,000	30%	1,200
$5,000	50%	2,500
Total		$ 4,200

Next, the $ 4,200 must be discounted similar to above.
$4,200 x (factor: PV of 1, @ 6%, 4 years out)
$4,200 x (.792) = $3,326

Under SFAC No. 7, the fixed contract of $5,000 to be paid four years from today would be estimated in today's dollars at $ 3,326.

Notice how SFAC No. 7 works to improve the quality of information provided to the user. Prior to SFAC No. 7, the amount reported on the financial statement would be $3,415. The explicit assumption is that the 10 percent interest rate factor captured the entire risk of the possible cash flows. Using the expected cash flow approach, each fixed contract cash flow possibility is weighted into the present value computation of $3,326. As a result, the quality of information provided to the user improves because the range of possible outcomes is built into the computation. This approach also points to the conservative nature of accounting and financial reporting. The amount recorded for the sale is $3,326 under SFAC No. 7 guidelines, and $3,415 prior to its adoption.

B.3 CONCLUDING REMARKS

This appendix shows that the FASB developed concept statements as a guide to meeting the users' needs for information that is useful in decision making. Defined specifically are the objectives of financial reporting, the qualitative characteristics of accounting information, recognition and measurement attributes and approaches, and elements of the financial statements. Knowledge of basic accounting theory enables you to have a clearer understanding of the content and limitations of financial accounting and reporting.

Questions for Review

1. Established by the FASB, the Statements of Financial Accounting Concepts provide a descriptive theoretical framework for establishing financial accounting rules and standards. How has this framework improved financial reporting over the pre-1973 system?

2. According to SFAC No.1, what are the primary objectives of financial reporting? Users of financial reporting information should also be aware of the limitations of this information. Give a specific example of a limitation of financial reporting information.

3. In order to be useful in decision making, accounting information must be both relevant and reliable. In making a decision on whether to extend credit to a company, give an example of information that may be reliable yet *not* relevant to the creditor's decision.

4. What is the difference between comparability and consistency? Why are these qualities important to the users of accounting information?

5. How does the size of a company affect the concept of *materiality* as it affects accounting information?

6. To be recognized or recorded and disclosed in the financial statements, information must meet what general guidelines according to the FASB?

7. The realization principle governs when to recognize revenue. What conditions must be met in order for a company to recognize revenue according to this principle?

8. What is accrual basis accounting? How does it differ from cash basis accounting? Why does SFAC No. 6 endorse accrual basis accounting for financial reporting purposes?

Internet Exercises

1. SFAC No. 6 identifies the following 10 financial statement elements: assets, liabilities, equity, revenues, expenses, gains/losses, net income, investments by owners, and distributions to owners. Locate the financial statements of a company you are interested in on the Internet. For each of the above 10 elements, describe briefly the information disclosed for your selected company including where (on which financial statement) the information appears.

   Example: Assets—includes current, property, plant and equipment, other... found on the Balance Sheet.

2. Locate an article that deals with *revenue recognition* issues by searching the Internet. Write a well-developed essay summarizing the issues in the article.

Index